PERGAMON INTERNATIONAL LIBRARY
of Science, Technology, Engineering and Social Studies

*The 1000-volume original paperback library in aid of education,
industrial training and the enjoyment of leisure*

Publisher: Robert Maxwell, M.C.

A Geography of the Soviet Union

THE PERGAMON TEXTBOOK
INSPECTION COPY SERVICE

An inspection copy of any book published in the Pergamon International Library will gladly
be sent to academic staff without obligation for their consideration for course adoption or
recommendation. Copies may be retained for a period of 60 days from receipt and returned
if not suitable. When a particular title is adopted or recommended for adoption for class use
and the recommendation results in a sale of 12 or more copies, the inspection copy may be
retained with our compliments. If after examination the lecturer decides that the book is not
suitable for adoption but would like to retain it for his personal library, then a discount of
10% is allowed on the invoiced price. The Publishers will be pleased to receive suggestions
for revised editions and new titles to be published in this important International Library.

Pergamon Oxford Geographies

General Editor: W. B. FISHER

Other Titles of Interest

CLARKE, J. I.
Population Geography, 2nd edition

CLARKE, J. I.
Population Geography and the Developing Countries

CLOUT, H. D.
Rural Geography: An Introductory Survey

CLOUT, H. D.
The Geography of Post-war France: A Social and Economic Approach

COOKE, R. U. & JOHNSON, J. H.
Trends in Geography: An Introductory Survey

COPPOCK, J. T.
Second Homes: Curse or Blessing?

COPPOCK, J. T. & SEWELL, W. D.
The Spatial Dimensions of Public Policy

JOHNSON, J. J.
Urban Geography, 2nd edition

KERR, A.
The Common Market and How It Works

McINTOSH, I. G. & MARSHALL, C. B.
The Face of Scotland, 3rd edition

O'CONNOR, A. M.
The Geography of Tropical African Development, 2nd edition

SUNDERLAND, E.
Elements of Human and Social Geography

A Geography of the Soviet Union

by

JOHN C. DEWDNEY, M.A. (EDIN.)

Reader in Geography in the University of Durham

THIRD EDITION

PERGAMON PRESS

OXFORD · NEW YORK · TORONTO · SYDNEY · PARIS · FRANKFURT

U.K.	Pergamon Press Ltd., Headington Hill Hall, Oxford OX3 0BW, England
U.S.A.	Pergamon Press Inc., Maxwell House, Fairview Park, Elmsford, New York 10523, U.S.A.
CANADA	Pergamon of Canada, Suite 104, 150 Consumers Road, Willowdale, Ontario M2J1P9, Canada
AUSTRALIA	Pergamon Press (Aust.) Pty. Ltd., P.O. Box 544, Potts Point, NSW 2011, Australia
FRANCE	Pergamon Press SARL, 24 rue des Ecoles, 75240 Paris, Cedex 05, France
FEDERAL REPUBLIC OF GERMANY	Pergamon Press GmbH, 6242 Kronberg-Taunus, Pferdstrasse 1, Federal Republic of Germany

First edition 1965

Reprinted 1968

Second edition 1971

Reprinted 1974 (with corrections)

Reprinted 1976

Third edition 1979

British Library Cataloguing in Publication Data

Dewdney, John Christopher
A geography of the Soviet Union.—3rd ed.
(Pergamon Oxford geographies).
(Pergamon international library).
1. Russia—Description and travel—1970–
I. Title
914.7   DK29   78-40992

ISBN 0-08-023739-8 (Hard cover)
ISBN 0-08-023738-X (Flexi cover)

*Printed and bound at William Clowes & Sons Limited
Beccles and London*

CONTENTS

LIST OF FIGURES

LIST OF TABLES

EDITOR'S FOREWORD

At the present time there is no need to explain or justify a choice of the Soviet Union as a subject for geographical study. Yet in spite of the significance of the U.S.S.R. as a major world power we possess very few books in English that offer a comprehensive and overall view of Russian geography within the compass of a small-scale text usable by senior pupils in schools. Over the last few years there have appeared a number of large-scale studies of the Soviet Union, but these have been either in greater part for reference or else designed in style and treatment, for the relatively advanced student.

It is the aim of Mr. Dewdney's book to present the salient geographical elements of the contemporary U.S.S.R. for pupils in schools, at fifth- and sixth-form level, and as an outline or introductory text for first-year university students. Moreover, a feature in many schools and universities is the increasing attention given to geography as part of the background to studies of language and literature; and it is hoped that the present work will thus also be of use to the small but growing numbers who study Russian as a major language.

Reflecting possibly what has now become a trend in certain university geography departments—and undoubtedly the case in Durham—the author's treatment is on a systematic basis, by topic rather than by region. Whilst appropriate consideration is given to physical elements, there is somewhat more extended treatment of economic aspects. This is perhaps only proper in dealing with the U.S.S.R. Regions as such are discussed, but on a minor scale, since in the opinion of some geographers the subject is now in the process of moving to consideration of conditions and problems—human, economic and political—posed by the various geographical features, with regions an incidental, though not negligible, factor. The traditional method in geography, that of erecting regional subdivision as a dominant element must thus be replaced by new treatment. Natural regions and associated concepts have for long been a useful approach and a sound framework, but more advanced ideas are now necessary, since growth of modern communications has in some ways destroyed what we can call traditional regional units, and the activities of man are creating at accelerating speed new situations, new human groupings, new problems and opportunities. All these to some extent render outdated the idea of a fixed regional pattern delimited by physical features. It is now the function of modern geography to offer an assessment of the part played by environment in fostering and influencing not only these changes but their resulting challenges in human existence. For few areas can this be better seen than in the Soviet Union.

Mr. Dewdney has first-hand experience of those parts of the U.S.S.R. that a foreigner may visit. His study attempts to show how human ingenuity and activity have transformed a major segment of the earth's surface, despite the handicaps imposed by great distances, a harsh climate, and by a turbulent historical past both within and on the frontiers of Russia, that has produced revolution, devastation and consequent slowness in development. This is why such topics as territorial administration and transport are regarded as sufficiently important to have separate chapters; and why there are no chapter headings on a purely regional basis.

Statistics are not always easy to come by or sufficiently informative when obtained; and comparison on a basis of proportion may not always convey the real position, even though its arithmetic can be wholly sound. In terms of economic development, it is a very different matter to increase by 50 per cent or even double an activity that is in its first stages, as compared with one that is already a large and efficient producer. To double one only adds another one; whereas doubling a thousand involves effort on a totally different scale. This tendency to compare by proportional growth leads to some difficulty both within the U.S.S.R., where there are some areas in an early stage of growth and others much more advanced, and also when Russian achievements are set alongside those of other countries. Nevertheless, sufficient statistics are now available to allow a better and more detailed picture of developments in the Soviet Union than we in the West often appreciate, and it will be obvious that the present book is based wherever possible on actual facts and figures rather than upon impressions or comparison. Objective knowledge of the U.S.S.R. has so far been rather lacking in our schools and universities—for many reasons we should know more of this interesting, remarkable and different country.

W. B. FISHER

PREFACE TO THE THIRD EDITION

In the seven years which have elapsed since the publication of the second edition, further rapid change has occurred in the scale and structure of the Soviet economy, necessitating a major revision of this book. The general arrangement and contents remain the same but, apart from the earlier physical and historical sections, much has been re-written. All the tables have been updated to the most recent year possible, and all the maps and diagrams have been re-drawn. Above all I have attempted to give as accurate a picture as possible of the current situation and the economic trends of the late 1970s.

Durham   JOHN C. DEWDNEY
1978

PREFACE TO THE SECOND EDITION

More than five years have elapsed since the first edition was written, a period during which rapid expansion of the Soviet economy has continued. For this second edition the maps, tables and other statistics have been brought as far up to date as possible. The general arrangement and contents of the book remain the same, but there has been a considerable amount of revision of both fact and emphasis to take account of the changes which have occurred over the past few years.

Durham   JOHN C. DEWDNEY
1971

PREFACE TO THE FIRST EDITION

Contacts with teachers in schools and universities who are concerned with teaching the geography of the Soviet Union have convinced me that there is a real need for a compact, up-to-date systematic treatment of the subject, which will provide basic information and serve as a starting point for further study. Such are the intentions of this book. I should like to express my thanks to Mr. G. McWhirter, who prepared the final drawings for many of the illustrations, and to Miss S. J. Pennington who typed the manuscript. I should also like to place on record my gratitude to Professor W. B. Fisher for his constant help and encouragement.

Durham   JOHN C. DEWDNEY
1965

ACKNOWLEDGEMENTS

I wish to pay a special tribute to the many members of the secretarial and technical staff of the Department of Geography, University of Durham, both past and present, who have contributed so much to the various editions of this book.

Figures 3 and 5 are based on maps appearing on pages 10 and 13 of *the Economic Geography of the U.S.S.R.* by Bal'zak, Vasyutin and Feigin, copyright, 1959, by the American Council of Learned Societies, used with the permission of the Macmillan Company. Figure 36 is based on a map by R. E. Lonsdale and J. H. Thompson appearing in *Economic Geography*, 36, No. 1, January 1960, page 42, with the authors' and editor's permission. Table 15 is based on data given on pages 37–41 of the *Geographical Digest 1977*, copyright George Philip & Son Ltd., with the publisher's permission.

INTRODUCTION

The most obvious yet at the same time one of the most significant facts about the Soviet Union is its enormous size. The country covers an area of 22.4 million sq km (8.6 million sq miles) approximately one-sixth of the earth's land surface. From the western frontier to the Bering Strait is a distance of nearly 10,000 km (6000 miles) and the maximum latitudinal extent, from the Arctic Ocean to the borders of Afghanistan, is 4800 km (over 3000 miles). No other political unit in the world approaches the size of the U.S.S.R., which is more than twice as large as China, nearly three times as big as the United States or Australia, and no less than ninety-three times the size of the United Kingdom (Fig. 1). However, the population of the Soviet Union, which on 1 July 1977 stood at 259 million, is a good deal less impressive than its area, being greatly exceeded by those of China (850 million) and India (623 million). The United States has 217 million

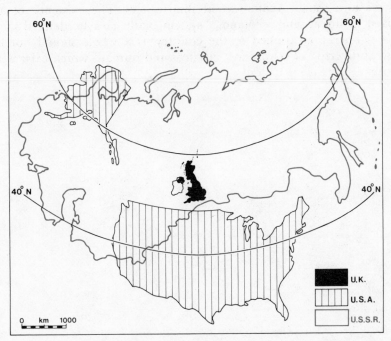

FIG. 1. A comparison of the relative sizes of the U.K., U.S.A. and U.S.S.R. The three countries are shown in their correct latitudinal positions.

inhabitants. The overall population density in the U.S.S.R. is approximately 11.6 per sq km (30 per sq mile), less than half the world average. This low figure suggests another important fact, the reasons for which will become apparent as we proceed, namely that a great deal of the Soviet Union is very thinly peopled; much of it can be described as virtually uninhabited. While this state of affairs is largely a result of the very harsh physical environment which exists over large areas, there are at the same time considerable stretches of territory which could, and no doubt eventually will, support much larger numbers of people than they do at present.

A country of such enormous size must be expected to have a great variety of physical conditions within its boundaries and this is certainly the case with the Soviet Union. At the same time, the individual physical regions are so large that monotonous uniformity of landscape over wide areas is as characteristic as the great contrasts between one region and another. To variety in the various aspects of physical geography must be added variety in the racial, historical and cultural backgrounds of the people and in their way of life. The contrasts between the sophisticated town-dwellers of Moscow, Leningrad and other great cities of European Russia and the nomadic pastoralists of Soviet Central Asia or the primitive tribes of the Arctic are as great as those between, say, the Londoner and the inhabitant of Iran or Alaska. Despite the rapid and far-reaching changes which have taken place in the Soviet Union over the past sixty years, these contrasts still exist; indeed in some ways they have become more marked, since modern economic development, particularly in the industrial sphere, has affected some areas to a much greater extent than others. The existence of a highly centralized political and economic system with clearly defined aims and methods of operation applied to the country as a whole should not blind us to the great diversity of conditions, physical and human, which exist within the boundaries of the Soviet Union.

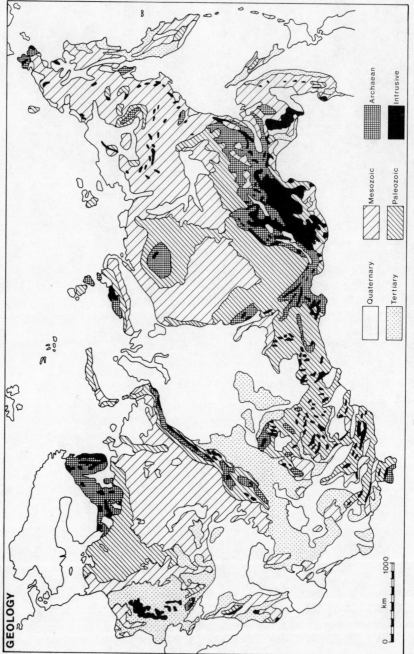

Fig. 2. Simplified geological map.

CHAPTER 1

STRUCTURE AND RELIEF

It is not possible in a book of this size to give a full and detailed account of the geological structure of the Soviet Union (Fig. 2) and in this chapter our attention must be concentrated on the main relief features. Nevertheless, some knowledge of the basic structural elements is necessary and these are best understood if we recall the main features of the structure of the world as a whole. Basically, there are two major elements, stable blocks or "continental platforms" and orogenic belts or zones of mountain building. The continental platforms are composed of extremely tough igneous and metamorphic rocks which were formed at great depth beneath the surface during mountain-building episodes in very early (Archaean or pre-Cambrian) geological times. These hard materials have proved resistant to all later fold movements and, although they have been faulted, raised and lowered *en masse* by epeirogenic earth movements and subjected to long periods of sub-aerial denudation, their structures are quite different from those of the intervening orogenic belts. The latter are zones of the earth's crust where, on various occasions, great thicknesses of sedimentary rocks, derived from the denudation of adjacent "platforms", have been thrown into folds by vigorous lateral orogenic or mountain-building earth movements.

The Soviet Union contains two stable blocks, the East European and Siberian platforms, between and around which have developed fold mountain systems from each of the major orogenic periods, the Caledonian, Hercynian, Mesozoic and Alpine. The distribution of these elements is shown on the map of tectonic zones (Fig. 3). This map divides the Soviet Union into zones according to the geological period during which the last main folding took place. Thus, in the area marked pre-Cambrian (Archaean), there has been little folding since the pre-Cambrian era, in that marked Caledonian there has been little since the Caledonian orogeny, and so on. It will be observed that these tectonic zones do not in every case correspond with the relief regions indicated in Fig. 4. This is because, at the present time, structures formed in the earlier periods are not everywhere visible at the surface. In many areas they have been worn down by denudation and covered by younger sedimentary rocks which lie nearly horizontally and remain at low elevations above sea-level. The Ural Mountains and the West Siberian Lowland, for example, are both part of the Hercynian zone because folding took place in both these areas in Hercynian times. However, the Hercynian structures of the West Siberian Lowland are buried beneath younger sedimentaries, while those of the Urals are exposed at the surface, so that the two regions, while they are parts of the same *structural* zone, are quite

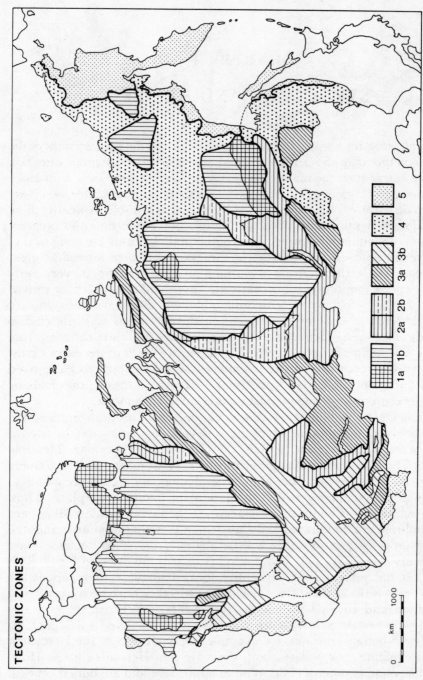

TECTONIC ZONES

1a   1b   2a   2b   3a   3b   4   5

Fig. 3. Tectonic zones: 1a, Archaean (exposed); 1b, Archaean (concealed); 2a, Caledonian (exposed); 2b, Caledonian (concealed); 3a, Hercynian (exposed); 3b, Hercynian (concealed); 4, Mesozoic; 5, Alpine. For explanation see text. (Based on a map appearing on page 10 of *Economic Geography of the U.S.S.R.* by S. S. Bal'zak, V. F. Vasyutin and Y. G. Feigin. Copyright 1949 by the American Council of Learned Societies. Used with the permission of the Macmillan Company.)

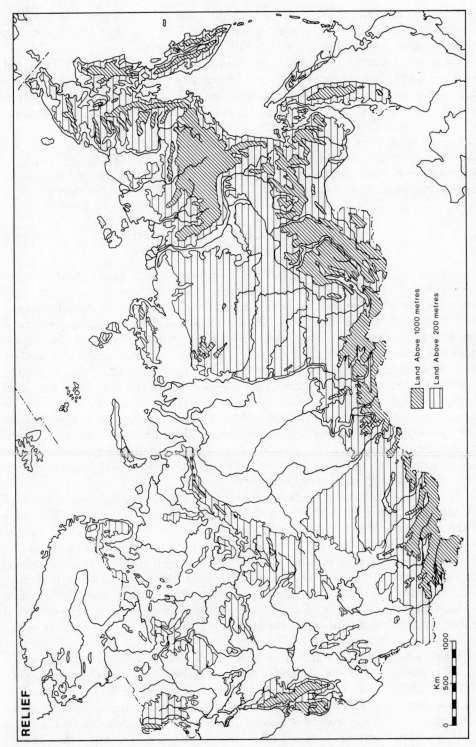

RELIEF

Land Above 1000 metres

Land Above 200 metres

Km
500   1000
0   500   1000

Fig. 4. Generalized relief map. Note the large areas less than 200 m above sea-level and the limited extent of areas above 1000 m.

different in their *relief*. The map of tectonic zones therefore distinguishes areas in which the structures of the periods named are exposed at or near the surface from areas where they are buried beneath later materials.

The general arrangement is fairly simple. There are, as already indicated, two pre-Cambrian platforms, the East European and the Siberian. Major areas of Caledonian folding are found in association with the latter, one belt occurring on its south-western side and another running in a south-west to north-east direction which cuts the Siberian platform into two parts. Hercynian structures occupy a wide area between the two platforms while belts of Mesozoic and Alpine folding run along the southern side of the East European platform, the Hercynian zone and the Siberian platform and continue around the eastern edge of the latter.

VOSTOCHNO–EVROPEYSKAYA PLATFORMA
(THE EAST EUROPEAN PLATFORM)

This occupies the bulk of the Soviet Union west of the Urals, but the resistant rocks of which it is composed outcrop at the surface over very limited parts of the area: the **Fenno-Scandian** or Baltic Shield in the north and the **Podol'sk-Azov** or Ukrainian Shield in the south. Elsewhere, the ancient rocks are covered by younger sedimentaries. The thickness of the sedimentary cover varies a great deal since the underlying platform has been considerably warped and faulted, and the surface rocks become progressively younger from north to south. The relief of this area, the **Vostochno-Evropeyskaya (Russkaya) Ravnina** (East European (Russian) Plain), is extremely gentle. Only in a very few places do heights exceed 300 m and even land above 200 m is limited in extent. A large part of the plain was affected by the Pleistocene glaciation and features of glacial deposition occur widely. In a region of this sort, small differences in height assume considerable importance and a number of distinct relief features, several of them of glacial origin, may be observed.

The Russian section of the **Baltic Shield** occupies the area between the Gulf of Finland and the White Sea, extending northward into the **Kol'skiy Poluostrov** (Kola Peninsula). Here, the ancient rocks are exposed at the surface and, although the relief is low, the area was near the centre of ice dispersion and shows features of glacial erosion. The surface has been swept bare of superficial deposits, but at the same time glacial drift accumulated in hollows so that there is an alternation of bare, ice-scraped rock with shallow depressions which often contain lakes and marshes. The greatest altitudes, over 1000 m, are reached in a few places in the **Khibiny Khrebet** (Khibin Mountains), but the bulk of this region lies well below 300 m.

The Baltic Shield is bounded on its southern side by a faulted trough which contains the Gulf of Finland, **Ladozhskoye Ozero** and **Onezhskoye Ozero** (Lakes Ladoga and Onega). South of this trough, the sedimentary rocks of the East European Plain begin. Here, Paleozoic materials dip south and south-eastwards towards the **Moscow Basin,** and have been eroded to give a series of escarpments and intervening lowlands. The most prominent scarp is that formed by the Carboniferous limestone which gives rise to the **Valdayskaya Vozvy-shennost'** (Valday Hills), running in a north-east to south-west direction from the southern end of Lake Onega to the northern frontier of the Belorussian Republic. These hills appear to have acted as a temporary barrier to ice movement and are capped by a moraine which raises their height to a maximum of 347 m. At one stage in the ice retreat, drainage north-westward from the Valday Hills was blocked by the ice front and large pro-glacial lakes accumulated between the glacier and rising ground. **Il'men' Ozero** (Lake Ilmen) is a remnant of one such lake. Another morainic ridge of considerable importance is the **Smolensko-Moskovskaya Vozvyshennost'** (Smolensk–Moscow Ridge), which runs in a north-easterly direction to pass just north of the capital. This zone of morainic ridges and large pro-glacial lakes is confined to the area covered by ice during the later of the two major advances which have left traces in the region, that of the *Würm* period. Here, as elsewhere in Europe, the Pleistocene ice age involved a number of separate advances of which the last two, the *Riss* and *Würm*, have definitely been identified in the U.S.S.R. The ice-sheets reached their greatest extent during the *Riss* advance and the final, *Würm*, advance reached only to the approximate latitude of Moscow. North of the line marking the maximum extent of the *Würm* ice-sheet, the features of glacial deposition are very fresh and have been relatively little modified by post-glacial river erosion. South of this dividing line, however, though features of glacial origin are by no means absent they are much less clearly marked and the pre-glacial relief is more readily visible. South of the latitude of Moscow, there is an east–west alternation of low plateaux and still lower valley plains. The **Sredne Russkaya Vozvyshennost'** (Central Russian Elevation) rises to a maximum of 286 m above sea-level and marks the south-western edge of the Moscow Basin. The plateau is bounded on its western side by the plains of the upper Dnepr and on the east by those of the upper Don. The latter in turn give way eastward to the **Privolzhskaya Vozvyshennost'** (pre-Volga Heights). This arrangement affected the movement of the *Riss* ice-sheet (older but more extensive than that of the *Würm*), which sent lobes of ice down the two valleys but left most of the Central Elevation and pre-Volga Heights clear of ice. The features resulting from deposition by the *Riss* ice-sheet have been largely removed by river action or covered by fluvio-glacial outwash, *loess* and *limon* laid down south of the *Würm* ice-front. However, the lowlands of the upper Dnepr and Don were areas in which large quantities of glacial melt-water accumulated and they remain very poorly drained. This is particularly the case in the **Poles'ye** or Pripet Marsh area.

Still further south, the presence of the Ukrainian Shield is reflected in the surface relief. The Archaean rocks reach the surface over a considerable part of the western Ukraine in the area known as the **Volyno-Podol'skaya Vozvy-shennost'** (Volyno-Podolsk Upland). This plateau diminishes in height eastwards across the Dnepr, but rises again to 325 m in the **Priazovskaya Vozvyshennost'** (pre-Azov Heights). The whole area is covered with *loess* or *limon*. Topographically, but not structurally, the pre-Azov Heights are continuous with the **Donetskiy Kryazh** (Donets Heights) which lie to the north-east. The latter, however, represent an area lying just north of the Ukrainian Shield in which the Archaean rocks are far below the surface and a great thickness of sedimentary materials (including Carboniferous deposits) was folded in Hercynian times. The resultant ridges in places exceed 350 m above sea-level.

South of the Ukrainian Massif, broad, gently sloping plains of *loess*-covered Tertiary sediments reach into the south-west Ukraine and the Crimean peninsula, where they are terminated by the Tertiary fold mountains of the Crimean range. In the **Azov–Caspian Depression,** the surface rocks are of Quaternary age.

The eastern section of the plain must now be considered, though in a little less detail. The major uplands are the **Timanskiy Kryazh** (Timan Range), a Caledonian fold system extending north-westward from the Urals to the Arctic Ocean, and the **Ufa Plateau,** a *horst* block on the western side of the Ural ranges. The bulk of the remainder of the area is composed of near horizontal sedimentary rocks among which the Permian is the most widespread outcrop. This zone is drained in the north by the Severnaya Dvina (Northern Dvina) river system and in the south by the Kama–Volga. While the former is an area of widespread glacial deposition, the latter for the most part escaped glaciation since the ice-sheets halted further north here than in the west. These eastern areas, which form the most monotonous part of the European plain, give way in the south to broad expanses of Quaternary lowland which extend north of the Caspian and mark the former limits of that sea.

URAL'SKIY KHREBET (THE URAL MOUNTAINS)

During the Paleozoic era, a depression developed in the earth's crust between the European and Siberian platforms. In this depression were deposited great thicknesses of sedimentary rocks derived from erosion of the East European and Siberian platforms to the west and east respectively. At the end of the Paleozoic, these sediments were thrown into folds by the Hercynian earth-movements and a vast mountain system came into being, stretching from the site of the present Urals to the Yenisey River. Sub-aerial denudation eventually reduced the whole area to a peneplane but in Tertiary times a relatively narrow western strip of territory was re-elevated and it is the subsequent erosion of this strip which has produced the present landforms of the Urals. The modern Ural Mountains thus represent only a small fraction of the Hercynian orogenic belt and owe their height to the Tertiary uplift and not to the original folding.

It is common practice to distinguish three subdivisions of the Urals. The **Severnyy Ural** (Northern Urals), extending from the Arctic Ocean to latitude 58°N., are the narrowest part of the system and consist of a single major ridge with subsidiary ridges parallel to it. The main ridge is composed of resistant materials and heights above 1500 m are reached in a few places. The **Sredniy Ural** (Central Urals), between latitudes 58° and 55°N., are developed on weaker rocks and are much lower, with a maximum height of only 800 m. In the **Yuzhnyy Ural** (Southern Urals), the system is a good deal wider than in either the centre or the north and comprises a series of ridges and valleys which fan out towards the south. One of these ridges contains the highest point in the whole system at 1638 m.

Despite their role as the traditional boundary between Europe and Asia, the Urals are in no way a serious barrier to movement between the two sections of the country. Maximum heights of little more than 1500 m are by no means impressive and the system takes the form of a series of parallel ridges separated by longitudinal depressions and broken by transverse valleys. As a result, low passes are plentiful, particularly in the central section which has long been the main gateway from Europe to Siberia. The importance of the Urals, as we shall see later, lies in their rich mineral resources which occur where ancient rocks have been exposed at the surface by long periods of erosion.

ZAPADNO-SIBIRSKAYA NIZMENNOST'
(THE WEST SIBERIAN LOWLAND)

This is the most remarkable single relief feature in the Soviet Union. For a distance of 1600 km from the Urals to the Yenisey, and for over 1900 km from north to south, the land never rises more than 180 m above sea-level. The Paleozoic basement, with its Hercynian structures, is buried by younger sedimentary rocks to depths as great as 1500 m. The area has been submerged for long periods on several occasions since the Paleozoic era and the sediments are everywhere horizontal or extremely gently tilted. By far the greater part of the surface is composed of Quaternary materials and only in the south-west, towards the border of Kazakhstan, are Tertiary rocks at all widespread. However, the Quaternaries vary a good deal in their composition. In the south, they include fluvio-glacial and *loess* deposits laid down beyond the margins of the ice-sheet; in the centre they are largely morainic; in the north they are marine, the product of an extensive advance of the sea in post-glacial times.

The region as a whole is extremely poorly drained, having a very gentle northward slope, and there are large areas of marsh and bog as well as innumerable lakes. The rivers, of which the Yenisey, Ob' and Irtysh are the most important, are wide and slow-flowing. Their shallow valleys are as much as 120 km across in places and the flood plains are up to 40 km in width. The south-western Tertiary zone is appreciably drier for climatic as well as topographic reasons, and it is here that the bulk of the settlement and agricultural land is to be found.

KAZAKHSKIY MELKOSOPOCHNIK (THE KAZAKH UPLAND)

This feature borders the West Siberian Lowland on its southern side. Folding took place in both Caledonian and Hercynian times, but the whole region, like the Urals, was reduced to a peneplane by sub-aerial denudation and re-elevated in more recent geological times so that it now consists of a series of plateaux and low hill-ranges. The highest elevations, about 1400 m, are found in the centre of the region, but the greater part lies between 450 and 900 m. Although in places a few patches of Mesozoic materials have been preserved, most of the surface is composed either of Paleozoic sedimentaries or pre-Cambrian metamorphic and igneous rocks. The ancient rocks have been exposed by long-continued denudation and are often very rich in minerals. The Kazakh Upland lies in the semi-desert and desert zones and permanent surface water is rare.

TURANSKAYA NIZMENNOST'
(THE TURANIAN (OR TURKESTAN) LOWLAND)

The Kazakh Upland is connected to the southern Urals by the **Turgayskaya Stolovaya Strana** (Turgay Plateau), an area of horizontally bedded Tertiary materials standing between 180 and 270 m above sea-level. Through the centre of the plateau runs a narrow corridor, the **Turgayskiye Vorota** (Turgay Gate), which forms a link, below 90 m, between the West Siberian and Turanian Lowlands. The latter, which occupies the greater part of Soviet Central Asia, is continuous, on its western side, with the Caspian Lowland, but is closed in on the north, east and south by the Urals, the Kazakh Upland and the young fold-mountain systems. Apart from the areas close to the Caspian which are, of course, below world sea-level, the most low-lying districts are found around the **Aral'skoye More** (Aral Sea). The largest rivers of the region, the Amu-Dar'ya and the Syr-Dar'ya, flow from the southern mountains into this sea which is the centre of a closed system of inland drainage. Several sizeable rivers, the Sarysu and the Chu, for example, disappear into the desert without even reaching the centre of the basin. The Aral Sea is a fairly shallow water-body: though the greatest depth is rather more than 60 m, most of it is less than 30 m deep. A second centre of inland drainage with a much smaller catchment area is provided by **Ozero Balkhash** (Lake Balkhash), whose average depth is only about 6 m.

A number of contrasting physiographic regions go to make up the **Turanskaya Nizmennost'**. Tertiary outcrops give rise to a number of low plateaux with steep, scarped edges where they overlook the more low-lying Quaternary areas. The **Plato Ustyurt** (Ust-Urt Plateau) stands at heights of 150–210 m between the Caspian and Aral Seas and is continued southward by the **Krasnovodskoye Plato** (Krasnovodsk Plateau), which in places reaches 300 m. The **Ravnina Bet-Pak-Dala** (Bet-Pak-Dala Plain), between the southern edge of the Kazakh Upland and the Syr-Dar'ya River, is largely between 270 and 300 m above sea-level.

The Turanian Lowland lies within the semi-desert and desert zones, mostly in the latter, and desert landforms predominate over the greater part of it. These are most clearly seen in a number of large sand deserts, which include the area south of Lake Balkhash, the **Peski Muyun-Kum** between the Chu River and the southern mountains, the **Peski Kyzyl-Kum** between the Syr-Dar'ya and Amu-Dar'ya and the **Peski Kara-Kum** between the latter river and the Caspian. In all these areas sand dunes, largely fixed by a scanty vegetation cover, alternate with clayey depressions where, because of surface accumulations of salt, vegetation is virtually absent.

The valleys of the major rivers form another distinctive region, with numerous river terraces and broad alluvial flood plains. These, together with the basins lying between the southern mountain ranges, offer great potentialities for the development of irrigated agriculture.

SIBIRSKAYA PLATFORMA
(THE SIBERIAN PLATFORM)

This is a zone in which structures are particularly complex and where relationships between structure and relief are by no means simple. It will be seen from the map of tectonic zones (Fig. 3) that the platform is divided into two parts by a belt of Caledonian folding which affected lower Paleozoic sediments laid down in a deep trough developed across the platform. To the west and north-west of this Caledonian belt is the **Anabar Shield.** Archaean materials are exposed at the surface over a small area in the north, but elsewhere lie deeply buried under sedimentary rocks. In the north-eastern part of the shield, and thence southwards to the upper Lena, these are lower Paleozoic in age, but over a wide area in the west they become much thicker and range from Lower Paleozoic to Permian, the latter outcropping over a very large area in the **Tunguska** (Tungus) Basin. The relief of this part of Siberia, however, bears little relation to the structural arrangement just described. The **Sredne-Sibirskoye Ploskogor'ye** (Central Siberian Plateau) is in fact a series of plateaux at various heights between 300 and 750 m, developed indiscriminately across Permian, Paleozoic and Archaean outcrops alike. The plateaux are in fact erosional features and represent uplifted erosion surfaces or peneplanes. In a few places, mountain ranges of particularly resistant rock rise above the general level, notably the **Gory Putorana** (Putoran Mountains), which reach above 2000 m. The plateau is dissected by river systems tributary to the Yenisey and Lena, which flow northwards below its western and eastern edges respectively. These include the Vilyuy in the east and the Nizhnaya (Lower) Tunguska, Podkamennaya (Stony) Tunguska and Angara in the west.

The plateau gives way northward to the **Severo-Sibirskaya Nizmennost'** (North Siberian Lowland) or Khatanga Depression, an eastward extension of the West Siberian Lowland. This in turn is bounded on its northern side by the Hercynian and Caledonian uplands of the **Poluostrov Taymyr** (Taymyr Peninsula).

Along the south-western edge of the plateau, the **Yeniseyskiy Kryazh** (Yenisey Ridge), Caledonian in origin, runs in a north-west to south-east direction, rising abruptly to more than 900 m from the eastern bank of the Yenisey River. The Caledonian fold ranges continue south-eastward into the **Sayanskiy Khrebet** (Sayan Range), whence they turn abruptly north-eastward to run along the south-eastern flank of the Anabar Shield. In this region, the mountain system has been subjected to peneplanation followed by re-elevation. The latter took the form of block faulting to give *horst* and *graben* country on a massive scale. The summits of the uplifted blocks often rise to more than

1800 m and are separated from the rift valleys by extremely steep fault scarps. One of the valleys contains **Ozero Baykal** (Lake Baykal) which is well over 600 km long and about 48 km across. While the mountains on either side reach 2000 m, the bottom of the lake is 1300 m below sea-level, a total height range of 3300 m. This is the world's deepest lake (maximum depth of water 1752 m) and has its own unique fauna.

The Caledonian belt as a whole decreases in altitude northwards and eventually passes into the **Middle Lena Basin** or **Tsentral'no-Yakutskaya Nizmennost'** (Central Yakut Basin), where the ancient structures are concealed beneath sedimentary rocks and where the surface is largely of Jurassic materials. This basin forms a lowland stretching nearly 900 km in an east–west direction between the eastern edge of the Siberian plateau and the mountains of the Far East.

East of the Caledonian belt, between the Middle Lena Basin and the Manchurian frontier, is the **Aldan Shield** over much of which Archaean metamorphic and igneous materials are exposed at the surface to give mountainous country of strong relief. The highest mountains are those of the **Stanovoy Khrebet** (Stanovoy Range) which rise to 2460 m.

THE SOUTHERN AND EASTERN MOUNTAIN RANGES

The remainder of the territory of the Soviet Union is occupied by complex fold-mountain systems. These are discussed together here, since they form a continuous barrier along the southern frontier and behind the Pacific coast, but it should be realized that they vary a great deal in their date of origin, rock type and landforms. As the map of tectonic zones (Fig. 3) indicates, the Caledonian system is most widespread in the southern part of eastern Siberia, where it forms an arc around the southern edge of the Anabar Shield, but also occurs on a smaller scale in Soviet Central Asia. Hercynian structures are found to the south of the Caledonian zone in both eastern Siberia and Central Asia, as well as in the Urals, and lie at depth in a structural trough, now generally low-lying, which runs from the Donbass, through the Azov–Caspian depression and across the Caspian into the western part of Central Asia. The Mesozoic system occupies much of the Far Eastern region to the east and south-east of the Siberian Platform. Mountains of Tertiary (Alpine) origin include the **Karpaty Khrebet** (Carpathians), the **Krymskiye Gory** (Crimean Mountains), the **Kavkazskiy Khrebet** (Caucasus) and the southernmost part of Central Asia. To the east of the last region they run outside Soviet territory, but recur along the Pacific coast and in Sakhalin and Kamchatka, where they form part of the great circum-Pacific ring of young fold mountains. There are important contrasts between the Caledonian and Hercynian mountain systems, on the one hand, and, on the other, those formed in Mesozoic and Alpine times. The former, having been exposed to the forces of sub-aerial denudation for long periods, are generally of fairly low elevation, with gentle slopes and broad, open valleys. Where steep slopes do occur, these are often the result of recent block faulting. One valuable result of the geological history of these areas, is the exposure at or near the surface of mineral-rich metamorphic and igneous rocks. The younger mountain zones, and particularly those produced by the Alpine orogeny, have not been denuded to anything like the same degree, though they have of course been vigorously dissected by rivers and glaciers. As a result, they stand at much greater heights and have sharper landforms and steeper slopes. Since they are composed of tightly folded sedimentary rocks they rarely contain an abundance of mineral wealth. In the account which follows, attention will be concentrated on the relief and landforms of the various mountain areas rather than on their geological structure.

Karpaty Khrebet (*The Carpathians*)

Since the addition to the Soviet Union after the Second World War of the former Czech province of Ruthenia (the sub-Carpathian Ukraine), a small section of the Carpathian Mountains with a maximum elevation of 1800 m is now included in Soviet territory.

Krymskiye Gory (*The Crimean Mountains*)

In comparison with the other great mountain systems of the U.S.S.R., these are a small mountainous belt some 32 km wide and 100 km long, backing the southern coast of the Crimean peninsula. There are three parallel ridges of which the southernmost is the highest reaching a little above 1500 m.

Kavkazskiy Khrebet (*The Caucasus*)

This is a much more complex system, which occupies the large isthmus between the Black Sea and the southern part of the Caspian. There are three major subdivisions: the **Bol'shoy Kavkaz** (Greater Caucasus or Main Caucasian Range), the Trans-Caucasian Depression and the **Malyy Kavkaz** (Lesser Caucasus).

Bol'shoy Kavkaz (The Greater Caucasus). A major anticlinal axis, structurally continuous with that of the Crimea, covers a distance of 1100 km from Novorossiysk on the Black Sea to the Apsheron peninsula on the Caspian. The western part of this anticline has been breached by erosion to expose a central core of granites and metamorphic rocks, flanked on either side by zones of folded Mesozoic materials. The crest of this core area exceeds 3600 m over a considerable distance, the highest point of all being **Gora El'brus**, Mt. Elbruz (5633 m). The eastern half of the anticline remains unbreached and Mesozoic rocks are continuous right across it. Here the main crest is somewhat lower (2100–2700 m), but a number of peaks rise much higher, reaching a maximum of 4477 m. The Greater Caucasus are flanked on their northern side by a zone of Tertiary plateaux which reach their widest extent in the **Stavropol'skiy**

Vozvyshennost' (Stavropol' Plateau) 570–780 m) which projects northward to separate the low-lying plains of the Kuban' and Terek rivers.

The Trans-Caucasian Depression itself falls into three parts. In the west is the **Kolkhida** (Rioni Lowland), a triangular plain with its base along the Black Sea and its apex about 100 km inland. This is separated by the granitic **Suramskiy Khrebet** (Suram Massif) from the much larger **Kura Lowland,** which runs from Tbilisi to the Caspian, a distance of about 500 km, and is 160 km across at its widest part.

Malyy Kavkaz (The Lesser Caucasus) is a good deal more varied in its structure than is the main range. On its northern side, numerous fold ranges, rising to about 3000 m, overlook the Rioni and Kura plains. To the south of these ranges is the **Armyanskoye Nagor'ye** (Armenian Plateau). Here, the original fold structures have been broken up by large-scale block faulting to give a series of plateaux and high-level basins. The picture is further complicated by the presence of vast spreads of Tertiary lavas, poured out in association with the rifting. **Ozero Sevan** (Lake Sevan) (1412 sq km) lies in a basin whose exit has been dammed by lava flows. The Lesser Caucasus fall away southward to the Araks valley which forms the Soviet frontier with Turkey and Iran.

The Mountains of Soviet Central Asia

The major fold axis represented by the Main Caucasian Range is continued to the east of the Caspian in the **Khrebet Bol'shoy Balkhan** and **Khrebet Kopet Dag** ranges. The latter, which form the northern edge of the Iranian Plateau, rise to heights of more than 2700 m along the southern frontier of the Turkmen Republic.

A vast and complex system of mountain ranges, basins and plateaux occupies the south-eastern part of Soviet Central Asia. The major elements are listed below.

Gory Pamir (The Pamirs) form part of the "Pamir Knot", a focal zone in the Alpine fold system from which high ranges stretch north-eastward along the Soviet-Chinese frontier, south-eastward into Kashmir and Tibet and westward into Afghanistan. The Soviet section occupies the eastern part of the Tadzhik Republic and contains the two highest points in the U.S.S.R.: **Pik Lenina,** (Lenin Peak) (7126 m) and **Pik Kommunizma** (Mt. Communism) (7500 m).

The Alay mountain system is separated from the Pamirs by the Surkhob valley. Its ranges run westward from the Chinese frontier and form the watershed between the Syr-Dar'ya and Amu-Dar'ya river systems. The crests exceed 3000 m in the Kirgiz and Tadzhik republics but further west, in Uzbekistan, they become progressively lower, terminating in a series of disconnected hills, 600–750 m high, rising above the Kyzyl-Kum desert.

The Basin of the Upper Amu-Dar'ya forms the southern frontier of the Uzbek and Tadzhik republics. Numerous south-flowing tributaries join the main river and are separated by high mountain chains which diverge southward from the Alay range.

The Basin of the Upper Syr-Dar'ya (Ferganskaya Dolina or Fergana Basin) is a fault-bounded trough standing between 300 and 450 m above sea-level. Being virtually surrounded by abrupt mountain slopes, this is a very well-defined physiographic unit.

The Tyan' Shan' (Tien Shan) mountain system is represented in the Soviet Union by a belt of territory between the Syr-Dar'ya and Balkhash basins. Here, as in the Alay, a broad complex of mountain ranges, rising well above 3000 m, declines towards the west. The system is prolonged north-westward into the desert by the **Kara-Tau** range. **Ozero Issyk-Kul'** (Lake Issyk-Kul) is a high altitude moraine-dammed lake.

The Balkhash Basin, between the Tyan' Shan' and the Kazakh Upland is a plateau, largely desert, between 300 and 360 m above sea-level.

The Upper Irtysh Basin occupies the north-eastern part of Kazakhstan and lies between the Kazakh Upland and the Altay Mountains.

From this brief description, it is readily apparent that the south-eastern part of Soviet Central Asia is an area of extreme diversity in relief. The mountains, save where they contain workable mineral deposits, are of relatively little value to mankind. The plateaux, basins and mountain-foot plains, however, with their fertile soils derived from *loess* and alluvium, are of great agricultural importance, especially where a plentiful supply of water is available.

The Mountains of Southern Siberia and the Far East

The alignment of the main mountain ranges in these regions is indicated in Fig. 5. Detailed description of the whole of this area is impossible within the compass of this volume and we must confine ourselves to a summary of the major elements.

The Altay and **Sayan** ranges constitute the southern part of Siberia from the Irtysh valley to Lake Baykal. The Altay system, between the Irtysh and Yenisey rivers, rises in places to more than 4500 m and its northward-projecting ridges enclose the **Kuznetsk** and **Minusinsk** basins. Beyond the Yenisey, the Sayan ranges form a barrier between Siberia proper and the Tuvinian Autonomous Republic.

Pribaykal'ye and Zabaykal'ye (Pre- and Trans-Baykalia) is a region of block-faulted mountain ranges and basins whose general features have already been commented upon. The major range in this region is the **Yablonovyy Khrebet** (Yablonovy), which forms a water divide between the Arctic and Pacific drainage basins.

Beyond the Yablonovy Mountains, two mountain systems diverge. One runs north-eastward around the eastern edge of the Siberian platform and fans out to occupy the whole area between the Lena and the Pacific Ocean. A second system occupies the southern part of the Far Eastern region between the Pacific and the Manchurian frontier.

The Far North-east. The Lena Basin is separated from areas draining into the Sea of Okhotsk by the **Stanovoy** and **Dzhugdzhur** ranges. The latter

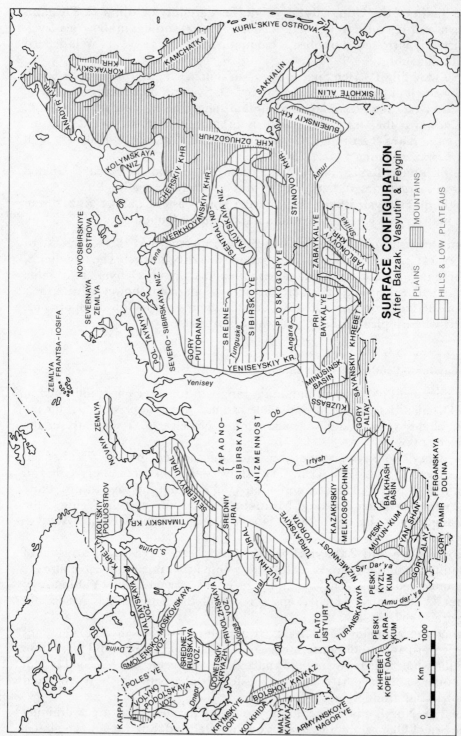

Fig. 5. Surface configuration. Most of the relief features mentioned in Chapter 1 are on this map. (Based on a map appearing on page 13 of *Economic Geography of the U.S.S.R.* by S. S. Bal'zak, V. F. Vasyutin and Y. G. Feigin, copyright 1949 by the American Council of Learned Societies. Used with the permission of the Macmillan Company.)

List of physical features, which appear on Figure 5 in vernacular form with their conventional English equivalents.

Vernacular	*Conventional English*
Alay, Gory	Alay Mts.
Altay, Gory	Altay Mts.
Amu-Dar'ya	Amu-Darya
Anadyr' Khrebet	Anadyr Range
Armyanskoye Nagor'ye	Armenian Plateau
Bol'shoy Kavkaz	Main Caucasus Range
Bureinskiy Khrebet	Bureya Range
Cherskiy Khrebet	Chersky Range
Donetskiy Kryazh	Donets Heights
Dzhugdzhur, Khrebet	Dzhugdzhur Range
Ferganskaya Dolina	Fergana Basin
Frantsa-Iosifa, Zemlya	Franz Josef Land
Karpaty	Carpathian Mts.
Kazakhskiy Melkosopochnik	Kazakh Upland
Kolkhida	Rioni Basin
Kol'skiy Poluostrov	Kola Peninsula
Kolymskaya Nizmennost'	Kolyma Lowland
Kopet Dag, Khrebet	Kopet Dag Range
Koryakskiy Khrebet	Koryak Range
Krymskiye Gory	Crimean Mts.
Kuril'skiye Ostrova	Kurile Islands
Malyy Kavkaz	Lesser Caucasus
Novosibirskiye Ostrova	New Siberian Islands
Pamir, Gory	Pamir Mts.
Peski Kara-Kum	Kara Kum Desert
Peski Kyzyl-Kum	Kyzyl Kum Desert
Peski Muyun-Kum	Muyun Kum Desert
Poles'ye	Polesye
Pribaykal'ye	Pre-Baykalia
Privolzhskaya Vozvyshennost'	Pre-Volga Heights
Putorana, Gory	Putoran Mts.
Sayanskiy Khrebet	Sayan Range
Severnaya Dvina	Northern Dvina
Severo-Sibirskaya Nizmennost'	North Siberian Lowland
Sikhote-Alin'	Sikhote Alin
Smolensko-Moskovskaya Vozvyshennost'	Smolensk-Moscow Ridge.
Sredne-Sibirskoye Ploskogor'ye	Central Siberian Plateau
Sredne Russkaya Vozvyshennost'	Central Russian Elevation
Stanovoy Khrebet	Stanovoy Range
Syr-Dar'ya	Syr-Darya
Taymyr, Poluostrov	Taymyr Peninsula
Timanskiy Kryazh	Timan Mts.
Tsentral'no-Yakutskaya Nizmennost'	Middle Lena Basin
Turanskaya Nizmennost'	Turanian Lowland
Turgayskiye Vorota	Turgay Gate
Tyan' Shan'	Tyan Shan (Tien Shan) Mts.
Ural, Severnyy	Northern Urals
Ural, Sredniy	Central Urals
Ural, Yuzhnyy	Southern Urals
Ustyurt, Plato	Ust Urt Plateau
Valdayskaya Vozvyshennost'	Valday Hills

Vernacular	*Conventional English*
Verkhoyanskiy Khrebet	Verkhoyansk Range
Volyno-Podol'skaya Vozvyshennost'	Volyno-Podolsk Upland
Yablonovyy Khrebet	Yablonovy Range
Yeniseyskiy Kryazh	Yenisey Mts.
Zabaykal'ye	Trans-Baykalia
Zapadnaya Dvina	Western Dvina
Zapadno-Sibirskaya Nizmennost'	West Siberian Lowland

is continued north-westward by the **Verkhoyanskiy** Mountains which reach the Arctic Ocean close to the Lena Delta. To the east of this system, the **Cherskiy** and **Kolymskiy** (Gydan) ranges enclose the northward-facing **Kolymskaya Nizmennost'** (Kolyma Basin). The **Chukotskiy (Anadyr')** Mountains are a separate system occupying the most remote north-eastern part of the Soviet Union, while the **Koryakskiy** (Koryak) and **Kamchatskiy (Sredinnyy)** ranges are part of an axis of folding which is continued southward through the Kurile Islands into Japan.

The Far South-east. A somewhat confused mountain zone in which the **Tukuringra** and **Bureinskiy** (Bureya) ranges are the most important, occurs between the Stanovoy ranges and the River Amur. Between the **Amur–Ussuri Lowland** and the Sea of Japan are the **Sikhote-Alin'** which reach a maximum height of nearly 3000 m.

In contrast to conditions over the Soviet Union as a whole, southern Siberia and the Far East are regions in which mountain territory predominates. The largest lowlands are in high latitudes of extremely harsh climate and extensive lowlands in more temperate latitudes are confined to the valleys of the Amur–Ussuri drainage system.

In conclusion, attention may be drawn to the simple map of surface configuration (Fig. 5) which divides the Soviet Union into areas of plain, hill or plateau and mountain. The major features of the country's relief are immediately apparent. True mountain territory is confined to the southern and eastern parts, the only exception being that provided by the Urals, while plains are virtually continuous over the European and West Siberian sections and over much of Soviet Central Asia.

CHAPTER 2

CLIMATE, SOILS, VEGETATION

CLIMATE

In all regional studies of climate, three major factors must be taken into account. These are latitude, altitude and distance from the sea.

Latitude

The Soviet Union stretches through a wide latitudinal range. Discounting the islands in the Arctic Ocean, Soviet territory extends from latitude 78°N. (Taymyr peninsula) to 36°N. (southern Turkmeniya). However, since the country widens northwards and has its greatest longitudinal extent close to the Arctic Circle, the bulk of the U.S.S.R. is situated in high latitudes. Three-quarters of the country is north of the 50th parallel and when we recall that the whole of the U.S.A. (with the exception of Alaska) is south of latitude 49°N., we can see that the U.S.S.R. is at a great disadvantage in this respect.

Latitudinal Distribution of the Land Area of the U.S.S.R.

	%
North of 70°N.	5.2
60–70°N.	34.3
50–60°N.	40.0
40–50°N.	16.8
South of 40°N.	2.8

Altitude

As the previous chapter has shown, the Soviet Union is predominantly a low-lying country, some three-quarters of which is less than 500 m above sea-level. As a result, districts in which the local climate is fundamentally affected by altitude are relatively restricted in extent. Mountainous zones are confined to southern and eastern parts of the country, where they form strong barriers between the U.S.S.R. and the outside world. In contrast, the interior is open northward to the Arctic Ocean and westward towards the Atlantic without the intervention of any major relief feature. This arrangement is extremely important in the effect it has on climatic conditions.

17

Distance from the Sea

The vast size of the Soviet Union ensures that some 75 per cent of its territory is more than 400 km from the sea, this distance reaching a maximum of nearly 2500 km in parts of southern Siberia. The longest coastline is that of the Arctic Ocean, frozen for more than half the year, while the Pacific shore is washed by cold currents and separated from the interior by high mountain ranges. As a result, maritime influences from these two water bodies are of limited importance, and it is the Atlantic which has most effect, its influence being discernible to a slight degree as far east as the Yenisey.

The combination of these three factors—high latitude, low altitude and great distance from the sea—means that the greater part of the Soviet Union has a continental climatic régime characterized by great extremes of temperature and relatively small amounts of rainfall. Only in a few peripheral areas such as the Crimean coast, Transcaucasia, parts of Central Asia and the Far East are other varieties of climate to be found.

Pressure and Winds (Fig. 6)

In the winter months, rapid cooling of the Asiatic land mass results in the development of an intense high-pressure system in the heart of the continent. This is generally centred in the vicinity of Lake Baykal where barometric pressure remains above 1030 millibars (mb) for long periods. A ridge of high pressure extends westward, roughly along latitude 50°N., and from this ridge there is a marked pressure gradient north-westwards toward the Icelandic low-pressure system. The ridge acts as a wind divide, winds to the north of the ridge being predominantly from the west or south-west while those to the south of the ridge come mainly from the east or north-east. Since westerly winds are, relatively speaking, mild and those from the east are cold, the temperature differences which one would expect to occur with latitude are much reduced. To the east of the Siberian high pressure there is a pressure gradient towards the low-pressure system developed in the area of the Aleutian Islands and winds blow from the north or north-west throughout the Soviet Far East. As a result, the ameliorating effect of the Pacific Ocean, which is in any case reduced by the presence of cold currents offshore, is confined to a narrow coastal strip.

In the summer months, pressure conditions are completely reversed. The Siberian high is replaced by a low-pressure system which is centred over Baluchistan, but extends north-eastward to the shores of the Arctic Ocean. Within the Soviet Union the depression is shallow (minimum 1000 mb) and pressure gradients are gentle. A weak ridge of high pressure extends eastward into the country along latitude 50°N. and this has some effect on wind direction. Over the European plain and western Siberia, winds are from the west and north-west, in Central Asia they blow from the north and north-east. Along the shores of the Arctic, they are mainly from the east. In the Far East, the prevailing winds are those of the south-easterly summer monsoon which affects the whole of the Pacific shore of Asia.

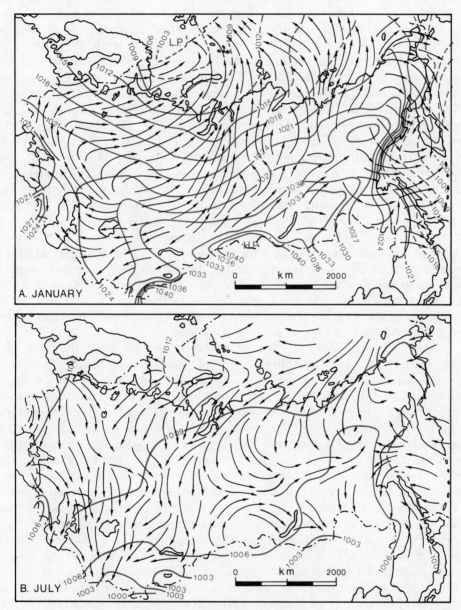

Fig. 6. Pressure conditions (red) and prevailing winds (black) in (A) January, and (B) July. Isobars at 3 mb intervals.

Temperature (Fig. 7)

In the winter, the influence of the Atlantic, carried by the prevailing westerlies, extends to the Yenisey and isotherms run from north-west to south-east over the European plain and the West Siberian Lowland, showing that in these regions the oceanic influence is more important than that of latitude, despite the big differences in insolation from north to south. The temperature of the coldest month at Arkhangel'sk (lat. 65°N.) is within one degree of that at Kazan' (lat. 55°N.). Conversely, there is a rapid falling-off of temperatures eastward along any given latitude, the lowest monthly means being −3°C at Kaliningrad, −10°C at Moscow, −14°C at Kazan' and −20°C at Tomsk in south-west Siberia. This gradation is continued eastward to beyond the Lena where Verkhoyansk (January mean −50°C) claims the distinction of the lowest temperature ever recorded outside the Antarctic, namely −70°C (or 126 degrees of frost on the Fahrenheit scale). Beyond this zone of extremely low temperatures, the isotherms again curve round to run from north to south, reflecting the slight warming effect of the Pacific. Even here, however, the term "warm" is wholly relative. Petropavlovsk-Kamchatskiy registers a January mean of −8°C, Okhotsk −25°C and even Vladivostok, which is in the same latitude as Florence, has a January mean of only −9°C. In fact there are very few areas in the U.S.S.R. where the coldest month has a mean above freezing point. These include the Crimean coast (Yalta 4°C) and Transcaucasia (Batumi 6°C). Most of Soviet Central Asia has low winter temperatures (Turtkul' −5°C). There is a small area along the southern margin with no monthly mean below zero, but even here frosts are a common occurrence.

In summer the effect of latitude on temperature does make itself felt and isotherms run in an east–west direction across most of the country. However, the moderating influence of the sea is apparent in the eastern and western extremities. In the Baltic region and over the European plain generally, isotherms trend towards the south-west, while in the Far East they turn abruptly southward, indicating the lowering of temperatures associated with the strong onshore winds of the summer monsoon. The lowest summer temperatures are recorded along the Arctic shores, where the 10°C July isotherm runs parallel to the coast (Sagastyr 5°C; Malyye Karmakuly 7°C). The highest July means are found in Soviet Central Asia where values exceed 25°C over large areas (Tashkent 27°C; Turtkul' 28°C). In the west the moderating influence of the Atlantic is reflected in the figures for Leningrad and Kaliningrad (both 17°C). On the Pacific coast, Vladivostok has an August mean of 20°C, but further north the summer is little warmer than it is along the shores of the Arctic (Petropavlovsk 11°C; Okhotsk 12°C). Summer temperatures vary much less from one part of the country to another than do those of winter. The highest and lowest July means are those of Tashkent (27°C) and Sagastyr (5°C), a difference of 22°C, whereas in January the range is from 6°C at Batumi to −50°C at Verkhoyansk, a difference of 56°C.

A characteristic of continental climates, which is well illustrated in the U.S.S.R., is the large temperature range between the hottest and coldest months.

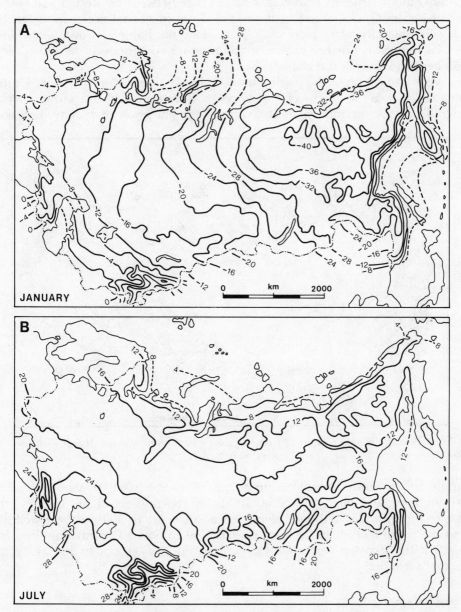

Fig. 7. Temperature conditions in (A) January, and (B) July. Isotherms at 4°C intervals. Note the very small areas with January temperatures above freezing.

Since winter temperatures vary more than those of summer, it follows that variations in the temperature range are largely a product of differences in the winter means. Thus the temperature range is at its maximum in the interior of eastern Siberia, where Verkhoyansk has a range between the hottest and coldest months of 65°C, the largest in the world. Even in coastal areas, however, the range is generally large, more than 17°C along the Baltic and over 34°C along the Pacific coast. Further details of temperature conditions at various stations will be found later in this chapter.

As an indication of the predominance of cold climates in the Soviet Union, mention should be made of the average duration of the frost-free period (Fig. 8). In the extreme north an average year has fewer than sixty days with

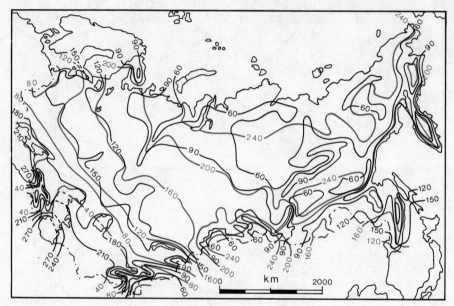

Fig. 8. Average annual number of frost-free days (black) and average duration of snow cover in days (red).

temperatures wholly above freezing point, the number rising to about 100 along the southern boundary of Siberia. In the European part of the country, the range is from about 120 days along the north coast to 200 on the Black Sea and a maximum of 340 in the southern Crimea. In Soviet Central Asia there is a north–south increase from about 150 in central Kazakhstan to 300 along the southern frontier.

Precipitation (Fig. 9)

The low relief and continental character of the U.S.S.R. ensure that precipitation over most of the country is moderate or light. The greater part of the inhabited area receives between 400 and 500 mm annually, figures typical of much of the European plain and West Siberian Lowland. Areas receiving larger

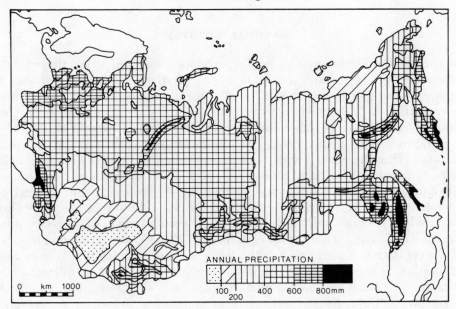

FIG. 9. Average annual precipitation (millimetres). Note the relatively small areas which receive more than 600 mm per annum.

amounts do so for a variety of reasons. The north-western part of the European plain (Riga 600 mm) shows the effect of the Atlantic maritime influence brought by the prevailing westerly winds which are also responsible for totals above 500 mm recorded along the western flank of the Urals. The higher parts of the mountains of Soviet Central Asia and south-west Siberia illustrate the effect of altitude on precipitation, amounts ranging from 400 mm in the foothills to 1250 mm or more on the higher peaks. In the Far East, the summer monsoon is responsible for heavy rain on the Sikhote-Alin' and in the Kamchatka peninsula. The highest totals of all are recorded on the south-western flank of the Caucasus where a combination of moist winds from the Black Sea and steep relief gives 2367 mm at Batumi.

There are large areas receiving less than 400 mm and these occur in two zones. The first comprises eastern Siberia and the interior lowlands of the Far East. Here there is a decline in precipitation northward towards the Arctic Ocean; lowlands from the Lena eastwards receive less than 200 mm, Sagastyr recording 82.5 mm. In the second area, Soviet Central Asia, there is a progressive diminution towards desert conditions in the centre of the region (Turtkul' 60 mm).

Throughout most of the Soviet Union, precipitation shows the marked summer maximum associated with the continental climate or, along the Pacific coast, with the onshore monsoon. The most important exception to this general rule is provided by the area along the eastern Black Sea coast from the Crimea to the Turkish frontier, where the predominance of winter depressions passing through the Black Sea gives a winter rainfall maximum. This is also the case in the interior of Central Asia, though here amounts in all seasons are, of course, small.

NATURAL REGIONS

The close interrelationships between climate, soils and vegetation make it imperative that these three elements in the physical environment should be considered together in any discussion of natural regions. The effect of climate on vegetation is fairly obvious. Any plant or group of plants can only grow within a certain, often quite limited range of climatic conditions, the most important elements in this respect being temperature, precipitation, humidity and wind. Thus the major vegetation belts are closely allied to the major climatic zones. Similarly, plants have certain requirements in the form of moisture and both inorganic and organic chemical compounds which they can only obtain from the soil so that the relationship between vegetation and soil type is equally close. Plants in turn affect the soil in which they grow particularly in so far as its organic content is concerned. That the major soil types (Fig. 10) are themselves largely a product of climate is, perhaps, a rather less familiar idea which may require some elaboration. It is particularly fitting that this concept should be discussed here since it was originally formulated by Russian soil scientists, notably by Dokuchayev. Dokuchayev and his contemporaries, working in the great European plain of Russia in the late nineteenth century, clearly demonstrated that the major soil belts are arranged in roughly parallel zones, running from east to west across the country, and are closely related to the major climatic zones. Soil is, in fact, the end product of the weathering processes and, since the character of these processes depends largely on climate, it is not surprising that soil and climate should be closely related. Precipitation and evaporation, by affecting the movement of soluble chemical compounds within the soil, have a profound effect on the chemical composition of the various soil layers or *horizons* which make up the vertical section or *profile* of the soil. Under a given set of climatic conditions, a major soil type (*zonal* soil) will develop, regardless of the parent material from which that soil is derived. Conversely, a particular rock type will break down into a variety of zonal soils in different areas according to the climatic conditions prevailing within each area. Within each major soil region, however, special local conditions of parent material and drainage may exert a strong enough influence to create a local soil type (e.g. a marsh soil) which differs appreciably from the zonal type. Such soils are said to be *intrazonal*. In areas where the fully mature soil profile associated with a particular climate has not yet developed (e.g. in areas of recent glacial deposition or of continuing alluvial deposition) an *azonal* soil type may be found. This too differs considerably from the mature, zonal soil. Thus the correspondence between climate, soil and vegetation belts is by no means exact in every respect. As a result, it is often expedient to choose one element only for the delineation of natural regions and, since it is the element most easily recognized on the ground, the choice frequently falls on vegetation. If vegetation regions are defined (Fig. 11), one can confidently expect them to reflect local conditions of soil and climate. This is the procedure adopted in this book where the following natural regions will be discussed in turn:—

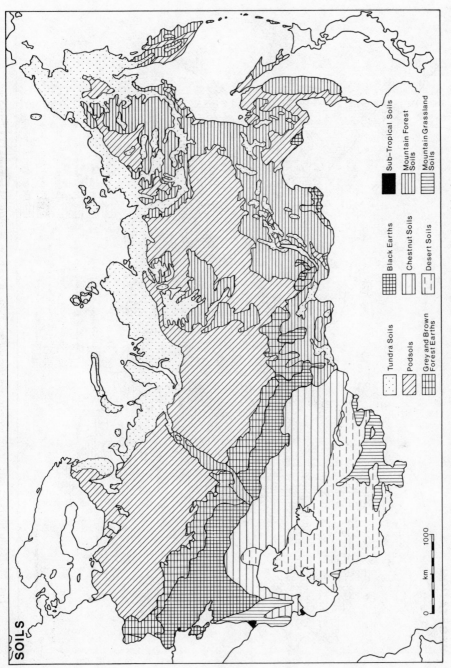

SOILS

Tundra Soils

Podsols

Grey and Brown
Forest Earths

Black Earths

Chestnut Soils

Desert Soils

Sub-Tropical Soils

Mountain Forest
Soils

Mountain Grassland
Soils

km   0   1000

Fig. 10. Soils. Only the major (zonal) soil types are distinguished.

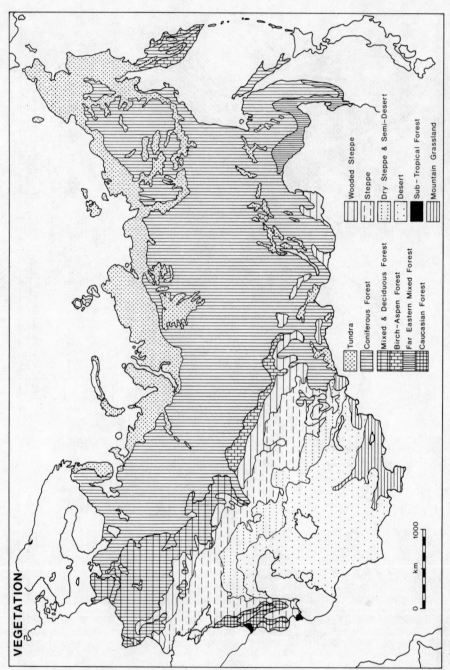

1. Tundra.
2. Coniferous forest.
3. Mixed and deciduous forest.
4. Wooded steppe.
5. Steppe.
6. Dry steppe and semi-desert.
7. Desert.
8. Humid sub-tropics.
9. Southern mountain areas.

1. Tundra

The tundra region, which occupies about 15 per cent of the area of the U.S.S.R., lies to the north of the 10°C July isotherm so that summers are cool as well as being short. Winters are cold, though less so than further inland, and become increasingly severe towards the east. Precipitation is light, ranging from about 375 mm along the shores of the Barents Sea to less than 100 mm near the Lena delta. The greater part falls as summer drizzle. Snow may occur at almost any time of the year, but snow cover is limited in extent and depth partly because of the limited precipitation and partly because of the strong winds which often sweep the surface clear. Atmospheric humidity is high, the sky is clouded over for at least 75 per cent of the time and coastal fogs are common.

Sagastyr (73° N., 125° E., 3 m a.s.l.)*

	J	F	M	A	M	J	J	A	S	O	N	D	Yr
Temp. (°C)	−37	−38	−35	−22	−15	0	5	3	1	−14	−20	−35	
Pptn. (mm)	2.5	2.5	0.0	0.0	5.1	10.2	7.6	35.6	10.2	2.5	2.5	5.1	83.8

* The position of climatic stations used as examples is shown in Fig. 12.

In all but the extreme western parts of the tundra region, the subsoil is permanently frozen, the top few feet thawing out in the summer months (permafrost layer: see below). As a result, drainage is extremely poor, particularly in flat, low-lying areas. Under these conditions, the decay of organic matter is slow and soils are highly acid. Where steeper slopes occur and drainage is better, leached podsols (see below) are found, but these are quite rare. Conditions are highly unfavourable to plant growth and the natural vegetation is very restricted in its range. In the northernmost area (*arctic tundra*) it is confined to lichen and mosses. Further south, in the *shrubby tundra*, stunted willow and birch occur together with bilberry and some grasses, but lichens and mosses remain widespread. The shrubby tundra gives way southward through a transitional zone where trees occur along river courses to the *wooded tundra*, in

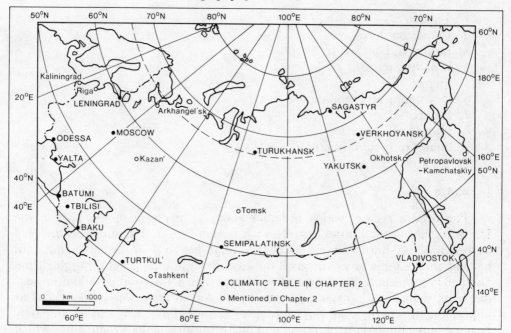

Fig. 12. Location of climatic stations for which data are given in Chapter 2.

which forest is common on interfluves as well as in valleys and sphagnum peat bogs become extremely widespread.

Permafrost is ground in which the moisture below the surface is permanently frozen and the permafrost zone covers no less than 10 million sq km, some 45 per cent of the territory of the U.S.S.R. The thickness of the permafrost layer varies from about one metre along the southern boundary to more than 350 m along the shores of the Arctic Ocean. The permanently frozen subsoil is covered by a layer which freezes in winter and thaws in summer, the depth to which it thaws depending on local conditions of climate, vegetation, relief and drainage. Permafrost is not continuous throughout the zone (Fig. 13), which falls into a number of subdivisions. These include islands of permafrost in thawing ground and islands of permafrost outside the main mass, some of them in the high mountain areas of the south. Thick seams of fossil ice 10–12 m below the surface of the ground, together with the preserved bodies of mammoth and hairy rhinoceros in the permafrost, indicate that it is a relic of the Pleistocene ice age and has been continuously in existence since that period. The total area of permafrost is now declining as the southern boundary retreats slowly northward, but the climate in the north of the zone is such as to ensure its persistence there for a long time to come. Permafrost is a major obstacle to the development of much of Siberia. Mining, transport development and any form of building works have to adopt special techniques which add appreciably to the cost of construction.

It should be noted that tundra conditions of climate, soil and vegetation occur on many high mountain areas of Siberia outside the main tundra zone.

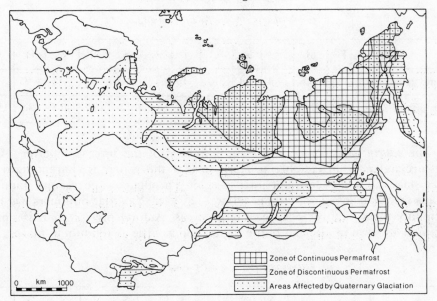

Fɪɢ. 13. The limits of the Quaternary glaciation and the extent of present day permafrost conditions.

2. Coniferous Forest (Taiga)

This is by far the largest and most continuous of the natural regions, occupying the European and West Siberian Lowlands north of latitudes 56–58°N. as well as the greater part of the U.S.S.R. east of the Yenisey. Over such a vast area there are considerable differences of climate, soil and vegetation, but the region has a basic unity derived from its extreme continentality, its podsolic soils and the predominance of coniferous forest. The taiga is usually divided into western and eastern sections along the line of the River Yenisey, reflecting the fact that temperature conditions become more extreme and rainfall diminishes from west to east.

In the *western taiga*, cyclonic influences from the Atlantic make themselves felt throughout the year. The total precipitation exceeds 500 mm over much of the European section and is between 400 and 500 mm in the West Siberian Lowland. More than 30 per cent falls as snow in the winter months. Summers are warm, with July means between 10° and 18°C; winters are long and cold, January means ranging from −8°C at Leningrad to −27°C along the middle Lena.

Leningrad (60° N., 30° E., 9 m a.s.l.)

	J	F	M	A	M	J	J	A	S	O	N	D	Yr
Temp. (°C)	−8	−8	−4	3	9	14	17	15	11	5	−1	−6	
Pptn. (mm)	22.9	20.3	22.9	22.9	43.2	45.7	68.6	68.6	50.8	43.2	35.6	30.5	475.2

Turukhansk (66° N., 88° E., 46 m a.s.l.)

	J	F	M	A	M	J	J	A	S	O	N	D	Yr
Temp. (°C)	−27	−20	−16	−8	1	10	15	12	−4	−5	−19	−25	
Pptn. (mm)	22.9	15.2	15.2	25.0	27.9	58.4	48.3	68.6	61.0	45.7	30.5	22.9	442.0

The *eastern taiga* comes under the influence of the intense Siberian high-pressure system from October to April so that the winter is characterized by clear skies, light snowfall and intense cold. Throughout the region, January means are far below zero, falling below −45°C in Yakutia. Summers are hot, with July means above 18°C over large areas. Annual precipitation is small: less than 400 mm in all parts of the region and as little as 100 mm in places.

Verkhoyansk (68° N., 133° E., 100 m a.s.l.)

	J	F	M	A	M	J	J	A	S	O	N	D	Yr
Temp. (°C)	−50	−45	−30	−13	2	12	15	11	2	−14	−37	−47	
Pptn. (mm)	5.1	2.5	0.0	2.5	5.1	12.7	30.5	22.9	5.1	5.1	5.1	5.1	101.7

Yakutsk (62° N., 130° E., 100 m a.s.l.)

	J	F	M	A	M	J	J	A	S	O	N	D	Yr
Temp. (°C)	−43	−37	−23	−9	5	15	19	15	6	−9	−30	−40	
Pptn. (mm)	22.9	5.1	10.2	15.2	27.9	53.3	43.2	66.0	30.5	35.6	15.2	22.9	348.0

The soils characteristic of the taiga zone are the *podsols* which, together with the modified podsols of the mixed and deciduous forest zone to the south, cover rather more than 50 per cent of the U.S.S.R. These soils are formed under a climate in which, over the year as a whole, precipitation exceeds evaporation and the movement of soil moisture is predominantly downward through the soil profile. The coniferous trees give rise to a highly acid raw humus layer at the surface, which decomposes slowly, producing soluble humic acids. These percolate through the soil, dissolving the iron and calcium minerals which are "leached out" of the upper horizon. The latter becomes pale in colour and highly acid. Soluble materials are redeposited at lower levels where an iron-rich hardpan often forms, impeding drainage in the upper horizons. In areas of low relief, particularly where the soil is heavy and impermeable, decomposition of organic matter and the process of leaching are hindered so that highly organic bog peat soils develop. This is particularly the case in the northern parts of the European and West Siberian Lowlands. East of the Yenisey, where the land is higher and precipitation less heavy, these conditions are generally limited to river valleys.

The character of taiga vegetation varies appreciably from one part of the zone to another. In the European section, spruce and pine are dominant but birch is also widespread. In the West Siberian Lowland, pine and larch are the main species over large areas but birch again occurs widely, particularly in the Yenisey valley, and rises to dominance along the southern fringe, where it forms an intermediate belt between the taiga and the wooded steppe (see below). Beyond the Yenisey, throughout both mountain and lowland areas, the larch is by far the most important species. Spruce is the main secondary species and is particularly widespread on the southern part of the central Siberian Plateau.

Although the taiga contains some of the world's largest areas of continuous forest it is by no means completely tree-covered. Large stretches of bog vegetation occur in badly drained lowland areas while, on the higher mountains, coniferous forest gives way to mountain tundra.

3. Mixed and Deciduous Forest

South of the taiga lies a belt of mixed forest in which deciduous trees become progressively more important, rising to dominance in the southern part of the zone. The climate of this region, which is virtually confined to the European part of the Soviet Union, is appreciably less severe than that of the taiga. Winters are still cold and there is heavy snowfall, but temperatures fluctuate a good deal so that, in the western part of the zone at least, temporary thaws sometimes occur. In summer, the mean temperature of the hottest month is everywhere below 21°C but midday shade temperatures above 35°C are common. Annual rainfall totals range from about 625 mm on the Baltic coast to less than 400 mm at Kazan'. Moscow, which is roughly in the centre of the zone, may be taken as showing fairly typical conditions.

Moscow (56° N., 38° E., 146 m a.s.l.)

	J	F	M	A	M	J	J	A	S	O	N	D	Yr
Temp. (°C)	−10	−8	−4	4	13	16	19	17	11	4	−2	−7	
Pptn. (mm)	27.9	22.9	30.5	38.1	48.3	50.8	71.1	73.7	55.9	35.6	40.6	38.1	533.5

The soils of the zone show a transition from true podsols in the north to *grey–brown forest earths* in the south. As temperatures become higher towards the south, evaporation increases and the leaching process becomes weaker. Thus the soils are less acid than those of the taiga and, because plant growth is more luxuriant, the organic content of the upper horizons is greater.

The predominant trees over the zone as a whole are oak and spruce, though a wide variety of other species also occurs including hornbeam, ash, maple, linden, birch and aspen. The zone becomes progressively narrower towards the east as winter temperatures become lower and rainfall diminishes so that the warmth- and moisture-loving deciduous trees disappear one by one. Thus the hornbeam, an indicator of particularly mild conditions, occurs only in the south-west, the oak and maple extend to the western foothills of the Urals, while only the birch and aspen, which are especially resistant to winter cold, are found beyond those mountains. As already indicated, a narrow belt of birch–aspen forest separates the taiga from the wooded steppe in the West Siberian Lowland.

The mixed and deciduous forest belt west of the Urals has been extensively cleared for agriculture.

Far Eastern mixed forest. Mixed forests also occur in the Amur and Ussuri valleys and along the southern coastal lowlands of the Far East. The climate here is transitional between the monsoon of the Pacific seaboard and the continental interior type, showing heavy summer rainfall and low winter temperatures for the latitude.

Vladivostok (43° N., 132° E., 143 m a.s.l.)

	J	F	M	A	M	J	J	A	S	O	N	D	Yr
Temp. (°C)	−14	−10	−3	4	9	14	18	20	17	9	−1	−10	
Pptn. (mm)	7.6	10.2	17.8	30.5	53.3	73.7	83.8	119.4	109.2	48.3	30.5	15.2	599.5

The vegetation is rich and varied including both deciduous and coniferous trees. Oak, birch, ash, pine, elm, linden and maple are all found in this region, the actual species being different from those of the European mixed forests. Along the river valleys there are stretches of rich grassland on black, alluvial soils.

4. Wooded Steppe

This zone, as its name suggests, is transitional between the forests to the north and the true steppe to the south. Its presence reflects the southward increase in temperatures and decline in precipitation across the European plain. The soils are usually described as *degraded chernozems* or *leached and podsolic black earths* and mark a further stage in the transition from true podsol to chernozem (see below). The leaching process is still present but is much weaker than in the forest soils to the north.

Vegetation in this zone is an alternation of deciduous woods and grassland. The tree cover gradually becomes less continuous and more open until, along the southern margins, woodland is confined to valley sides. The wooded steppe zone is continued across the West Siberian Lowland, but in eastern Siberia this type of vegetation is found only in relatively small lowland basins.

5. Steppe

This covers about 15 per cent of the U.S.S.R., stretching in a continuous belt from the western frontier to the Altay Mountains. In eastern Siberia it occurs in several lowland basins close to the southern frontier. The climate is both warmer and drier than in the forested zone to the north. Rainfall varies between 200 and 400 mm, decreasing towards the east and south, and there is a pronounced summer maximum. The later part of the summer, however, is usually rather dry, with low relative humidity and rapid evaporation. Summers are hot; the July mean temperature is between 20 and 25°C throughout the region. In winter there are three to five months with average temperatures below freezing point. The limited precipitation results in a thin and discontinuous snow cover so that the ground is exposed to the full effect of severe frost for a considerable period.

Odessa (46° N., 31° E., 64 m a.s.l.)

	J	F	M	A	M	J	J	A	S	O	N	D	Yr
Temp. (°C)	−3	−2	3	8	15	20	23	22	17	11	4	0	
Pptn. (mm)	22.9	17.8	27.9	27.9	33.0	58.4	53.3	30.5	35.6	27.9	40.6	33.0	408.8

Semipalatinsk (50° N., 80° E., 180 m a.s.l.)

	J	F	M	A	M	J	J	A	S	O	N	D	Yr
Temp (°C)	−16	−15	−10	3	14	19	22	19	13	3	−6	−13	
Pptn. (mm)	12.7	5.1	10.2	10.2	20.3	22.9	27.9	10.2	15.2	15.2	15.2	20.3	185.4

The steppelands are characterized by Black Earth (*chernozem*) soils. These take their name from their very dark-coloured upper horizon which is due to a high humus content, a direct result of the climatic conditions prevailing in the region. Winter frost and hot, dry summers* slow down the decomposition of organic matter, while the high summer evaporation rates prevent leaching so that the humus accumulates. Organic matter is derived from the rich cover of herbaceous vegetation typical of the steppe in its natural state and a humus-rich upper horizon more than 2 feet thick is characteristic throughout the Black Earth zone. Such soils are highly fertile but, being very friable, are liable to suffer soil erosion during the heavy downpours of convectional rain.

* Although summer is the season of maximum rainfall, this comes in heavy convectional downpours separated by lengthy periods of drought. Amounts of rain are in any case quite small over most of the region.

In European Russia there are very few areas in which the natural grassland of the steppe is preserved, vast stretches having been ploughed up during the last 200 years. The largest stretches of untouched steppe are found in south-west Siberia and northern Kazakhstan, the scene of the "virgin lands" project (see p. 75), where the cultivated area has been much extended since 1954. Pockets of steppeland also occur further east in Siberia.

6. Dry Steppe and Semi-desert

Southward from the steppe, rainfall continues to decrease and summer temperatures become higher in the dry steppe and semi-desert zone which runs eastward from a line midway between the Black Sea and the Caspian. Rainfall nowhere exceeds 250 mm, falling below 200 mm along the southern border. As a result, the vegetation cover becomes progressively poorer southward, the humus content of the soil decreases and chernozem is replaced by lighter-coloured *chestnut-brown soils*. These are often highly alkaline owing to the intense evaporation drawing salts to the surface, and in places saline soils (*solonets* and *solonchak*) develop. These carry a few grasses and shrubs adapted to conditions of high alkalinity.

7. Desert

This extends from the northern and eastern shores of the Caspian to the foothills of the Alay and Tyan' Shan' mountains. A combination of low annual rainfall, cold but short winters and long, extremely hot summers with intense evaporation results in highly alkaline soils and a poor, thin vegetation cover.

There are several different types of desert. Sand desert, interspersed with stony areas, is the most common, as in the Muyun-Kum, Kyzyl-Kum and

Turtkul' (41°N., 61°E., 80 m a.s.l.)

	J	F	M	A	M	J	J	A	S	O	N	D	Yr
Temp. (°C)	−5	−2	6	14	22	26	28	26	19	11	4	−1	
Pptn. (mm)	7.6	10.2	12.7	15.2	5.1	0.0	0.0	2.5	0.0	2.5	2.5	2.5	60.8

Kara-Kum. Grasses of various kinds, together with the saxaul "tree", make up the scanty natural vegetation. Around the shores of lakes, however, and along the courses of the few rivers that cross the desert, there are dense thickets of poplar and tamarisk. Clay deserts are the poorest of all with wide stretches virtually devoid of vegetation. These are most widespread on the Ustyurt and Bet Pak Dala plateaux and to the north of Lake Balkhash. The grey clay soils are interspersed with salt-encrusted *solonets* and *solonchak* areas.

8. Humid Sub-tropics

Sub-tropical conditions are found in two regions: the Black Sea coast of Transcaucasia (the Kolkhida or Colchis Lowland) and the smaller Lenkoran' Lowland adjoining the Persian frontier west of the Caspian. The climate of these areas is characterized by mild winters, hot summers and heavy rainfall with a winter maximum.

Batumi (42° N., 42° E., 6 m a.s.l.)

	J	F	M	A	M	J	J	A	S	O	N	D	Yr
Temp. (°C)	6	7	8	11	15	20	23	23	20	16	12	9	
Pptn. (mm)	259.1	152.4	157.4	127.0	71.1	149.9	152.4	208.3	302.3	223.5	309.9	254.0	2367.3

Soils are the *red and yellow earths* typical of the moist sub-tropics, and the dominant vegetation is broad-leafed forest of oak, hornbeam, beech and poplar. In the Kolkhida Lowland there is a dense undergrowth of evergreen bushes including holly, laurel and rhododendron as well as giant ferns, lianas and bamboo. Though small in area, these districts are of considerable agricultural importance, permitting the cultivation of crops that can be grown nowhere else in the country.

9. Southern Mountain Areas

With the exception of the humid sub-tropics, the natural regions so far described form vast belts of territory sweeping virtually without interruption across the plains and low plateaux which make up so much of the surface of the U.S.S.R. Along the southern borders of the country, however, a number of high mountain areas, by reason of their great altitudinal range, introduce more diversity, giving rise to numerous relatively small natural regions in close proximity to each other.

The smallest mountain area, that of the *southern Crimea*, can be dismissed quite briefly. The south coast of the peninsula has the nearest approach to a Mediterranean type of climate found in the Soviet Union though the marked summer drought typical of that climate is not present.

Yalta (44° N., 34° E., 41 m a.s.l.)

	J	F	M	A	M	J	J	A	S	O	N	D	Yr
Temp. (°C)	4	4	6	11	16	20	24	24	19	14	9	6	
Pptn. (mm)	45.7	40.6	40.6	33.0	27.9	38.1	33.0	22.9	35.6	43.2	50.8	76.2	487.6

The natural vegetation to a height of about 300 m above sea-level is of the Mediterranean forest type, with cypress, laurel, cork oak and Italian pine and shrubs such as myrtle, oleander and acacia. Above this is a belt of juniper–oak forest which in turn gives way to Crimean pine and then to beech. On the summit plateau there is mountain meadow grassland.

The Caucasus is a particularly complex region and nowhere else in the Soviet Union is there so great a diversity of physical conditions within such a relatively small area. This variety is a result partly of the position of the region between the Black and Caspian Seas and partly of the great range of altitude. There is a marked contrast between the western and eastern parts. The former is strongly influenced by the Black Sea, which produces, on the lower slopes at least, warm,

Tbilisi (42° N., 45° E., 412 m a.s.l.)

	J	F	M	A	M	J	J	A	S	O	N	D	Yr
Temp. (°C)	0	3	7	12	17	21	24	24	19	14	7	3	
Pptn. (mm)	15.2	20.3	27.9	53.3	73.7	68.6	53.3	40.6	50.8	33.0	27.9	20.3	484.9

Baku (40° N., 50° E., 0 m a.s.l.)

	J	F	M	A	M	J	J	A	S	O	N	D	Yr
Temp. (°C)	3	4	6	11	17	22	25	25	22	17	11	7	
Pptn. (mm)	33.0	22.9	20.3	20.3	15.2	7.6	5.1	5.1	20.3	30.5	30.5	30.5	241.3

moist conditions (see Batumi above). The Caspian, on the other hand, has little or no moderating effect on climate and the eastern Caucasus has dry climates with a large temperature range, conditions approaching those found in Soviet Central Asia.

In addition to contrasts between east and west, there is a strongly marked vertical zoning of natural conditions. Considerations of space prevent a full description of the many natural regions of the Caucasus but the description which follows gives the general picture.

The northern slope of the main Caucasian range shows clearly the effects of both altitude and the west–east diminution of rainfall. In the west, the steppe of the Don–Kuban lowlands gives way southward to a wooded steppe zone, which reaches its maximum extent on the Stavropol' Plateau. Above this is a belt of deciduous forest, which eventually grades upwards into the coniferous forests, alpine meadow and bare rock of the high mountains. In the east, in Dagestan, where conditions are much drier, the lowlands to the north of the main range are semi-desert. In the foothills, there is a belt of grassland with xerophytic shrubs which gives way to a narrow zone of deciduous forest.

Humid western Transcaucasia includes the sub-tropical Kolkhida Lowland (see above, p. 35). This is succeeded inland by the deciduous forest zone. North-westward, along the Black Sea coast, conditions become progressively drier and the vegetation on the lower slopes takes on the general character of the xerophytic Mediterranean forest. At intermediate levels between the latter and the coniferous forest of the higher areas is a zone of deciduous forest in which the beech is predominant.

Dry eastern Transcaucasia is roughly coincident with the basin of the Kura River. Beech forest occurs at intermediate levels on the north side of the basin and below these conditions become progressively drier towards the east, giving a gradation from steppe through semi-desert to desert along the Caspian shore.

The Armenian Plateau is largely under mountain grassland, though some of the heights rising above the general level are covered with coniferous forest. South-ward, diminishing precipitation brings a transition to dry steppe and semi-desert in the Yerevan basin.

Mountains of Soviet Central Asia. Here, again, vertical zoning is an obvious feature, precipitation increasing with altitude above the desert, while at the same time conditions at any particular height become progressively drier towards the east. Thus, basins within the mountain ranges, particularly those in the eastern part of the region, are very dry. Forest is not at all widespread, generally occurring at intermediate levels between the desert and dry steppe of the lowlands and foothills and the mountain grasslands of higher altitudes. It is the latter which form the most common vegetation type of the region. They include mountain meadows with a luxuriant grass cover in the better-watered districts and mountain steppe and semi-desert in the drier parts. Above the grasslands are zones of alpine flora, bare rock and perpetual snow.

The Altay Mountains show a basically similar arrangement. The steppeland of south-west Siberia rises, in the foothills, to heights of 350–600 m and is interspersed, in the higher parts of this zone, with coniferous forests of pine, fir, spruce and larch. Above this, mountain meadows rise to about 2700 m where they give way to mountain tundra.

Mountains of Siberia and the Far East. Over most of Siberia, the mountain slopes are covered with coniferous forest (see p. 30) and require no further description. In the Stanovoy and Sikhote-Alin' ranges of the Far East, however, deciduous forest extends to 450 m above sea-level, while in Kamchatka birch forest is widespread below 600 m.

CHAPTER 3

HISTORICAL GEOGRAPHY—
THE GROWTH OF THE RUSSIAN STATE

THE ESTABLISHMENT OF THE RUSSIAN STATE

The Soviet Union as it exists today covers a vast area of territory and includes within its boundaries a great variety of natural conditions. Having examined the physical geography of this enormous country, we must now turn our attention to its historical geography, tracing the stages by which so large an area has been brought within the frontiers of a single political unit.

Archaeological evidence points to the widespread occurrence of prehistoric settlement in what is now the southern part of European Russia, but we must begin our story at the point where the Slav people first appeared on the historical scene as a distinct and recognizable group, an event which took place in the middle Danube area a century or more before the birth of Christ. Early in the second century A.D., the Slavs suffered a serious defeat at the hands of the Romans and migrated north-eastwards through the Carpathians to establish themselves along the northern flank of those mountains. By the sixth century, they were in control of an area between the Vistula and Dnestr rivers which included the greater part of the Galician Plateau. From this early homeland, the Slavs spread out in several directions becoming divided, in the process, into three major groups. The west Slavs, represented today by the Poles, Slovaks and Czechs, at one time penetrated central Europe as far as the Elbe but were later driven eastward by the Teutonic peoples. A south Slav group developed in the Balkans, now the home of the Serbs, Croats and Slovenes, while the east Slavs advanced into the area which we now refer to as European Russia. It is this last group with which we are chiefly concerned.

By the ninth century A.D., the eastern Slavs had colonized much of the East European Plain, their zone of occupation extending as far north as Lake Ladoga and eastward to the upper reaches of the Volga. In extending their settlement over this area, the Slavs submerged the indigenous peoples, most of them Finno-Ugrian in origin (see below, p. 52), though traces of the latter remain in the make-up of the present-day population of the area. The southern limits of Slav settlement were roughly coincident with the boundary between forest and steppe. The steppelands at this time formed a zone of instability occupied by predominantly nomadic pastoral peoples who, on a number of occasions, burst out from their homeland in the interior of Asia and swept westward across the steppe into central Europe. The relationship of these pastoral peoples to their Slav neighbours varied. At times, the latter were left in peace, subject only to the nominal overlordship of the steppe-dwellers. On other occasions, particularly when a new wave of migrants arrived from the east, Slav settlements were attacked and trade disrupted. The steppe separated the Slav agriculturalists of the forest zone from the Black Sea coast where numerous small towns had been established by Greek settlers as early as the second century B.C. and were now under the control of the Byzantine Empire.

Slav settlement at this stage was virtually confined to the mixed forest and wooded steppe zones, areas which offered a number of distinct advantages to the early communities. Although the soils were not, in their natural state, so fertile as those of the steppe, they could be used to produce crops of grain, to rear cattle and to grow flax for the manufacture of linen cloth. At the same time, the virtually unlimited supply of timber was a vital source of both fuel and building material for settled agricultural communities, commodities in short supply in the open steppe. Furthermore, the forests and marshes were a natural defensive barrier against the recurrent danger of attack by the pastoral nomads, who in any case would have little interest in occupying an environment so dissimilar from that to which they were accustomed.

From the earliest days, the Slavs' economy was by no means wholly agricultural; indeed, some writers hold that agriculture was of relatively minor importance, at least in the early stages. The hunting of forest animals for their furs and hides and the collection of wax and honey were major activities, and trade in these commodities soon became widespread. Here, again, the mixed forest belt offered peculiar advantages. From the area to the west of the Moscow basin, the great rivers of the plain diverge towards the Baltic, Black and Caspian seas, their headwaters separated by short portages across low watersheds. These routes had been used in the days of Ancient Greece and were now revitalized by the eastern Slavs, who took a lively interest in the trade which flowed along them and particularly in contacts with Byzantium, via the Black Sea ports. A number of trading posts grew up along these routes and each became the centre of a loosely defined Slav principality. Such were Novgorod, Pskov, Smolensk, Chernigov and Kiyev, all of them on or near the major routeway which ran from the Gulf of Finland via the Neva, the Volkhov, Lake Il'men, the Lovat and the Dnepr to the Black Sea. Novgorod, near the northern end of the route, and Kiyev, towards the southern limit of the Slav domain, became the most important centres and, for a while, rival contenders for leadership.

From the second half of the ninth century onwards, there was considerable infiltration into the Slav settlement zone of Scandinavian elements, known variously as the Varangians or "men of Rus", who came as warriors and merchants and stayed to rule. The advent of the Varangians coincided with a period when the Slavs were under pressure from the steppe peoples and when it appeared that the trade routes to the south might be cut. The newcomers succeeded in organizing the Slavs sufficiently to enable them to resist these attacks and individual Scandinavian rulers came to power in the various Slav principalities. In A.D. 950, these came together in a loose federation known as Kiyevan Rus, with Kiyev as its capital. The word Rus, originally applied only to the Varangian minority, now came to be used for the population as a whole and it is from this term that the word Russia is derived. As time passed, the Scandinavian element was in any case assimilated into the majority. Kiyevan Rus survived for some three hundred years, throughout which period it traded extensively with Byzantium (Constantinople). As early as A.D. 998, Vladimir, Prince of Kiyev, was converted to Christianity by missionaries from Byzantium, an event which won Russia to the Eastern Orthodox Church in contrast to the lands along her western border which were Roman Catholic. Monasteries and schools were established, art and literature flourished and Russia was, for the first time, strongly influenced by the higher civilizations of the Mediterranean. Although trade was a major element in the economy of Kiyevan Rus, this early Russian state also engaged in agricultural pioneering. Large areas of the wooded steppe were cleared and cultivated and the settled areas of the forest zones were much expanded.

Towards the end of the twelfth century, however, the power of Kiyevan Rus began to wane. Struggles for supremacy between the rulers of the various principalities, occasioned in part at least by growing pressure on land resources, weakened the confederation whose headquarters at Kiyev was dangerously exposed to attack by the nomads of the steppe. The thirteenth century witnessed the most devastating outburst of nomadic peoples from the east, that of the Tatars. Kiyev fell and was sacked in 1240, Kiyevan Rus was destroyed and the greater part of European Russia came under Tatar control as part of a vast Tatar–Mongol empire stretching from eastern Europe to the shores of the Pacific Ocean.

The fall of Kiyev stimulated increased migration northward, a process which may be looked upon as a retreat by the Russians away from their vulnerable southern frontier into a zone of relative security. Protected by the barriers of swamp and forest from the ravages of the Tatar horsemen, the Russians led their own life, subject only to a general Tatar overlordship expressed mainly in the payment of tribute to the Khans. Over the years, the Russian population steadily grew and there was a sustained expansion of the area settled and cleared for agriculture. In such a situation, Russia was cut off from the mainstream of European civilization for more than two centuries. The Russian princes acted as tax-collecting agents for their Asiatic overlords and as such their authority over their own people was recognized and, indeed, encouraged by the Tatars, who often went as far as to allocate small bodies of troops to the various Russian rulers to assist them in collecting taxes. As a result, the power of the Russian princes increased until eventually they were able to assert their full independence from the Tatars.

One of the areas most affected by these developments was the district known as Suzdal', situated between the upper Volga and its tributary the Oka. Protected by strong natural frontiers of marsh, forest and river, Suzdal' attracted a particularly numerous population and soon became the most densely settled part of the European plain. At the same time, it was particularly well suited to engage in trade, lying as it did within easy reach of the headwaters of numerous navigable rivers. It was this area which became the heart of the Principality of Moscow (Muscovy).

As the wealth and power of Muscovy increased, its rulers gradually expanded its frontiers, gaining control over neighbouring, rival principalities either by treaty or by conquest. Muscovy was the first to assert its independence from the Tatars and thus took the lead in freeing European Russia from Tatar rule. By the sixteenth century, the ruler of Moscow was by far the most powerful of the Russian princes, and in 1547 Ivan the Terrible was proclaimed "Tsar of all the Russias", setting the seal on his supremacy. Meanwhile the power of the Tatars had greatly declined. Not only had they lost control of most of the forest zone, they had also suffered from a good deal of internal strife and their domain had been split into a number of Khanates such as those of Kazan', Astrakhan' and the Crimea. At the same time they had lost territory in the west to the expanding Kingdom of Lithuania, which had advanced south-eastward to the Black Sea, occupying, among other places, Kiyev itself.

Muscovy, as it emerged in the mid-sixteenth century, was the direct ancestor of the modern Russian state. It was hemmed in on all sides by rival powers: the Tatars to the south and east, the Lithuanians and Poles to the west and south-west and the Swedes, periodically penetrating across the Baltic, to the north-west. The history of Russia from this time forward may be considered as the process of expansion outwards from the core area of the Moscow principality (Fig. 14). Thus it is now convenient to examine this expansion in each direction in turn rather than to attempt a chronological description of the process as a whole.

THE EAST

The first stage of this expansion took place under Ivan the Terrible (1533–84). Striking out south-eastward to the middle Volga, he captured Kazan' in 1552 and four years later had extended Russian power to the Caspian Sea, taking Astrakhan' in 1556. The southern steppelands of European Russia were thus cut off from Central Asia by a belt of Russian-held territory along the Volga. In the ensuing hundred years, Russia devoted most of her attention to rapid expansion eastward into Siberia. Russian settlers had reached the western flank of the Urals in the thirteenth century and, by the sixteenth, had crossed to the eastern side, opening routes into the vast unexplored territories beyond.

Asia north of the Himalayas contains two very different geographical zones. In the south, high mountain ranges separate steppe and desert basins which were the homes of nomadic pastoralists and groups of oasis cultivators. To the north, covering the bulk of the area known as Siberia, were vast stretches of forest and marsh, occupied by numerous small, primitive tribes, engaged in hunting, trapping and stock-rearing with little in the way of settled agriculture. To the Tatars, these northern forests had been a forbidding area which they left strictly alone, but to the Russians they provided an environment which, though more harsh, was basically similar to that of their European homeland. Russian penetration of this zone, once begun, proceeded rapidly, meeting little or no

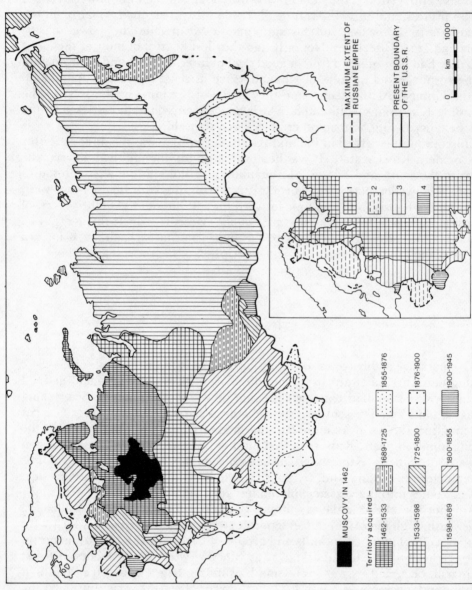

Fig. 14. Territorial expansion of the Russian Empire and the U.S.S.R. from 1462 to the present. The inset shows twentieth-century changes along the western frontier: 1, areas which have remained under Russian/Soviet control throughout the present century (except during the two world wars); 2, areas lost after 1913 and never regained; 3, areas lost after 1913 and regained 1939–45; 4, areas gained in 1945 which had never before been

resistance from the unorganized and ill-equipped indigenous peoples. The main lines of movement were along the great Siberian rivers, with occasional use of the difficult Arctic sea route between their mouths. Tobol'sk, near the southern edge of the forest, was the scene of the final defeat of the Tatars in 1587. The Russians reached the Yenisey in 1609, the Lena in 1630, Yakutsk in 1632 and Okhotsk, on the Pacific, in 1649. By the end of the seventeenth century, Russia was in control of more than 3000 km of the Pacific coast. The Russian penetration of Siberia bears many similarities to the opening up of the forested zone of North America. First came the explorers, closely followed by hunters, trappers, mineral prospectors and traders. As the area of colonization was extended and the indigenous peoples subdued, the new lands were taken over and organized by the State, which established military posts and provided garrisons and administrative personnel. Siberia also came to be a useful place of exile for criminals and political dissidents who were set to work in the mines, as well as a refuge for religious minorities and for small numbers of agricultural settlers freed or escaping from serfdom. It was not until much later, however, that Russian power extended southward into the wooded steppe and steppe zones of south-west Siberia, the most favourable area for agriculture, and large-scale peasant colonization did not take place until the nineteenth century.

In the far north-east, expansion continued virtually unchecked. Kamchatka and the Anadyr peninsula were annexed in the eighteenth century and the impetus of Russian exploration carried settlers across the Bering Strait into Alaska and southward along the eastern shores of the Pacific. These North American territories, however, were much too remote from the centre of Russian power ever to come fully under the control of Moscow and were finally abandoned in 1867 when Alaska was sold to the United States for $7,200,000, surely one of the best bargains in history.

Towards the southern limits of their Far Eastern domains, the Russians came into contact and conflict with rival powers. The Chinese Empire of the seventeenth century was expanding northward and was sufficiently powerful to put a stop to the southward expansion of the Russian Empire. In 1689 the Treaty of Nerchinsk fixed the boundary between the two roughly along the line of the Stanovy Mountains. With the decline of Chinese power in the nineteenth century, Russia was again able to expand. In 1858 the frontier was advanced to the lower Amur and in 1859 the area between that river and the Pacific coast was ceded by China. Vladivostok was founded in 1860. Sakhalin and the Kurile Islands were under joint Russo-Japanese control from 1854 until 1875 when, by an agreement between the two powers, Sakhalin passed to Russia and the Kuriles to Japan. From the mid-nineteenth century onwards, the main challenge to Russian expansion in the Far East was the growing strength of Japan and it was at the hands of the Japanese that Russia received her first major set-back. At the time of the Sino-Japanese War of 1895, Russia brought great pressure to bear on China, gaining a lease of the Kwantung peninsula (Port Arthur) and a "sphere of influence" in northern Manchuria. Between 1900 and 1904 much of Manchuria, in fact if not in law, was dominated by Russia, who was particularly interested in that country's industrial resources which appeared much greater than those of her own Far Eastern territories. It was, in fact, largely for control of Manchuria that the Russo-Japanese War was fought. This conflict resulted in a decisive victory for Japan, which established that country in the eyes of the world as a Great Power. Russia lost control of Manchuria, Port Arthur and the southern part of Sakhalin. The last of these was regained in 1945 together with the Kuriles, and Port Arthur was again leased from China until 1955. Manchuria, together with North Korea, in which the Russians at one time showed great interest, are now firmly within the Chinese sphere, the former as part of the Chinese Peoples' Republic and the latter as a close ally. Today, the Soviet Union and China, two of the world's largest powers in both territory and population, face each other along a frontier of some 3200 km.

Mention should be made at this stage of the Mongolian Peoples' Republic, formerly known as Outer Mongolia. This territory was within the Russian sphere of influence in the late nineteenth century but in 1911 became a province of China. In 1921 it became an independent Communist state and for the past forty years has had close economic and political links with Russia.

CENTRAL ASIA

We must now turn our attention to Russian expansion in a different direction, south-eastward from the European plain into Turkestan or Central Asia. South of the forested zone of western Siberia which, as we have already seen, came under Russian control in the seventeenth century, lies a fairly narrow belt of wooded steppe beyond which are the dry steppelands of northern Kazakhstan. These in turn are separated by the formidable natural barrier of the Central Asian deserts from the southern mountain zones which form the present frontiers of the Soviet Union. The foothills and basins of these mountains had, for many centuries before they came under Russian control, supported numerous populations, engaged mainly in intensive irrigated agriculture and organized into a number of Moslem Khanates centred on such ancient cities as Tashkent, Bukhara and Samarkand. Compared with the rapid Russian advance into Siberia, progress in this direction was slow. The wooded steppe belt was occupied during the seventeenth century and there were further small gains in the eighteenth, but as late as 1800 the frontier of the Russian Empire lay roughly along the present boundary of the Kazakh Republic. During the nineteenth century, however, the advance was much more rapid. The nomadic Kazakhs were no match for the warrior Cossacks who formed the spearhead of the Russian advance and, by 1850, the steppe and desert zones had been largely absorbed. The Khanates of the south now became the meeting ground of two spheres of influence, the Russian pressing southward, and the British reaching out from north-west India, each attempting to gain control of the area or at least to prevent it from falling into the other's hands. While the British confined their activities to political intrigue, the Russians mounted full-scale military expeditions across the desert and succeeded in subjugating the Moslem Khanates, despite the latter's attempts to maintain their independence by playing off one Great Power against the other. Tashkent fell to the Russians in 1865, Bukhara and Samarkand in 1868; and in

1888 an agreed frontier was demarcated between the Russian Empire and Afghanistan, the latter being supported by Britain as a buffer state on the north-west frontier of her Indian Empire. Some of the Khanates succeeded in maintaining at least a nominal independence as Russian "protectorates" well into the twentieth century. Bukhara and Khiva survived until after the Soviet Revolution, eventually joining the U.S.S.R. in 1920.

THE CAUCASUS

A rather similar series of events took place in the lands between the Black and Caspian Seas. Although the latter was reached by the Russians in the mid-sixteenth century, 200 years elapsed before they were established on the Sea of Azov; Rostov, at the mouth of the Don, was founded in 1761. At the end of the eighteenth century, the frontier of the Russian Empire lay along the northern flank of the Main Caucasian Range. The mountains themselves were the home of numerous small groups of Christian and Moslem peoples, fiercely independent and often engaged in fighting among themselves. In 1801 the Russians took control of the Kingdom of Georgia, when the last native king, George XIII, abdicated in favour of Tsar Alexander I, and parts of Azerbaydzhan and Armenia were annexed from Persia in 1828, but it took some fifty years of intermittent warfare before the last of the Caucasian tribes were overcome in 1864. The Russian frontier in Transcaucasia reached approximately its present position in 1878 and for a while extended westward to include the area around Kars which was ultimately returned to Turkey in 1921.

THE EUROPEAN WEST AND SOUTH

The reader will have noticed that, between the Treaty of Nerchinsk in 1689 and the beginning of the nineteenth century, there was little expansion of the Russian domain in Asia. The intervening eighteenth century was in fact a period during which the attention of the Tsars was concentrated on their European frontiers and it was during the eighteenth and nineteenth centuries that these frontiers reached, and in places extended well beyond, their present position. Although Russian power had extended rapidly from its centre in Moscow to its most distant limits along the Pacific coast, there had been no simultaneous advance to the west or south-west. Russia, at the beginning of the eighteenth century, was isolated from the rest of Europe by rival powers and in particular had access to neither the Baltic nor the Black Sea. This lack of contact with the outside world does much to explain the backwardness of Russia compared with other European powers. She was, for example, virtually untouched by the Renaissance or the Reformation which did so much to mould the modern civilizations of western Europe. West European traders and explorers, such as the Englishman Chancellor in 1550, made contact with Muscovy by the long and difficult sea route round the North Cape to Arkhangel'sk, itself separated from the capital by nearly 1000 km of forest and swamp. Contact with the Mediterranean via the Black Sea was possible only through Turkish waters.

During the reign of Peter the Great (1689–1725) the position was greatly changed. His victory in the war against Sweden (1700–21) resulted in the annexation of much of Latvia, the whole of Estonia and the lands around the head of the Gulf of Finland. Here, in 1703, Peter founded his "window on the west", St. Petersburg, which remained the capital until 1918. Peter the Great travelled widely in western Europe, including England, was much impressed by what he saw there and made strenuous efforts to modernize Russia. He imported foreign technicians to assist in the development of industries, especially metal-working in the Urals and shipbuilding at St. Petersburg, and founded the Russian Navy. At the same time he set about reducing the powers of the turbulent Russian nobility and overhauled the archaic administrative system. The highly centralized autocratic government which characterized the last 200 years of Tsarist rule was largely a product of Peter's reforms.

To the west and south-west of Peter the Great's Empire, a belt of territory from Lithuania to the Ukraine was under Polish control. The central Ukraine, the Crimea and the Black Sea coast were nominally part of the Turkish Ottoman Empire, though local power was often in the hands of Cossack chieftains. During the eighteenth century, these areas were brought within the Russian Empire. The capture of Sevastopol' in 1783 and Odessa in 1792 established Russian power along the northern shores of the Black Sea, a process completed with the annexation of Moldavia from Turkey in 1812. The western frontier was slowly advanced until, by 1800, it had reached approximately its present position. Advances beyond this line involved the annexation of Finland from Sweden in 1809 and the occupation of the Duchy of Warsaw as a result of the Vienna Settlement of 1815, which followed the Napoleonic Wars.

Russia's defeat at the hands of Germany in the First World War and her weakness in the period immediately after the Bolshevik Revolution resulted in large losses of territory in the west. By the Treaty of Brest Litovsk (March 1918), the whole of the Ukraine, much of Belorussia and the Baltic provinces were ceded to Germany, though the latter's collapse eight months later prevented the treaty from coming into effect. Nevertheless, the Soviet Union as it finally emerged in 1921 was a good deal smaller than the Russian Empire of 1913. A resurrected Poland had pushed its frontier well to the east, Lithuania, Latvia, Estonia and Finland had become independent states and Bessarabia had been lost to Romania.

Growing Soviet power was accompanied by renewed westward expansion. The "winter war" of 1939–40 between the U.S.S.R. and Finland was followed by Russian annexation of the Karelian isthmus and frontier areas further north. The three Baltic states were incorporated into the Soviet Union in 1940 and Bessarabia and Bukovina transferred from Romania in the same year. Following the defeat of Germany in 1945, the frontier with Poland was moved some 240 km westward (roughly to the so-called Curzon line, the Russo-Polish frontier agreed by the Allied Powers in 1919). The northern part of East Prussia, annexed from Germany, part of former Polish Galicia and Ruthenia (the sub-Carpathian Ukraine), transferred from Czechoslovakia, were the only territories gained in 1945 which had not at some time been part of the Russian Empire, so that the

U.S.S.R. today remains appreciably smaller than the Russian Empire at its maximum extent.

It is highly significant that the most important changes in the Russian frontiers during the present century have taken place in the west. Here, where no natural boundaries exist and where rival powers have faced the U.S.S.R. across the great plains of eastern Europe, a weakened Soviet Union was obliged to retreat in the years immediately after the Revolution, only to advance again as her strength was renewed. The smaller states of east-central Europe have been obliged to play the role of buffer states between the U.S.S.R. and the Western powers. In the inter-war years their strongly anti-Communist governments were often supported by western European countries. In the post-war period, as Communist "Peoples' Republics" they have generally been aligned with the Soviet Union against the west. It is this western frontier which has been the danger zone for the U.S.S.R. since 1917 and events along this frontier have received most attention from the Soviet rulers. With the growing strength of China and the recent demonstration that her relations with the U.S.S.R. are not at all times completely friendly, we may expect to see more attention paid in the future by the Soviet Union to events along her Asiatic frontiers.

CHAPTER 4

THE PEOPLES OF THE SOVIET UNION

In the last chapter we saw how, by a process of expansion lasting some 400 years, the Russian Empire spread out from its original small nucleus in the Moscow basin to cover more than one-third of Europe and nearly half of Asia. As a result of this expansion, many different peoples were brought within the boundaries of the Russian Empire, and the Soviet Union, inheriting the latter's widespread territorial possessions, also inherited its extremely diverse population. The various peoples of the U.S.S.R. differ in their racial, cultural, historical and religious backgrounds, and in the languages they speak. The census of 1970 recognized the existence, within the Soviet Union, of no fewer than 104 different national groups. Since the distinguishing feature of nationality is the possession of its own language, we can best examine the distribution of the peoples of the U.S.S.R. on the basis of linguistic groupings.

Many of the 104 nationalities are, of course, very small, no fewer than twenty-seven having less than 10,000 members each. A further twenty-eight are between 10,000 and 100,000 strong and there are twenty-four of 100,000 to 500,000. This does, however, leave twenty-five sizeable groups of people, each numbering more than half a million. These are listed in Table 1.

The fact that these many nationalities live within a single political unit has, of course, made it possible for them to migrate and to become intermingled to a progressively greater degree, particularly during the present century. Thus, individual groups are no longer restricted, if indeed they ever were, to clearly

TABLE 1. *Major nationalities of the U.S.S.R. population (000's) at the census of 1970*

Russians	129,015		
Ukrainians	40,753	Germans	1,846
Uzbeks	9,195	Chuvash	1,694
Belorussians	9,052	Turkmen	1,525
Tatars	5,931	Kirgiz	1,452
Kazakhs	5,299	Latvians	1,430
Azerbaydzhanians	4,380	Mordovians	1,263
Armenians	3,559	Bashkirs	1,240
Georgians	3,245	Poles	1,167
Moldavians	2,698	Estonians	1,007
Lithuanians	2,665	Udmurts	704
Jews	2,151	Chechens	613
Tadzhiks	2,136	Mari	599

defined settlement areas of their own. Nevertheless, there are still particular districts in which one or other nationality is in a strong majority among the local population and such areas are generally recognized as the homelands of the various groups (see below, Chapter 5).

The present-day distribution of national groups within the Soviet Union (Fig. 15) is the product of historical processes already examined (Chapter 3) and of prehistoric migrations about which much less is known. The distribution is further complicated by the fact that the U.S.S.R. contains representatives of at least two of the world's major language families which now occupy areas of territory so intricately inter-mixed that it is impossible to draw a simple dividing line between them. The larger of these language families is the *Indo-European*, which originated somewhere between central Europe and central Asia and spread outwards to occupy a zone stretching from the Atlantic to India. The second and much smaller family is known as the *Ural-Altaic*. This, too, is a regional name indicating an origin in the steppe zone which stretches across south-west Siberia from the Urals to the Altay, whence it spread not only north-eastward through Siberia to the Pacific but also westward into Europe and south-westward into the Middle East.* As they spread out from their original centres, these linguistic families became differentiated into groups and the groups into individual languages, eventually resulting in the great diversity of tongues now spoken in the U.S.S.R.

THE INDO-EUROPEAN LANGUAGES

The largest representative of this family is the *Slav* group of tongues, spoken by more than three-quarters of the total population. By far the most numerous Slav-speakers are the **Russians** (Great Russians) who account for some 54 per cent of the Soviet people. Russians are in a majority over most, though not all, the forest belt of Europe. Since it was they who played the leading role in the expansion of the Empire, they are also in a majority in areas which, before they came under Russian control, were quite thinly populated, notably a belt of territory running across south-west Siberia and along the southern frontier to the Pacific. As a result of continued migration, particularly to areas of recent agricultural and industrial development, Russians are now to be found in practically all inhabited parts of the country, particularly in the towns, where they form a small but influential minority of the local population. The second largest national group are the **Ukrainians** (Little Russians), with about 17 per cent of the total, who began to emerge as a distinct group from the thirteenth century onwards. While the Great Russians, in their northward colonization of the forest zone, merged to a considerable degree with the indigenous Finnic

---

* The migrations which resulted in the diffusion of these early languages took place in remote prehistoric times when the physical environment of the regions involved was very different from that of the present day. Large areas which are now semi-desert, for example, were probably at that time steppe or even wooded steppe and offered no barrier to movement.

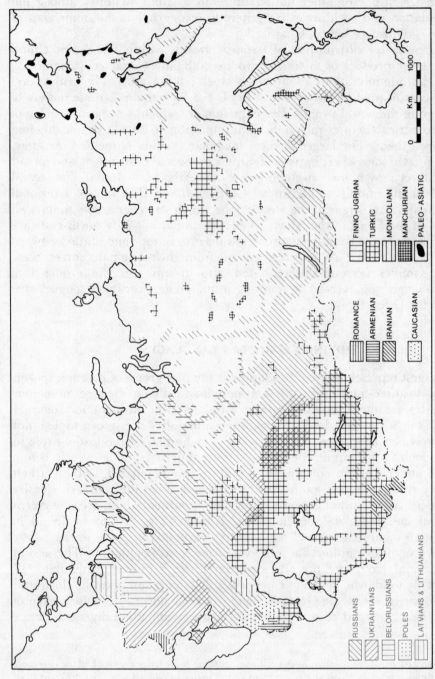

FIG. 15. Nationalities of the U.S.S.R. on a linguistic basis. Slav and Baltic groups are shown by red shading, others by black.

peoples (see below), the Ukrainians, centred on the wooded steppe, received an admixture of Turkic blood as a result of the Tatar invasions. However, the Ukrainians remain basically European, speaking a Slav language closely allied to Great Russian. With the Russians they played an important part in the later stages of the colonization of Siberia where they are widely distributed, particularly in rural areas. The **Belorussians** (White Russians) are a much smaller group, accounting for less than 4 per cent of the Soviet population. They too are an offshoot of the original Slav stock, in this case much influenced by contacts with the Poles and Lithuanians to the west.

Another Slav group of significant size within the Soviet Union are the **Poles**, found mainly in western parts of the Ukraine and Belorussia, which were at various times under Polish control and where the population is a mixed one.

Thus, even among the Slav majority in the Soviet Union, there is considerable linguistic variety, to which must be added differences in culture, particularly religion. Before the Revolution at least, the Slavs were all nominally Christian. Practically all Russians and the majority of Ukrainians and Belorussians were Greek Orthodox, a result of the conversion of Kiyevan Rus in the tenth century, but large numbers of Ukrainians, together with the Poles, were Roman Catholic.

There are a number of non-Slav, Indo-European peoples within the European part of the Soviet Union. The *Baltic* group includes two peoples, the **Lithuanians** (Roman Catholic) and the **Latvians** (Protestant) whose cultures, including their languages, are quite distinct from those of the Russians. They have been much affected by contacts with the Poles and Baltic Germans respectively and (like their Estonian neighbours) still use the Roman as distinct from the Russian (Cyrillic) script. In the extreme south-west live the **Moldavians** of Bessarabia, linguistically allied to the Romanians, speaking a Romance language derived from Latin but adhering predominantly to the Orthodox church. It is perhaps surprising to find the **Germans** among the larger nationalities of the U.S.S.R. There was a considerable immigration of German-speaking farmers and artisans, often refugees from religious or political persecution, from the eighteenth century onwards. Before the Second World War there was a sizeable concentration of Germans along the Volga River near Saratov. During the war, however, they were accused of collaboration with the invaders and dispersed to other parts of the country. There are very few Germans living in that part of East Prussia occupied by the Soviet Union since 1945. The local German population migrated to the west and was replaced by Russian settlers.

The number of **Jews** in the Soviet Union is much below its pre-war level as a result of German attempts at their extermination in the occupied territories and, more recently, some emigration. The majority of Jews, however, are still to be found in the European part of the country, though there are also small Jewish communities of very ancient origin in the Caucasus and Central Asia. The Jewish Autonomous Oblast (see below, Chapter 5), established in the Far East in 1934 as a national home for Soviet Jews, contains less than 5 per cent of the Jewish population.

THE URAL-ALTAIC LANGUAGES

European Russia contains a number of peoples who speak languages belonging to the *Finno-Ugrian* subdivision of the Ural-Altaic family. These peoples were in possession of much of the forest zone before it was settled by the Slavs and, although in many places they were assimilated by the latter, there are still areas where they remain a distinct group. Finno-Ugrian peoples are found in two main areas. In the extreme north-west of the country, they are represented by the **Estonians,** who have been much affected by contacts with German speakers, as well as the less numerous **Karelians,** who are closely related to their Finnish neighbours. A second predominantly Finno-Ugrian zone stretches south from the Arctic Ocean to the middle reaches of the Volga. The **Nentsy** occupy northern Siberia roughly between longitude 45° and 110°E. To the south of them are the **Komi** on the west side of the Urals and the **Khanty** and **Mansi** on the east. These are small and rather primitive groups. The **Mordovians, Mari** and **Udmurts,** however, who occupy an area stretching from west of the Volga to the flanks of the Urals, total about $2\frac{1}{2}$ million. Though Asiatic in physical appearance and retaining their Finno-Ugrian languages, these peoples are more advanced than their northern cousins. They are predominantly Orthodox Christian in religion and are for the most part settled farmers.

A second language group derived from the Ural-Altaic root is the *Turkic* whose speakers form the largest group in the Soviet Union after the Slavs, totalling more than 30 million. Moslem in religion, Turkic peoples occupy the greater part of Soviet Central Asia, where they are represented by the **Uzbeks, Turkmen, Kirgiz** and **Kazakhs.** As is the case with other Moslem peoples of the Middle East, these groups include both nomadic pastoralists and settled farmers, the latter now in the majority. Turkic speakers have spread out in several directions from their early homeland. To the west they have penetrated via northern Iran into the Caucasus (and, of course, into Turkey) where they are represented by the **Azerbaydzhanians.** To the north-west, the area between the Volga and the southern Urals is the home of the Turkic-speaking **Bashkirs, Tatars** and **Chuvash.** They have also moved north-eastward into Siberia. The **Khakass, Altays** and **Tuvinians** in the south and the **Yakuts** of the Lena valley and beyond also belong to the same group.

The peoples of Soviet Central Asia are Moslems. Most of them speak Turkic languages, but the **Tadzhiks** speak a language belonging to the *Iranian* subdivision of the Indo-European.

The Caucasus is a zone of extraordinarily complex linguistic patterns. A Turkic language is spoken by the Moslems of Azerbaydzhan, while the **Armenians,** who belong to the Gregorian Church, and the **Osetins** speak languages belonging to the Indo-European family. The other peoples of the Caucasus speak languages which are quite unrelated to either the Indo-European or the Ural-Altaic family. These languages also differ widely from each other, and their classification presents great difficulties. The *Iberian* group includes **Georgian** and several other closely related south Caucasian languages. The Georgians are Greek Orthodox and have a literary tradition dating back to the Middle Ages.

The Georgians and Armenians each have their own highly distinctive alphabet and script which are totally different both from each other and from the Cyrillic and Roman. There are literally dozens of other mutually unintelligible languages spoken in the Caucasus, especially among the various tribes of Moslem mountaineers living north of the main range. Among these we may note the *Circassian* group including **Cherkess, Abkhazian** and **Kabardinian,** which have clearly marked similarities, and the languages spoken by the **Chechen-Ingush** and **Lesghian** tribesmen, which resemble neither the Iberian, the Circassian nor each other.

NATIONALITIES OF THE U.S.S.R. ON A LINGUISTIC BASIS

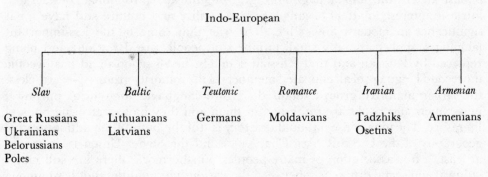

Slav	*Baltic*	*Teutonic*	*Romance*	*Iranian*	*Armenian*
Great Russians	Lithuanians	Germans	Moldavians	Tadzhiks	Armenians
Ukrainians	Latvians			Osetins	
Belorussians					
Poles					

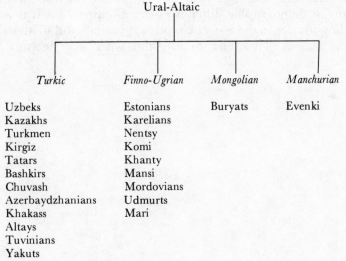

Turkic	*Finno-Ugrian*	*Mongolian*	*Manchurian*
Uzbeks	Estonians	Buryats	Evenki
Kazakhs	Karelians		
Turkmen	Nentsy		
Kirgiz	Komi		
Tatars	Khanty		
Bashkirs	Mansi		
Chuvash	Mordovians		
Azerbaydzhanians	Udmurts		
Khakass	Mari		
Altays			
Tuvinians			
Yakuts			

Caucasian groups belonging to neither of the two major families: Georgians, Chechen-Ingush, Cherkess, Kabardinians, Abkhazian, Lesghian

Paleo-Asiatic groups: Ainu, Koryaks, Chukchi

Note. Only peoples mentioned in the text are shown in this table. Those omitted are, however, of little importance.

Mention should also be made of a number of Asiatic peoples whose languages are probably of Ural-Altaic origin but are distinct from both Turkic and Finno-Ugrian groups. The **Buryats,** concentrated in the Baykal region, represent the *Mongolian* group. *Manchurian* languages are spoken by numerous small and rather primitive peoples of eastern Siberia and the Far East such as the **Evenki.** Finally, in the extreme east and north-east are the small groups often referred to as the *Paleo-Asiatics,* including the **Ainu** of Sakhalin, the **Koryaks** of Kamchatka and the **Chukchi** of the Arctic.

Enough has been said to indicate that the ethnic and linguistic composition of the Soviet population is extremely complex and difficult to describe in an orderly fashion. The diagram on page 53, while open to criticism, attempts to show the main relationships among the various groups whose actual distribution is illustrated by the map on page 50 (Fig. 15). Quite apart from their considerable intrinsic interest, matters of language, nationality and culture still have great significance in modern Soviet life. It is true that some of the less-important languages, spoken by only small numbers of people, are dying out and being replaced by Russian and that Russian is taught in all schools and has become the second language of all educated members of the minority groups. Nevertheless, the larger minority groups retain their own languages for official purposes; newspapers and books are published in them and they have a growing body of literature. The idea of the national territory is still the basis of the administrative geography of the U.S.S.R. (see Chapter 5) and the Soviet Union is, in theory at least, a free association of many peoples. Furthermore, there are still major cultural and social differences between the various nationalities, not least among which are major demographic differences (see Chapter 11). It is as inaccurate and misleading to refer to the Soviet Union as "Russia" and to all its inhabitants as "Russians", as it is to refer to England when one intends the United Kingdom.

CHAPTER 5

THE ADMINISTRATIVE STRUCTURE
OF THE U.S.S.R.

Our discussion, in the last chapter, of the linguistic composition of the Soviet people leads naturally to a consideration of the U.S.S.R.'s administrative structure since this is based, to a large degree, on the distribution of the various national groups. The country is divided into political–administrative areas of various kinds, the boundaries of which are intended to enclose the main settlement zones of the various national groups. These divisions are represented in the central organs of Soviet government; thus a brief description of the political organization of the country is relevant at this stage.

The highest legislative and administrative body of the U.S.S.R. is the *Supreme Soviet* which meets at least twice a year. This body elects a *Praesidium* which carries on the work of government between sessions though all its decisions are subject to the approval of the Supreme Soviet. The latter is divided into two chambers, the *Soviet of the Union* and the *Soviet of Nationalities*. The former is elected by the direct ballot of all citizens over the age of 18, and for this purpose the country is divided into electoral areas, each of which has some 300,000 inhabitants and elects one deputy to the Soviet of the Union. The Soviet of Nationalities, however, is elected on the basis of the various political units which make up the U.S.S.R. Each union republic sends 32 deputies to the Soviet of Nationalities, each autonomous republic sends 11, autonomous oblasts 5 and autonomous okrugs one each. Since all measures must be approved by both houses, the Soviet of Nationalities, in theory at least, acts as a regulating body which ensures that the interests of the smaller groups are not overridden in the interests of the larger ones. For example, the Estonian Republic, with a population of only 1.4 million, sends 32 deputies to this body, the same number as the Russian Republic, which has nearly 135 million inhabitants.

POLITICAL DIVISIONS

The various types of political unit based on nationality have been named in the preceding paragraph. In addition, there are a number of purely administrative units which are based on economic rather than on ethnic considerations. Our next task is to examine the political–administrative structure of the Soviet Union and the relationships between the different units. These can be arranged into a series of levels or grades, units in the lower grades being subordinate to those at higher levels, the degree of local autonomy diminishing down the scale. The arrangement is shown schematically in Fig. 16.

At the top of the tree are the full union republics, of which there are at present fifteen (Fig. 17). The Russian Republic, because of the large number of lower grade units within its boundaries, has been referred to as "a Union within a Union" and bears the cumbersome title of the **Rossiyskaya Sovetskaya Federativnaya Sotsialisticheskaya Respublika** (Russian Soviet Federative Socialist Republic (R.S.F.S.R.)). This covers the whole of the Russian homeland in Europe together with Siberia and the Far East where, as a result of the immigration of Russian settlers, people of Russian origin are in the overall majority. The other fourteen **Sovetskaya Sotsialisticheskaya Respublika** (Soviet Socialist Republics (S.S.R.s)) represent the more numerous and more advanced minority peoples of the Soviet Union. However, because under the Soviet constitution S.S.R.s have the right to secede from the Union, each must have a frontier with the outside world. Thus a number of nationalities of considerable size, the Tatars for example, can never attain full S.S.R. status since their secession would create the "political anomaly" of an independent state completely surrounded by Soviet territory. The fourteen S.S.R.s fall readily into three groups whose distribution reflects the pattern of nationalities already discussed. Six of them, the **Estonskaya** (Estonian), **Latviyskaya** (Latvian), **Litovskaya** (Lithuanian), **Belorusskaya** (Belorussian), **Ukrainskaya** (Ukrainian) and **Moldavskaya** (Moldavian) S.S.R.s, lie along the western frontier. Three more, the **Gruzinskaya** (Georgian), **Armyanskaya** (Armenian) and **Azerbaydzhanskaya** (Azerbaydzhanian) S.S.R.s are found in Transcaucasia, while Soviet Central Asia is divided among the **Kazakhskaya** (Kazakh), **Turkmenskaya** (Turkmen), **Uzbekskaya** (Uzbek), **Tadzhikskaya** (Tadzhik) and **Kirgizskaya** (Kirgiz) S.S.R.s.

It is interesting to note that the federal nature of the Soviet Union is to some extent recognized in international affairs. At the United Nations, Belorussia and the Ukraine have seats and voting rights in addition to those held by the U.S.S.R. as a whole.

Subordinate to the S.S.R.s are the **Avtonomnaya Sovetskaya Sotsialisticheskaya Respublika** (Autonomous Soviet Socialist Republics (A.S.S.R.s)) of which there are at present twenty. These are widely scattered but there are certain regions within which they are particularly numerous. A group of A.S.S.R.s in the area between the Volga and the Urals reflects the presence there of various Finno-Ugrian and Turkic minorities. The presence of numerous A.S.S.R.s in the Caucasus is a further indication of the mixed composition of the population of that area. Other autonomous republics are to be found in Central Asia and southern Siberia.

Those parts of the R.S.F.S.R. which do not have A.S.S.R. status, together with the larger S.S.R.s, are divided into *oblasts* and *krays* (see Fig. 16). These have no direct political significance—they send no representatives to the Soviet of Nationalities—but are purely administrative and economic in function. The oblast is the basic economic unit into which all but a few of the smaller

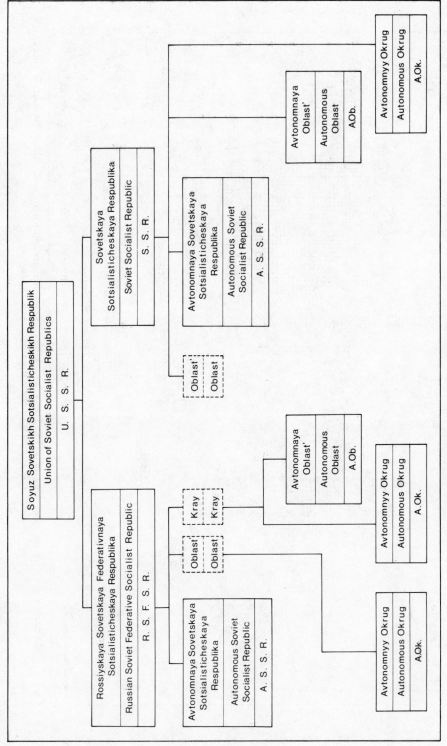

FIG. 16. The political–administrative structure of the U.S.S.R.

57

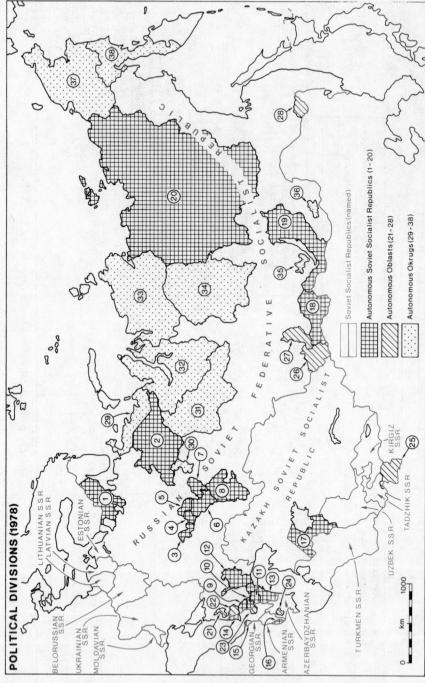

POLITICAL DIVISIONS (1978)

BELORUSSIAN S.S.R.
UKRAINIAN S.S.R.
MOLDAVIAN S.S.R.
LITHUANIAN S.S.R.
LATVIAN S.S.R.
ESTONIAN S.S.R.

RUSSIAN SOVIET FEDERATIVE SOCIALIST REPUBLIC

KAZAKH SOVIET SOCIALIST REPUBLIC

UZBEK S.S.R.
TADZHIK S.S.R.
KIRGIZ S.S.R.
TURKMEN S.S.R.

GEORGIAN S.S.R.
ARMENIAN S.S.R.
AZERBAYDZHANIAN S.S.R.

km 0   1000

Soviet Socialist Republics (named)
Autonomous Soviet Socialist Republics (1–20)
Autonomous Oblasts (21–28)
Autonomous Okrugs (29–38)

Fig. 17. Political divisions at the beginning of 1978. The fifteen Union Republics are shown in red, other divisions in black. For a full list of these divisions, *see facing page.*

S.S.R.s are divided. Its boundaries are usually drawn to embrace a variety of economic activities, each oblast having both an industrial and an agricultural element. The administrative centre is usually an industrial town which gives its name to the oblast. The kray is found only in the R.S.F.S.R. It is similar in function to the oblast but is usually much larger in size and occurs only in areas which are relatively thinly populated or recently developed. The kray is more directly subordinate to the central government than the oblast, the latter having a measure of local autonomy in economic matters. At present there are only six krays, those of Primorskiy and Khabarovsk in the Far East, Krasnoyarsk and Altay in Siberia, and Krasnodar and Stavropol' on the northern side of the Caucasus. Oblasts and krays are divided into *rayons* and these in turn into urban and rural districts.

Returning to our consideration of political as distinct from purely economic units, we find a third grade below the level of S.S.R.s and A.S.S.R.s. This is the **Avtonomnaya Oblast'** (autonomous oblast (A.Ob.)) of which there are eight. In the R.S.F.S.R. these are few in number and are subordinate to krays. Elsewhere they are subordinate to S.S.R.s. Finally, at the lowest level, are the **Avtonomnyy Okrug** (Autonomous Okrugs (A.Ok.s))*, numbering ten. These are found only in the R.S.F.S.R. where they are subordinate either to oblasts or to krays. These represent the homes of many of the smaller and less advanced of the Soviet peoples and are particularly numerous in Siberia.

The administrative structure of the Soviet Union is highly complex but at the same time is a great deal less rigid than that of many other countries. Boundary changes and regrouping of areas frequently take place, particularly

---

* Prior to 1977 these were known as **Natsional'nyy Okrug** (National Okrugs (N.O.s)).

FIG. 17. Political–administrative divisions of the U.S.S.R. at the beginning of 1978. Sovetskaya Sotsialisticheskaya Respublika (Soviet Socialist Republics, S.S.R.s) are named on the map in conventional English. The following is a list of the conventional English and vernacular forms: Armenian S.S.R. (Armyanskaya S.S.R.); Azerbaydzhanian S.S.R. (Azerbaydzhanskaya S.S.R.); Belorussian S.S.R. (Belorusskaya S.S.R.); Estonian S.S.R. (Estonskaya S.S.R.); Georgian S.S.R. (Gruzinskaya S.S.R.); Kazakh S.S.R. (Kazakhskaya S.S.R.); Kirgiz S.S.R. (Kirgizskaya S.S.R.); Latvian S.S.R. (Latviyskaya S.S.R.); Lithuanian S.S.R. (Litovskaya S.S.R.); Moldavian S.S.R. (Moldavskaya S.S.R.); Tadzhik S.S.R. (Tadzhikskaya S.S.R.); Turkmen S.S.R. (Turkmenskaya S.S.R.); Ukrainian S.S.R. (Ukrainskaya S.S.R.); Uzbek S.S.R. (Uzbekskaya S.S.R.); Lower grade-units are indicated by shading and key numbers: Avtonomnaya Sovetskaya Sotsialisticheskaya Respublika (Autonomous S.S.R.s): 1, Karel'skaya. 2, Komi. 3, Mordovskaya. 4, Chuvashskaya. 5, Mariyskaya. 6, Tatarskaya. 7, Udmurtskaya. 8, Bashkirskaya. 9, Kabardino-Balkarskaya. 10, Severo-Osetinskaya. 11, Checheno-Ingushskaya. 12, Kalmytskaya. 13, Dagestanskaya. 14, Abkhazskaya. 15, Adzharskaya. 16, Nakhichevanskaya. 17, Kara-Kalpakskaya. 18, Tuvinskaya. 19, Buryatskaya. 20, Yakutskaya. Avtonomnaya Oblast' (Autonomous Oblasts): 21, Adygeyskaya. 22, Karachayevo-Cherkessskaya. 23, Yugo-Osetinskaya. 24, Nagorno-Karabakhskaya. 25, Gorno-Badakhshanskaya. 26, Gorno-Altayskaya. 27, Khakasskaya. 28, Yevreyskaya (Jewish). Avtonomnyy Okrug (Autonomous Okrugs): 29, Nenetskiy. 30, Komi-Permyatskiy. 31, Khanty-Mansiyskiy. 32, Yamalo-Nenetskiy. 33, Taymyrskiy (Dolgano-Nenetskiy). 34, Evenkiyskiy. 35, Ust Ordynskiy Buryatskiy. 36, Aginskiy-Buryatskiy. 37, Chukotskiy. 38, Koryakskiy.

in the case of oblasts and krays, which are modified in response to changing economic patterns. Changes in the frontiers of the various political units are less common, but do take place: in 1963, for example, a considerable area of territory was transferred from Kazakhstan to Uzbekistan. As particular minority groups become culturally more advanced and economically more developed, they may move up the ladder of the political hierarchy. Thus, for example, the former Tuvinskaya (Tuvinian) Autonomous Oblast became an A.S.S.R. in the late 1950s. Conversely, under special circumstances, political units may be dissolved by the decision of the Supreme Soviet. In 1944 and 1945, a number of A.S.S.R.s suffered this fate, notably those of the Crimean Tatars, the Volga Germans and the Kalmyks and Chechen-Ingush of the north Caucasus, on the grounds that their inhabitants had collaborated with the Nazi invaders. Since the death of Stalin, the last two have been re-established. There is also one case of the demotion of a full Union Republic. The former Karelo-Finnish S.S.R. is now an A.S.S.R. within the Russian Republic.

ECONOMIC REGIONS (Fig. 18)

Mention has already been made of oblasts and krays as economic divisions of the U.S.S.R. which also have administrative functions as areas of local government. The subject of economic regions must be pursued a little further since these form the basis for Soviet planning and development and are widely used in published statistics. Each economic region is made up of a number of administrative areas which are grouped together. The boundaries of economic regions never cut across political boundaries and this has led to a number of anomalies of which the splitting of the Donbass coal-field between two economic regions is the most obvious. There is a certain conflict here between the recognition, in the Soviet form of government, of the existence of national groups and the desire to develop a logical pattern of economic regions.

In the 1950s and early 1960s there were several major changes in the arrangement of economic regions. Prior to 1957 there were fifteen major economic regions. The R.S.F.S.R. was divided into nine: North, North-west, Centre, Volga, North Caucasus, Ural, West Siberia, East Siberia and Far East. The Ukraine (with Moldavia), Belorussia and Kazakhstan were economic regions in their own right, while the smaller republics were grouped to form the Baltic, Transcaucasian and Central Asian regions. These fifteen major economic regions were both planning regions in the sense that long-range development plans were prepared for each as well as for the U.S.S.R. as a whole, and statistical regions in that many data in Soviet official publications were tabulated on that basis. Within each major economic region, oblasts, krays and A.S.S.R.s were subordinate "economic–administrative areas" with limited powers over local economic development. In 1957, as part of the general decentralization of Soviet organization associated with the Khrushchev period, a new type of economic–administrative body, the *Sovnarkhoz* (National Economic Council), was established with greatly enlarged powers and the country was divided into 105

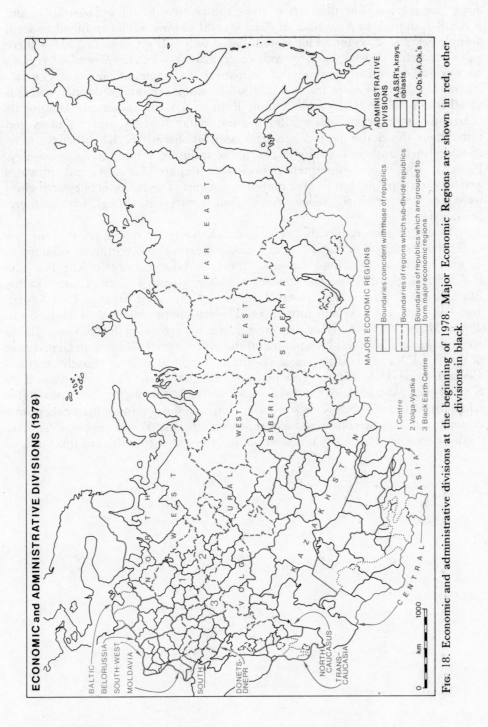

Fig. 18. Economic and administrative divisions at the beginning of 1978. Major Economic Regions are shown in red, other divisions in black.

Sovnarkhoz regions. The majority of these coincided with the oblasts, krays and A.S.S.R.s, though in a number of cases several oblasts were combined to form a single *Sovnarkhoz* region. This system lasted only a few years. In 1962–3 there was a pronounced swing back towards centralization when the *Sovnarkhoz* regions were consolidated into forty-seven "Industrial Management" regions. Centralization became still more marked in 1965–6, when regional economic councils at all levels below that of the Union Republics were abolished. Meanwhile central ministries, each responsible for a particular industry, which had existed throughout the Stalin period and had been abolished by Khrushchev, were re-established and took over the control of industry throughout the country. Plans for 1966–70 and subsequent periods were prepared for individual industries and for each republic but not for economic regions. The major economic regions were, however, retained, at least for statistical purposes, though with changed boundaries.

The pattern of economic regions, which has existed unaltered since the mid-1960s, is shown in Fig. 18, which also indicates the subordinate economic–administrative areas. There are now nineteen Major Economic Regions. The R.S.F.S.R. is divided into ten such regions—North-west, Centre, Volga-Vyatka, Black Earth Centre, Volga, North Caucasus, Ural, West Siberia, East Siberia and Far East; the Ukraine into three—Donets-Dnepr, South-west and South. Three Major Economic Regions are formed by groups of S.S.R.s—the Baltic Region (Estonia, Latvia, Lithuania and the Kaliningrad oblast, a detached part of the R.S.F.S.R.), Transcaucasia (Georgia, Armenia and Azerbaydzhan) and Central Asia (Uzbekistan, Tadzhikistan, Kirgiziya and Turkmeniya). Two S.S.R.s—Kazakhstan and Belorussia—are economic regions in their own right, while the Moldavian S.S.R. is a republic "outside the system of major economic regions" but may be considered as the nineteenth unit. Wherever possible, these Major Economic Regions have been used in the statistical tables in this book.

CHAPTER 6

AGRICULTURE

GENERAL BACKGROUND

A great deal of territory of the Soviet Union is highly unfavourable for agricultural development, mainly for climatic reasons. As we have already seen (Chapter 2), the high latitudes in which most of the country is situated, together with its land-locked character, result in a predominance of extreme continental conditions, characterized by intense winter cold and a short growing season. Large areas are, to all intents and purposes, useless for agriculture as a result. In addition, there are vast stretches of desert where, although the growing season is much longer, agriculture can only be carried on if water is supplied by irrigation works, a costly process. Further areas are marginal by reason of their low and unreliable rainfall. The Soviet policy of attaining self-sufficiency in food and other agricultural products has meant that many essential crops have to be grown in areas of climatic difficulty, a fact which considerably increases production costs. The short growing season characteristic of so much of the U.S.S.R. is an additional factor in raising costs, in that it demands the intensive use of a large labour force and much machinery during a restricted part of the year while these resources are underutilized throughout the winter months.

The basic facts concerning land use are apparent from Tables 2 and 3. The difficulties facing farming in the Soviet Union are clearly reflected in the fact that barely one-quarter of the territory is used for agriculture of any kind, while the area sown to crops is less than one-tenth of the total. The major uses of the sown area are shown in Table 3. Particularly striking is the large area devoted to cereals, wheat alone occupying well over a quarter of the whole sown area.

TABLE 2. *Major land use categories, 1976*

	Million of hectares	%
Total land area	2227.5	100.0
Area in farms	1047.5	47.0
Area used for agriculture	551.1	24.7
Grazing land	283.7	12.7
Arable land	225.7	10.1
Sown area	217.9	9.8

TABLE 3. *Major uses of the sown area, 1976*

	Million of hectares	%
Total sown area	217.9	100.0
Cereals	127.8	58.7
Technical crops	14.6	6.7
Potatoes and vegetables	9.3	4.3
Fodders and sown grasses	66.3	30.4

No other crop approaches it in importance. The generalized distribution of individual crops is shown in a series of maps (Figs. 19, 20 and 21), and their significance in the agriculture of different parts of the country is discussed in the section of this chapter which deals with agricultural regions (p. 68). Confining our attention for the moment to the more general aspects of land use, we may note the figures given in Table 4 which illustrates the great

TABLE 4. *Extent of the sown area (1975) by economic regions* (millions of hectares)*

Region	Total area	Sown area	Sown area as % of total area
U.S.S.R.	2227.5	217.7	9.8
R.S.F.S.R.	1707.5	126.5	7.4
North-west	166.3	3.1	1.9
Centre	48.5	14.6	30.1
Volga–Vyatka	26.3	7.1	27.0
Central Black Earth	16.7	11.0	65.9
Volga	68.0	28.5	41.9
North Caucasus	35.5	15.6	43.9
Ural	68.1	16.4	24.1
West Siberia	242.7	18.6	7.7
East Siberia	412.3	8.4	2.0
Far East	621.6	2.9	0.5
Ukraine	60.1	33.6	55.9
Donets–Dnepr	22.0	14.0	63.6
South-west	27.0	13.0	48.1
South	11.1	6.6	59.4
Baltic	18.9	5.3	28.0
Transcaucasia	18.7	2.5	13.4
Kazakhstan	271.5	35.7	13.1
Central Asia	127.9	6.5	5.1
Belorussia	20.7	6.2	30.0
Moldavia	3.4	1.8	52.9

* For boundaries of these regions, see Fig. 18.

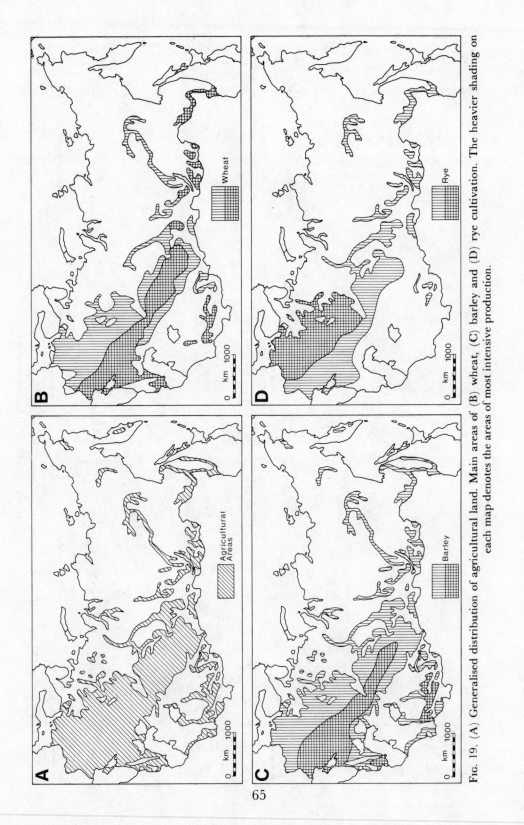

FIG. 19. (A) Generalised distribution of agricultural land. Main areas of (B) wheat, (C) barley and (D) rye cultivation. The heavier shading on each map denotes the areas of most intensive production.

65

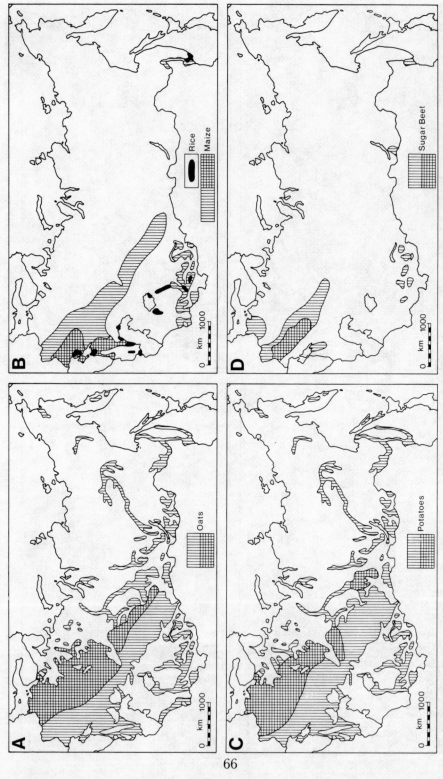

Fig. 20. Main areas of (A) oats, (B) maize and rice, (C) potatoes and (D) sugar-beet cultivation. The heavier shading on each map denotes the areas of most intensive production.

66

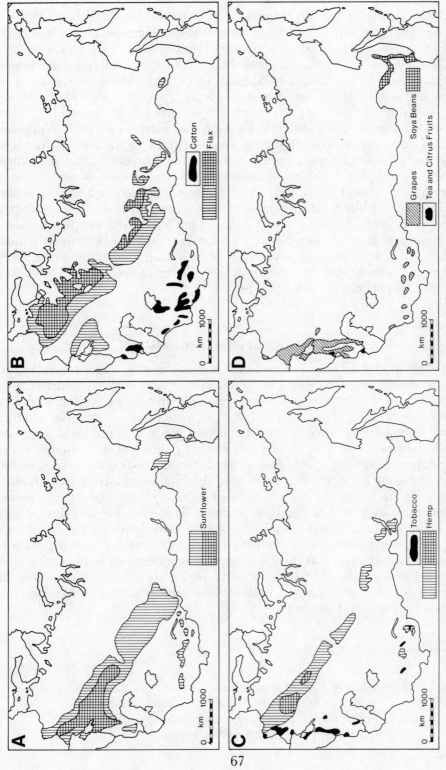

Fig. 21. Main areas of (A) sunflower, (B) cotton and flax, (C) tobacco and hemp and (D) grapes, tea and citrus fruits, and soya-bean cultivation. The heavier shading on each map denotes the areas of most intensive production.

67

variations that exist between regions in the size of the sown area. The uses to which that area is put in each region are shown diagrammatically in Fig. 22, which also indicates the scale of agricultural production in each region.

On the basis of the proportions of their total areas under crops, the regions listed above fall into a number of fairly distinct groups. The three regions of the Ukraine (Donets–Dnepr, South-west and South), together with Moldavia and the Central Black Earth region, stand out as districts with more than 50 per cent of their land under cultivation. To the east and south-east, in the Volga and North Caucausus regions, the proportion declines to 42 and 44 per cent respectively. Somewhat more northerly parts of the European plain, the Volga–Vyatka, Central, Ural, Baltic and Belorussian regions, have between 20 and 30 per cent of their land under crops. In Transcaucasia there is a further decline to 13 per cent, while West Siberia has rather less than the national average of 9.8 per cent. Central Asia has barely half and the North-west less than a quarter of the national average. East Siberia and the Far East, the two largest regions, have only 2 and 0.5 per cent respectively of their land under cultivation. These two regions, which together make up nearly half the area of the U.S.S.R., have only about 5 per cent of the whole sown area.

AGRICULTURAL REGIONS

The division of an area as large as the Soviet Union into agricultural regions presents serious problems to the economic geographer, not only in defining the regions themselves, but also in showing them on a map. Most Soviet textbooks of economic geography divide the U.S.S.R. into some twenty or thirty agricultural regions, naming each after its most important product or products. These are usually illustrated by a series of maps covering each major economic region separately and showing a great deal of detail. For this book it has been necessary to compress the great amount of detailed information available from Russian sources and to present a much simplified picture of the agricultural regions accompanied by a map of the whole country. This map (Fig. 23) distinguishes four major agricultural zones, each of which is divided into several regions, the latter numbering ten in all. It should be realized that each of these regions is by no means uniform and that there are considerable contrasts in the character of farming between different parts of a single region. It is felt, however, that the scheme presented here gives a reasonably accurate picture of the range of conditions to be found within the U.S.S.R.

The scheme is as follows:

Zone I. *Northern areas of low agricultural value*
    Region 1. Reindeer herding, hunting and coastal fishing
    Region 2. Forest exploitation, with small-scale agriculture
        (a) Yakut grain and livestock region

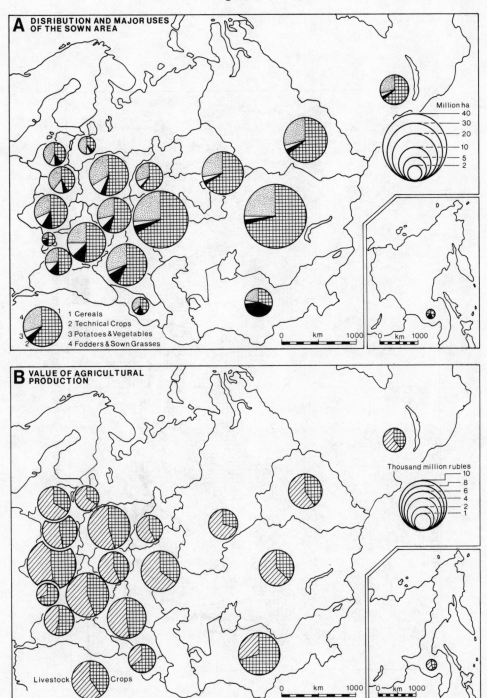

A DISRIBUTION AND MAJOR USES OF THE SOWN AREA

Million ha
40
30
20
10
5
2

1 Cereals
2 Technical Crops
3 Potatoes & Vegetables
4 Fodders & Sown Grasses

0 km 1000

B VALUE OF AGRICULTURAL PRODUCTION

Thousand million rubles
10
8
6
4
2
1

Livestock   Crops

0 km 1000

FIG. 22. (A) Extent and major uses of the sown area, by economic regions. (B) Value of agricultural production, by economic regions.

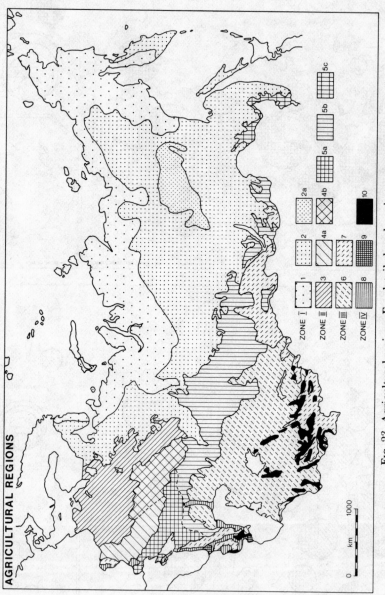

Fig. 23. Agricultural regions. For detailed explanation, see text.

Zone II. *Main agricultural belt*
    Region 3. Cereals, flax and dairying
    Region 4. Arable and livestock
        (a) western type
        (b) eastern type
    Region 5. Cereals and livestock
        (a) western, more intensive type
        (b) eastern, more extensive type
        (c) Far Eastern type

Zone III. *Southern areas of low agricultural value*
    Region 6. Desert and semi-desert stock-rearing
    Region 7. Mountain stock-rearing

Zone IV. *Southern areas of high agricultural value*
    Region 8. Horticulture, viticulture and tobacco production
    Region 9. Sub-tropical crops
    Region 10. Main areas of irrigated agriculture

It will be observed that there is a close correlation between the four agricultural zones and the major natural regions discussed in Chapter 2. Zone I coincides fairly closely with the extent of the tundra and taiga; zone II covers the mixed and deciduous forest belt together with the wooded steppe and steppe; zone III is coincident with the great deserts of Soviet Central Asia and the massive mountains of the south; zone IV is most widespread in the fringing belt between the mountain and the desert. We will now discuss each of the ten in turn.

Region 1. Reindeer Herding, Hunting and Coastal Fishing

Throughout this large region, which covers the tundra and the more northerly parts of the taiga zone, agriculture is virtually nonexistent and a considerable part of the small population is engaged in semi-nomadic reindeer herding. The people and their herds range widely in search of grazing for the animals on which they depend for their livelihood. In the brief northern summer, the best pastures are provided by the tundra vegetation, but in winter there is a general retreat southward into the open northern part of the taiga. Those who are not reindeer herders are, for the most part, engaged in such non-agricultural activities as fishing, hunting and trapping, lumbering and mining. Even the last two are little developed in this region, despite its considerable resources. In the absence of reliable transport links, many resources remote from the country's main centres of population and industry are as yet virtually untouched.

Region 2. Forest Exploitation with Small-scale Agriculture

As summer temperatures increase towards the south, the proportion of the land devoted to farming becomes a little greater. Cattle, pigs and sheep are raised, and cereals, mainly rye, oats and barley, are grown, together with potatoes and fodders. Even in this region, however, as its title suggests, agriculture is of secondary importance to lumbering, mining and trapping. Areas used for agriculture are small and scattered and farming is usually at its most intensive in the neighbourhood of lumbering and mining settlements. The most developed sections are in the European part of the country.

Set into this region, in the valleys of the middle Lena and its tributaries, is the grain and livestock farming area of the Yakut A.S.S.R. (2a). Here, owing to the more continental climate, soils are less heavily leached than in the rest of the taiga zone and support patches of grassland vegetation. The hot, though brief, summers permit the growing of crops; indeed, the Yakuts were one of the few indigenous peoples of Siberia to develop settled agriculture before the arrival of the Russians. Today the crops grown are cereals, including some spring wheat and barley as well as oats and rye, together with a variety of vegetables, but the emphasis is on cattle rearing, mainly for beef, and the livestock rely heavily on natural pastures. In recent years the area under crops has declined, whereas livestock numbers continue to increase.

The two regions just described cover at least half the territory of the Soviet Union and are of little or no agricultural value to the country as a whole. They certainly provide no food surplus beyond the needs of their scanty population and where occasional large towns do occur, Arkhangel'sk and Murmansk for example, these rely heavily on food brought in from other regions.

Southward from this negative zone is the agricultural "heartland" of the U.S.S.R. (Zone II). This is at its widest along the western frontier and narrows eastwards into the interior of the country. Beyond the Yenisey, it breaks up into a series of disconnected pockets or islands of farmland separated by broad expanses of forest. The range of crops grown in this zone is very wide, regional variations reflecting important variations in the physical environment. Put in the simplest terms, the latter involve an increase in summer temperatures and a lengthening of the growing season from north to south and a decrease in precipitation from north-west to south-east. At the same time, largely for historical reasons, the density of settlement and the general intensity of land use fall off rapidly to the east of the Volga and the Urals. Today, the great bulk of this zone is devoted to systems of mixed farming involving both crop growing and the raising of livestock. The types of crops grown and the relative importance of the arable and livestock elements are the features which distinguish regions 3, 4 and 5.

Region 3. Cereals, Flax and Dairying

This region occupies the southern part of the European taiga and the northern section of the mixed and deciduous forest belt, generally north of the latitude of Moscow (56°N.). Precipitation is a good deal more generous and temperatures less extreme than in many other parts of the country, but the acid podsolic soils are often rather poor and require heavy applications of lime and fertilizer. Drainage is a problem over much of the region, since there is a large excess of precipitation over evaporation and relief is gentle since this is an area of glacial deposition.

The traditional cereal of the region is rye, of which there is still a large acreage, but this crop is being slowly replaced by other cereals. Oats and sown grasses support large numbers of dairy cattle and there are extensive, though rather low-quality semi-natural pastures. Flax is another traditional crop of the region and is still widely grown although, as in the case of rye, the acreage is decreasing. Potatoes, grown as an industrial crop as well as for animal and human food, are a major element throughout the region. The most striking feature of recent years has been a big increase in the amount of arable land devoted to fodder crops and sown grasses, which has greatly increased the region's livestock-carrying capacity. This applies particularly in the northern and western parts of the region, where climatic conditions favour a dominance of livestock and the growth of dairying. Pig rearing is a well-developed subsidiary activity in these areas.

Throughout the region, much of the land has not yet been brought under cultivation and remains either forest or swamp. As might be expected, the underdeveloped area diminishes from north to south: whereas along the northern fringes of the region less than 10 per cent of the land is cultivated, in the south the proportion rises above 50 per cent.

Region 4. Arable and Livestock

This region covers the western part of the wooded steppe belt and the southern section of the mixed and deciduous forest zone. It may be subdivided into western (4a) and eastern (4b) sections, the latter being noticeably drier and cooler and rather less intensively farmed. The region as a whole has a wider crop range than region 3 consequent upon its higher temperatures and longer growing season. Most of region 4 is well suited to agriculture and little of the natural forest remains. Natural pasture, too, is much less extensive than in region 3, and over large areas the arable land is 50 per cent or more of the total. Hemp, mainly in the eastern section, replaces flax as the fibre crop, an indication of warmer conditions, and sugar-beet makes its appearance, especially in the west, where it is grown in rotation with wheat. The latter is the main cereal in the south of the region, where maize is also grown, but in the north it is secondary to barley and oats. Potatoes are widely grown, together with a variety of root crops for stock feeding. Livestock are predominantly dairy cattle although, as in most areas where modern dairy farming is carried on, pig rearing is an important subsidiary enterprise.

Regions 3 and 4 are areas of intensive mixed farming, where the production of crops and stock rearing are closely integrated. Prior to the opening up of the steppelands in the late eighteenth and early nineteenth centuries, they were the most important agricultural areas of the Russian Empire and they still make a major contribution, particularly on the livestock side. They are also important grain producers but are by no means as significant in this respect as the steppe-lands to the south which are, by a large margin, the country's most valuable cereal-growing area.

Region 5. Cereals and Livestock

This is the largest of the productive agricultural regions and its simple title conceals a good deal of local variation. It has, however, a basic unity derived from its close correlation with the steppe grassland vegetation belt and its extreme importance as a supplier of both grain and livestock products. The region is by no means devoid of physical problems. The advantages of higher temperatures are offset by low precipitation so that yields per hectare are often less than in the wooded steppe zone and irrigation is necessary for some crops in the drier parts. A major danger to crops is the *sukhovey*, a warm desiccating wind from the south-east which often affects the region in the summer months.

A major subdivision of the area occurs along a north–south line roughly along the Volga and thence midway between the Black and Caspian seas. To the west of this line, the climate is a good deal kinder than it is to the east: winter temperatures are appreciably higher, the growing season longer and precipitation more plentiful. Settlement and agricultural development took place much earlier to the west of the Volga than to the east and population densities are much higher, even if we discount the great urban agglomerations of the Ukraine. Consequently the intensity of land use is greater and the range of crops grown is wider, hence the division made on the map (Fig. 23) into "western, more intensive" and "eastern, less intensive" subregions.

Wheat is, of course, the dominant crop throughout region 5, though yields per acre diminish rapidly towards the east. West of the Volga, winter wheat predominates, but spring-sown varieties become progressively more important east of the Dnepr. East of the Volga, winter wheat disappears entirely, an indication of the harsher climate. Other cereals are also important and, though secondary to wheat, are produced in large quantities. These include rye and oats in the colder north-west, maize in the warm, moist south-west and barley and millet in the dry south-east. By the beginning of the present century, considerable parts of the European steppe were showing signs of soil deterioration as the result of long-continued cereal cultivation, and in places, particularly in the drier areas, soil erosion had become a serious problem. To combat these dangers and to increase the overall agricultural production of the region, farming has been greatly diversified. Industrial crops, notably sugar-beet in the damper north-west and sunflower in the east and south, have been introduced on a large scale as have root fodders and sown grasses. As a result, the number of cattle which can be supported has increased and output of meat and dairy produce has risen. In the moister areas, especially in the Ukraine, stock, including pigs as well as cattle, are closely integrated into the arable farming system and there is little natural pasture. Eastward towards the Volga and southward into the Crimea, the proportion of arable land declines and there is a greater reliance on grazing. In addition to the crops already mentioned, there is a good deal of vegetable production, particularly in the vicinity of large urban centres, and in several districts fruit and vines are important. Irrigation is used in some of the drier, southern parts, based on water from the Dnepr and Don rivers. Generally speaking, there is little possibility of any large-scale expansion of the cultivated area in that part of the region lying to the west of the Volga. Most of the suitable land has already been brought into use and any future increase in production will depend almost entirely on raising yields from land already farmed.

The steppelands to the east of the Volga are, as already indicated, a region where land is used much less intensively. Throughout this part of region 5, spring wheat is the main crop. In the north, where rainfall is higher and more reliable, oats and rye are also important and dairying is widespread, producing a surplus for use in other parts of the U.S.S.R. Southward, as rainfall becomes more scanty, the proportion of cultivated land declines. Spring wheat takes up an increasing part of the crop land and stock, among which beef cattle and sheep are more important than dairy cattle, rely to a higher degree on natural steppe pastures.

It is in this southern part of the region, straddling the boundary between southwest Siberia and Kazakhstan, that some 40 million hectares (100 million acres) were brought under the plough between 1954 and 1961 in the scheme for the reclamation of "virgin and long-fallow lands", a development involving the movement into the area of several hundred thousand volunteers from European U.S.S.R. Rainfall here is marginal for successful wheat cultivation, and yields per acre are low. However, thanks to a high degree of mechanization, output per worker is high and the virgin lands have become second only to the Ukraine in cereal production. Output has varied greatly from year to year, largely as a result of fluctuations in the amount of rainfall. The 1963 harvest was particularly poor, less than half that of the peak year, 1958. Serious problems of wind erosion have occurred in dry years and some of the land ploughed up in the 1950s has been abandoned. The initial resounding success of the scheme to some extent represented a rapid exploitation of the accumulated fertility of the natural steppe, a process which could not, by its nature, be continued indefinitely. The problems of the virgin lands (as they are still called) are now being tackled in a more realistic manner by Soviet agriculturalists: more attention is being paid to the need for crop rotation, and a more diversified type of agriculture, with fodder crops and cattle, is being introduced. Despite the difficulties experienced in the early 1960s, it now seems likely that a permanent major addition has been made to Soviet food supplies.

Pockets of wooded steppe and steppe, and thus of cereal and livestock farming, occur further east, along the southern edge of Siberia, notably on either side of the upper Angara and in Trans-Baykalia. In the Far East, in the lowlands of the Amur and Ussuri, bordering on Manchuria, conditions, are both warmer and wetter than in the Siberian steppe basins. Here (5c), the cereals include rice and maize as well as wheat and barley, and there is much fodder-crop production. The main non-cereal crop is soya bean.

Region 5, like regions 3 and 4, is now a mixed farming region. However the part played by cereals is very much greater than in more northerly areas and the integration of stock and crop farming much less close, particularly to the east of the Volga.

Region 6. Desert and Semi-desert Stock Rearing

As rainfall continues to diminish and summer temperatures to increase southward, the vegetation changes from steppe through semi-desert to desert, and arable land virtually disappears. Natural pastures become poor, indeed over large areas vegetation is practically absent and, as a result, stock densities are very low. This region is traditionally the home of nomadic sheep-herders, but under the Soviet régime true nomadism has declined in importance as a way of life. In the more favoured areas, fodder crops are grown to supplement the scanty natural grazings and permanent settlements have been established to house the population. From these, herdsmen set out with their flocks on their annual migrations which now follow regular circuits, returning eventually to the starting point. In any case, despite its tremendous size, this region makes but a small contribution to the Soviet agricultural economy.

Region 7. Mountain Stock Rearing

Steep slopes and severe climates limit the possibilities for arable farming in these areas, though stretches of cultivated land are frequently to be found in the valleys. Transhumance between low-lying winter and high-level summer pastures is still widespread. In the Caucasus, dairy cattle are now the most important type of stock, but in the mountains of Central Asia, which are much drier, the emphasis is on sheep with some beef cattle.

Region 8. Horticulture, Viticulture and Tobacco Production

This category includes a variety of areas of intensive cultivation benefiting from special local conditions. In Moldavia, vineyards are especially important and now account for about one-third of Soviet production. Fruit, vegetables and tobacco are also produced in large quantities. In the southern Crimea, particularly along the coast, a wide variety of fruits are grown, including peaches, apricots and figs as well as apples, pears and plums, together with tobacco and vines. Much the same can be said of the Caucasian areas falling into this category. Along the lower Volga, the presence of fertile alluvium, together with the availability of irrigation water, gives rise to a broad ribbon of fruit and vegetable production which contrasts vividly with the semi-desert on either side.

Region 9. Sub-tropical Crops

Though very small in size when compared with the other regions, these areas are extremely important in that they constitute the only parts of the country in which a combination of heavy summer rainfall and high temperatures permits the cultivation of sub-tropical perennial plants. This has become a region of intense specialization producing high value crops, the most important of which are tea, citrus fruits, tung nuts (a source of vegetable oil), tobacco, vegetables and maize.

Region 10. Areas of Irrigated Agriculture

These are to be found in the drier parts of Transcaucasia but reach their greatest extent in the Central Asian Republics where they occur in mountain basins, in the border zone between the mountain and the desert and along the river valleys which stretch out into the latter. The most valuable single crop is cotton, but these areas also produce large quantities of rice, sugar-beet, hemp, tobacco, vines and fruit. Lucerne, grown in rotation with cotton, encourages stock rearing, with *Karakul* sheep as a major product. Returns per acre of land are high and large surpluses are produced for use in other parts of the country. This applies particularly to fruit, vines and tobacco and, above all, to cotton, practically the whole of the U.S.S.R.'s supply coming from these districts. The rapid growth of population in these areas has been supported to a large degree by expansion of the irrigated area. The region is no longer self-supporting in basic foodstuffs, owing to the emphasis placed on industrial crops, and grain has to be brought in, mainly from northern Kazakhstan.

Throughout the country, pockets of particularly intensive agriculture occur in the vicinity of the main urban agglomerations, where vegetables, fruit and milk are the main products. These perishable, high value goods which are difficult and expensive to transport, are produced close to their markets and the distribution of areas of "suburban" farming depends on economic factors rather than on any particular conditions of soil or climate.

AGRICULTURAL ORGANIZATION

Some of the most striking changes which have occurred as a result of the Bolshevik Revolution have been those concerned with the ownership and organization of agricultural land. In the nineteenth century, most of the farmland of the Russian Empire was in the hands of large landowners and although, in the fifty years preceding the Revolution, many large holdings were broken up, big estates remained a major element in many areas. In 1913, of a total of 367 million hectares of agricultural land, 152 million hectares or 41 per cent were in large estates owned by the royal family, the nobility and the church. The remaining 215 million hectares were in the hands of some 20 million peasant families who held, on average, little more than 10 hectares each. Generally speaking, the peasant holdings were more intensively worked than the large estates and accounted for at least 70 per cent of agricultural production. After the Revolution, large holdings were expropriated and their lands distributed among the peasants. There followed a period of some ten years during which, although state and collective farms were set up in some areas, the bulk of the land remained in the hands of individual peasant proprietors. This, however, was only a temporary state of affairs and was fundamentally changed by the policy of collectivization, which was applied on a large scale from 1928 onwards. Under the new system, the land passed into the hands of two types of farm, the Collective Farm (*Kolkhoz*) and the State Farm (*Sovkhoz*). By 1940 virtually all farmland was worked by one or other of these organizations. Areas annexed by the U.S.S.R. as a result of the Second World War were organized along the same lines, the process being practically completed by the early 1950s.

The Collective Farm (*Kolkhoz*)

In this case the land, which like all land in the Soviet Union belongs to the state, is leased in perpetuity to the collective as a unit and worked as a single farm under the direction of a committee elected by the members of the collective. This management committee organizes the use of the collective's land and labour force, deciding what crops are to be grown, when harvesting should begin, what tasks are to be performed by individual members and so on. In the past, the managements of collectives were generally subject to directives from the central agricultural authorities, which often ran counter to local needs and led to inefficient production. Since the late 1950s, such interference has become less common and the individual collective now has much more freedom of action though the central authorities still influence decisions by laying down general guidelines of agricultural policy and by deciding the prices to be paid for specific commodities by the state purchasing agencies.

The collective as a unit is the owner of all agricultural equipment and farm buildings and is the tenant of the land allocated to it. However, each member of the collective retains a small plot of land and a few livestock for the use of himself and his family. Many observers see a basic contradiction in the existence, side by side, of both individual and communal farming and there can be little doubt that many peasants have tended to devote excessive attention to work on their own private plots at the expense of their duties to the collective.

The income of the collective is the produce of its lands and the management committee decides how the income shall be disposed of. In the past, compulsory deliveries of produce had to be made by each collective to the state at prices fixed by the latter, a process which could be considered the equivalent of rental or income tax payments in the capitalist world. The system of compulsory deliveries, which, in years when the harvest was poor, weighed very heavily on the collective farms, has now been modified and the collective negotiates with the state purchasing agencies both the amount of produce which it will sell to the state and the price which is to be paid. As a result of this change, farm incomes have greatly increased over the past decade. With the cash derived from these sales, the collective buys equipment and seed, maintains its buildings and provides communal facilities such as shops, libraries and recreation centres for its members. The remaining cash is divided among the members. The produce not sold to the state may either be sold on the open market, thus bringing in further cash for division among the members, or may itself be allocated to members as payments in kind. Thus each member has an income which may be in the form of cash, of agricultural produce or both. The actual size of the individual's income is determined by a complicated piece-work system based on the amount and nature of the work performed. This is evaluated in terms of "work-day units" which take into account not only the time spent at work but also the actual amount of work achieved and the degree of skill required for a particular operation. The produce and cash available for distribution among the members of the collective are divided up according to the number of work-day units accumulated by each individual. It has now become general practice for the collective farm worker to receive a basic monthly wage which is counted as an advance to be set against his eventual total income for the year. When the member of a collective receives part of his income in the form of produce he may either consume this produce, together with that derived from his personal land and livestock, or sell it on the open market. The complexity of this system, together with the built-in conflict between the interests of the collective as a whole and the interests of the individual member have led the Soviet authorities in recent years to look more favourably upon the alternative form of organization, that of the State Farm.

The State Farm (*Sovkhoz*)

As the name suggests, this type of farm is owned and operated by the state and its workers are paid employees as in other state enterprises. As well as being productive farms, state farms are also in many cases centres of agricultural research on which new farming techniques and new crops are first tried out. The ideas evolved on state farms are disseminated among nearby collectives and, with this end in view, state farms often function as agricultural schools, training farm workers, tractor drivers, mechanics and other specialists.

Until 1958 there was a third element in the organization of Soviet agriculture in the shape of the machine-tractor station (M.T.S). These owned and operated mechanical equipment such as tractors and combines which served the collectives in return for payments in kind. Thus the M.T.S. formed a channel through which a good deal of agricultural produce passed from the collective to the state. In 1958, however, it was decided to abolish the M.T.S., and their equipment was sold to the collectives which the skilled operators usually joined. A small number of M.T.S. have been converted into repair technical stations (R.T.S.) which act as service centres supplying repair facilities, spare parts and fuel. This change has resulted in a valuable addition of skilled labour to the collectives and has removed their need to pay for the hire of equipment and operatives. On the other hand, the collectives are now obliged to pay for the purchase, upkeep and operation of the machinery.

Important changes have also taken place since the Second World War in the number and size of state and collective farms. The number of collectives, which in 1928 was about 33,000, reached a peak of 237,000 in 1940, but by

1950 had fallen to 124,000. Since the latter date there has been a further rapid decline to 27,700 in 1976. This reduction in the number of collective farms results partly from the conversion of some into state farms, but mainly from a policy of amalgamating the collectives into larger and thus, in theory, more efficient units. The average *Kolkhoz* now has about 6600 hectares of agricultural land, including some 3700 ha of arable, carries about 4500 livestock and supports 486 families—roughly 1600 people. Altogether, about 44 million people live on collective farms.

State farms are, and always have been, considerably larger than collectives, though the difference is less great than formerly, and they continue to increase in number. In 1928 there were 1407 *Sovkhozy* and by 1950 they numbered 4988; in 1976 there were 19,600. Much of this increase has been due to the fact that the state farm has been the type of organization most used in the opening up of new lands. Consequently, state farms are almost universal in the Virgin Lands, and over Kazakhstan as a whole they occupy more than 80 per cent of the farmland; on the other hand, the *Kolkhoz* remains dominant in the older settled areas of the European U.S.S.R. In 1976 the average state farm had 18,100 ha of agricultural land, including 5900 ha of arable, carried about 6000 livestock and had a population of more than 2500.

As a result of these changes, about 52 per cent of the sown area of the U.S.S.R. is in the hands of state farms and 45 per cent belongs to collectives. There are significant differences in the contributions made by the two types of farm to the various branches of agriculture (Tables 5 and 6). State farms have more than half the land devoted to cereals, fodders and sown grasses but little more than a quarter of that under vegetables, potatoes and technical crops. On the livestock side, state farms have fewer cattle and pigs but more sheep and goats than collectives. In general terms, then, state farming is rather less intensive.

The part played by private plots held individually by members of collectives, by state farm workers or as allotments not forming part of farms, is out of all proportion to their size. Although such plots occupy only 2.7 per cent of the sown area of the country, and account for negligible proportions of the land under cereals, industrial crops and fodders, they include 45 per cent of the land devoted to potatoes and vegetables. Still more striking is their role in livestock

TABLE 5. *Sown area by type of holding, 1976*

	Sovkhoz		Kolkhoz		Private plots & allotments		Total
	Mill. ha.	%	Mill. ha.	%	Mill. ha.	%	Mill. ha.
Sown area	113.8	(52.2)	98.2	(45.1)	5.9	(2.7)	217.9
Cereals	70.7	(55.3)	56.2	(44.0)	0.9	(0.7)	127.8
Technical crops	4.0	(27.4)	10.5	(71.9)	0.1	(0.7)	14.6
Potatoes and vegetables	2.4	(25.8)	2.7	(29.0)	4.2	(45.2)	9.3
Fodders and sown grasses	36.6	(55.2)	28.9	(43.6)	0.8	(1.2)	66.3

TABLE 6. *Livestock by type of holding, 1976*

	Sovkhoz		Kolkhoz		Private plots & allotments		Total
	Mill.	%	Mill.	%	Mill.	%	Mill.
All cattle	39.7	(36.0)	47.8	(43.3)	22.8	(20.7)	110.3
Cows	13.1	(31.2)	15.5	(36.9)	13.4	(31.9)	42.0
Pigs	22.8	(36.1)	28.5	(45.2)	11.8	(18.7)	63.1
Sheep	65.0	(46.5)	50.3	(36.0)	24.5	(17.5)	139.8
Goats	0.8	(14.5)	0.5	(9.1)	4.2	(76.4)	5.5

farming. Private plots support 20 per cent of the cattle (including nearly one-third of the cows), and slightly smaller proportions of the pigs and sheep. In recent years, however, there has been a noticeable decline in the importance of the private plot. This has been due in part to the growth of the state farm sector (where the size and labour input of the private plot are more firmly controlled) and in part to the greater returns available to the collective farmer for his work on the collective lands.

AGRICULTURAL PRODUCTION

It is only since the mid-1950s that data on agricultural production in the Soviet Union have been available in any quantity. The lack of information characteristic of earlier periods reflects the fact, now admitted by the Soviet authorities themselves, that the achievements of the régime in the agricultural sphere have been much less impressive than those in industry. Data published in recent years now make it possible to examine the growth of agricultural production over the whole period since the Revolution, and the basic facts are set out in Tables 7, 8 and 9 and Fig. 24.

On the basis of these data, it would be fair to say that, until about 1950, the growth of agricultural output barely kept pace with population increase and that the amount of food available to each Soviet citizen in 1950 was little greater than it had been in 1913. Historical factors were in part responsible for this situation. The two world wars, the civil war which followed the Revolution and the forced collectivization of the 1930s all played havoc with agriculture. At the same time there can be little doubt that, in the planned development of the Soviet economy under Stalin, agriculture was neglected, receiving a relatively small share of the capital and effort devoted to economic development when compared with the industrial sector. Since the mid-1950s, the position has radically changed. Agricultural production has expanded more rapidly than ever before, and recent five-year plans have aimed at a continuation of this growth.

TABLE 7. *Expansion of the sown area, 1913–76*

	1913	1940	1950	1960	1976
(a) Area (mill ha)					
Sown area	118.2	150.4	146.3	203.0	217.9
Cereals	104.6	110.5	102.9	121.7	127.8
Technical crops	4.9	11.8	12.2	13.1	14.6
Potatoes and vegetables	5.1	10.0	10.5	11.2	9.3
Fodders and sown grasses	3.3	18.1	20.7	57.0	66.3
(b) Index nos. 1913 = 100					
Sown area	100	127	124	172	184
Cereals	100	106	98	116	122
Technical crops	100	241	249	267	298
Potatoes and vegetables	100	196	206	220	182
Fodders and sown grasses	100	548	627	1727	2009

As the figures show, when population growth is taken into account, the supply of grain and livestock products available per head was no greater in the early 1950s than it had been in 1913. The number of livestock of all kinds (except goats) was still appreciably below the pre-revolutionary level (Fig. 25), though well above that of the 1930s, when many farmers had destroyed their livestock in preference to handing them over to the new collective farms. The sown area had increased by about a quarter, but the area under cereals had remained almost stationary, the difference being accounted for by large increases in the areas devoted to industrial crops, vegetable crops and fodders. Output of sugar-beet, oilseeds, potatoes and vegetables were all more than double their 1909–13 levels, and production of cotton had risen fivefold. Flax, by contrast, was produced on a much smaller scale.

TABLE 8. *Increase in the number of livestock, 1913–76*

	1913	1940	1950	1960	1976
(a) Millions					
All cattle	58.4	47.8	58.1	74.2	110.3
Cows	28.8	22.8	24.6	33.9	42.0
Pigs	23.0	22.5	22.2	53.4	63.1
Sheep	89.7	66.6	77.6	136.1	139.8
Goats	6.6	10.1	16.0	7.9	5.5
(b) Index nos. 1913 = 100					
All cattle	100	82	99	127	189
Cows	100	79	85	118	146
Pigs	100	98	97	232	274
Sheep	100	74	87	152	156
Goats	100	153	242	120	83

TABLE 9. *Agricultural production, 1913–1975*
(millions of metric tons; annual average)

	1909–13	1940	1951–5	1961–5	1971–5
(a) Mill. tonnes					
Grain	72.5	95.6	88.5	130.3	181.6
Raw cotton	0.7	2.2	3.9	5.0	7.7
Sugar beet	9.7	18.0	24.0	59.2	76.0
Oilseeds	0.8	2.6	2.5	5.1	6.0
Flax	0.3	0.3	0.2	0.4	0.5
Potatoes	30.6	76.1	69.5	81.6	89.8
Vegetables	5.5	13.7	11.2	16.9	23.0
Meat	4.8	4.7	5.7	9.3	14.0
Milk	28.8	33.6	37.9	64.7	87.4
Wool	0.2	0.2	0.2	0.4	0.4
Eggs (000 mill.)	11.2	12.2	15.9	28.7	51.4
(b) Index nos.					
1909–13 = 100					
Grain	100	132	122	180	250
Raw cotton	100	314	557	714	1100
Sugar-beet	100	186	247	610	783
Oilseeds	100	325	313	638	750
Flax	100	100	67	133	167
Potatoes	100	249	227	267	293
Vegetables	100	249	204	307	418
Meat	100	98	119	194	292
Milk	100	117	132	225	303
Wool	100	100	100	200	200
Eggs	100	109	142	256	459
Population	100	126	123	146	162

During the 1950s and 1960s, however, the area under cereals and the output of grain increased rapidly, largely as a result of the Virgin Lands scheme, but the most striking development was the much greater attention paid to livestock farming. Since 1950 there have been large increases in the numbers of cattle, sheep and pigs, and the output of meat, milk, wool and eggs has more than doubled. The area under fodder crops has more than trebled over the same period. In the past, the Soviet farmer had devoted too much attention to grain production and the diet of the people had contained a very high proportion of cereals. The trends of recent years have increased the protein content considerably.

In the 1970s, further changes have occurred. The expansion of the sown area has virtually ceased (it increased by only 4.2 per cent between 1965 and 1976, as against a growth of 43 per cent between 1950 and 1965) and the increase in livestock numbers has slowed down (Fig. 25). These trends indicate that, whereas in the 1950s and 1960s rising agricultural production was achieved mainly by

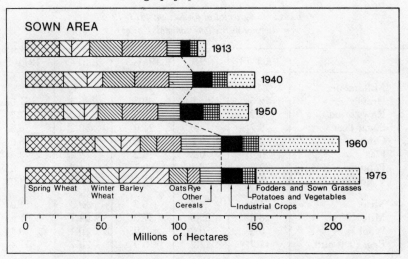

FIG. 24. Changes in the size and uses of the sown area, 1913–75.

increases in the national "stock" of arable land and animals, it now depends increasingly on intensification of agriculture and increasing yields from existing land and livestock.

The problems of agriculture have proved the most intransigent of all economic problems in the Soviet Union and have by no means been completely solved. Annual fluctuations in output, due primarily to annual climatic fluctuations, are still severe, particularly in the case of cereals (Fig. 26) and there have been

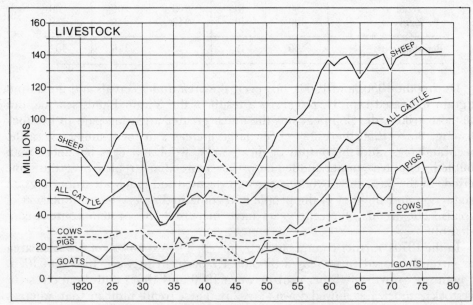

FIG. 25. Changes in the numbers of livestock, 1913–78.

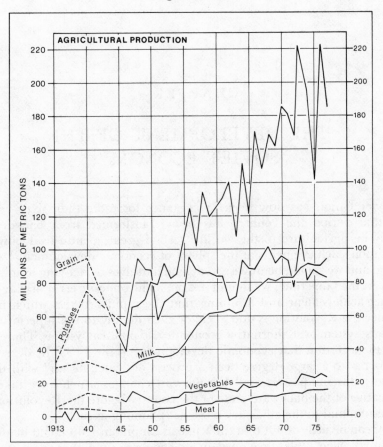

FIG. 26. Agricultural production, 1913–77.

several occasions on which the Soviet Union has been obliged to buy large quantities of grain on the world market to offset poor harvests at home.

Despite considerable advances, productivity in Soviet agriculture remains low, and the Soviet Union is unique among the major industrial powers in the large proportion of her population actually engaged in farming. At present, agriculture occupies something approaching 30 per cent of the Soviet labour force compared with only 10 per cent in the United States. Though the USSR may be overhauling other advanced countries in output per head of the population as a whole, it will be some time yet before she equals them in production per worker.

CHAPTER 7

THE DEVELOPMENT OF THE
SOVIET ECONOMY

THE Soviet Union has now been in existence for more than sixty years and during that period the country has been transformed from one depending primarily on agriculture to the world's second greatest industrial power. The Soviet Union's achievements in the sphere of economic development have been very great and we should be unwise to delude ourselves by denying or minimizing this fact. At the same time, we should not make the opposite error of exaggerating the Soviet achievement and assuming that the rapid progress which has been made since the Revolution is due solely or even mainly to the superiority of the Communist system over alternative economic and political systems. There is much truth in the assertion that economic development in the U.S.S.R. over the past fifty years has to a large degree been a process of "catching up" with the more advanced industrial powers and that the vast changes which have taken place are indicative of the backward state of the country before the Revolution rather than a testimonial to the efficiency of Soviet planning as such.

There can be little doubt that the Russian Empire in 1913 could be described as backward, even underdeveloped in its economy, and that, as a result, the living standards of the vast majority of her population were low, much lower than they should have been in the light of the country's vast natural resources and the techniques then in use in other parts of Europe which might have been applied to the development of those resources. This is not to say, as is sometimes believed, that all industrial growth is a product of the Soviet régime and that no progress at all was made before 1917. In fact, the last fifty years of the Tsarist period witnessed a considerable growth of several sectors of the Russian economy. Compared with the expansion which has taken place since 1917, however, progress was slow and, what is even more significant, it was a great deal less rapid than that taking place in other capitalist economies during the latter half of the nineteenth century. The industrial revolution came late to Russia and by 1913 she was lagging behind the more advanced industrial nations by an amount which has been estimated at between thirty-five and fifty years.

Pre-revolutionary Russia was a predominantly agrarian country with more than 80 per cent of her labour force employed on the land. The vast majority of her people depended on agriculture for their livelihood and agricultural products made up a large part of her considerable export trade. She was one of the world's major wheat exporters and also sold abroad large quantities of flax, hemp, timber and furs. The fact that Russia was a large-scale exporter of these primary products in itself suggests a backward economy in that, particularly in the case of grain, surpluses were only available because of the low living-standards of the people and their inability to consume these surpluses themselves. Similarly, the export of oil, metals and other industrial raw materials, which also took place, was indicative of a low degree of industrialization. The import of much machinery and manufactured goods was further evidence of the country's backward state.

The period between 1860 and 1913 saw expansion in a number of branches of industry and in a number of areas which have remained important to this day. During the fifty-year period, production of coal rose from less than 0.5 million tonnes* to 29 million, of pig iron from 0.4 to 4.2 million tonnes and of steel from practically nothing to 4.3 million tonnes. But this quite rapid growth still left Russia a long way behind other European countries. The U.K., for example, in 1913 produced 292 million tonnes of coal, 10 million tonnes of pig iron and 8 million tonnes of steel. Russian coal production was only 6 per cent of that of the United States and equivalent figures for other commodities were: oil 30 per cent, pig iron 13 per cent, and steel 14 per cent.

The limited industrial development which had taken place by 1913 relied heavily on foreign capital. The Russians themselves, even when they could afford it, had proved remarkably slow to invest in industry and at least half the investment capital had come from abroad, much of the modern equipment and many of the largest factories being in the hands of west European concerns. Management was generally far from efficient and the quality of the goods produced was low so that export was difficult and industry relied mainly on the internal market for the sale of its products. The general poverty and low living standards of the population resulted in restricted internal demand for manu-factured goods, and this was a very real hindrance to expansion.

Industry was not only limited in the range of goods it produced, it was also very restricted in its geographical distribution. Heavy industry was confined almost entirely to the eastern Ukraine where the coal of the Donbass and the iron of Krivoy Rog were the main supports of the iron and steel industry. The Urals, which in the late nineteenth century produced the bulk of Russia's iron and which had, in the eighteenth, made her one of the world's leading iron producers, were, by 1913, an area of stagnation and decline. The Ural iron industry, which depended almost entirely on charcoal for smelting, could not complete with coke-smelted iron from the Ukraine, which was in any case closer to the main centres of population in the European plain. By the eve of the First World War, the Ukraine was producing nearly 70 per cent of Russia's pig iron and 56 per cent of her steel as well as 87 per cent of her coal. Another major development of the late nineteenth century was the exploitation of the Baku oilfield on the western shore of the Caspian. Large-scale extraction began here in the 1870's and by 1900 the district was producing 95 per cent of

---

* Throughout the text, 1 tonne = 1 metric ton = 1000 kg = 2,205 lb = 0.984 long ton

Russia's oil, almost half the world output. Even in this item, Russia's leading position was lost by 1910, as output rose more rapidly in other countries.

A large part of the manufacturing industry was situated in the region centred on Moscow. The traditional activities of metal-working, on the basis of local iron deposits, and textiles derived from the position of flax as a major crop in the area, were modernized and expanded from the middle of the nineteenth century. The Moscow region came to be Russia's main engineering district and cotton textile manufacture became a major activity. The latter depended on foreign, largely American, sources for up to half its raw cotton, the remainder coming from Russian Central Asia.

Away from the regions mentioned above, industry, apart from local handicrafts, was on a very small scale. The only centres of any importance were a few large cities and ports, notably St. Petersburg, Odessa, Arkhangel'sk and Batumi (an oil-refining and exporting centre linked to Baku by pipeline).

The period since 1913 can be divided into a number of distinct phases. The First World War, which furnished striking proof of the economic and military weakness of the Russian Empire, together with the civil war which followed the Revolution, left the economy in ruins. The period 1917–20 is usually referred to as that of *War Communism* when the new régime, in addition to its struggles with internal anti-revolutionary forces and their foreign allies, attempted to establish state control over all forms of economic activity. Industry was nationalized and the large estates of private landowners were broken up and redistributed among the peasants, who were charged with compulsory deliveries of foodstuffs to the state. The strain on the economy was too great and by 1920 both industrial and agricultural production, in virtually all fields, were still well below the by no means impressive levels of 1913. In an attempt to remedy this situation there was introduced, in 1921, the *New Economic Policy* under which a considerable return to private enterprise was permitted. A good deal of manufacturing industry was denationalized, private trading was encouraged and compulsory deliveries of food by the farmers were stopped. As a result, production began to increase in both agriculture and industry and by 1927 had returned to their pre-war levels. However, the experiment was short-lived. It was, of course, contrary to the principles on which the Soviet state was based and was a temporary expedient rather than a long-term change in methods on the part of the Soviet rulers. From 1925 onwards, private enterprise was subject to increasing restrictions and 1928 marked a return to full state control under the system of *Five-year Plans*. From that date onwards, as the Soviet constitution puts it: "The economic life of the U.S.S.R. is determined and directed by a State Plan of national economy with the aim of increasing the public wealth, of steadily raising the material and cultural standards of the working people and of strengthening the independence of the U.S.S.R. and its capacity for defence."

The first three five-year plans were for the years 1928–32, 1933–7 and 1938–42 respectively, the last being abruptly terminated by the outbreak of war with Germany in 1941. These plans were particularly concerned with the wider exploitation of the country's fuel and mineral resources, the development of the heavy industrial base, improvements in communications and the expansion of the engineering and chemical industries. Some idea of the progress made in these branches can be obtained from the figures given in Chapters 8 and 9. The concentration of effort and resources on the development of heavy industry meant, inevitably, that much less was done in other branches of the economy, that is in the production of consumer goods and in agriculture. The production of such things as textiles, clothing, foodstuffs, furniture and domestic equipment increased much more slowly and on the eve of the Second World War levels of output in these commodities were still very low by comparison with the situation in other industrial countries. The fifth five-year plan (1946–50) was devoted very largely to the reconstruction of war-devastated areas in the west where a large part of the Soviet Union's inter-war industrial capacity had been destroyed. The sixth plan (1951–5) brought renewed rapid expansion, again with the emphasis on heavy industry and much the same can be said of the seventh (1956–60). In 1957, however, planning targets were revised and a seven-year plan devised for the period 1959–65. The latter, together with subsequent five-year plans (1966–70, 1971–75 and 1976–80) aimed at a more vigorous expansion in the production of consumer goods and foodstuffs than ever before. In the words of Kosygin in a speech delivered to the 23rd Congress of the Communist party of the Soviet Union in 1966:—

> For many years, the production rate of consumer goods lagged behind that of producer goods. The level of development achieved by the economy allows the new [i.e. the eighth] five-year plan to envisage a considerable growth in the rate of development of agriculture to bring it nearer the development rate of industry and, within industry, to narrow the gap between the rate of growth of consumer goods production and that of producer goods production.

These policies are reiterated in the current (tenth) five-year plan for 1976–80. Industrial output is scheduled to rise by 35–39 per cent, with the output of the "means of production" (i.e. capital equipment) rising by 38–42 per cent and that of consumer goods by 30–32 per cent (as against 14–17 per cent in agriculture). Growth targets in some of the more important branches of industry include: coal 15 per cent, oil 30 per cent, natural gas 50 per cent, electricity 33 per cent, iron ore 18 per cent, steel 19 per cent, engineering 55 per cent, light industry 27 per cent, food industries 27 per cent. Particular emphasis is laid on the need to increase labour productivity in the light of the current demographic situation (see Chapter 11) and it is intended that about 90 per cent of the increase in industrial production and the whole of the increase in agricultural production should be achieved by the increased productivity of labour. To reach these targets, large-scale investment will be necessary and the annual investment of capital in 1980 will be 25 per cent higher than in 1975.

CHAPTER 8

INDUSTRIAL RESOURCES

THE Soviet Union is extremely well endowed with industrial resources including both fuel supplies and most of the raw materials required by modern industry. The limited nature of the economic development achieved in the Tsarist period was a product of historical, social and economic factors and was in no way due to any lack of physical resources. Once a determined effort was made to carry out a full exploitation of the country's resource wealth and to build up the industrial side of the economy, it was almost inevitable that the U.S.S.R. should advance rapidly to achieve its present position as the world's second greatest industrial power. To give a complete list of Soviet raw material resources and their location would be a tedious exercise: reference should be made to the texts and atlases listed in the Bibliography (pages 159–162). In this chapter, attention will be concentrated on the distribution and development of major items and areas.

FUEL AND POWER

The U.S.S.R. is particularly rich in sources of power which are great enough to supply all her needs in the foreseeable future. The problems that do exist are concerned with the uneven distribution of these resources and the difficulties involved in exploiting them when they occur in thinly settled areas of harsh climate far removed from the main centres of population and industry.

Coal

This is the most important single energy resource in the Soviet Union. Estimates of coal reserves vary a great deal according to the method of evaluation used, but recent Soviet publications suggest a total of 8,760,000 millions tonnes of which 7,765,000 million tonnes are classed as workable. Of these, 65 per cent are in the form of hard coal (bituminous and anthracite) the remainder being brown coal or lignite. However, of the total estimated reserves, only about 3 per cent are proven; 11 per cent are classed as "probable" and the remaining 86 per cent as "possible". Even the 3 per cent proven reserves are sufficient to support the present output for close on 400 years. The exact calculation of coal reserves is, of course, a highly complex matter, and it is sufficient for our purposes to note that the Soviet Union's reserves are very large, probably as much as half the world total, and can supply all her needs for a long time to come.

Of much greater significance is the present situation as regards production and the contribution made to the total output by individual fields. The map of coal basins and deposits (Fig. 27) shows all known sources of coal, but many of these, particularly in the Asiatic part of the country, are virtually unworked. Included in this category, for example, are the vast Tungus and Lena coal-basins of eastern Siberia which together are believed to contain about half the Soviet reserves. Total coal production has increased nearly twenty-five-fold over the past sixty-five years, rising from 29 million tonnes in 1913 to 722 million tonnes in 1977 (Fig. 28). Of the latter total, about one-quarter was coking coal and another quarter in the form of lignite. The contrast with the situation before the First World War is seen by the fact that, whereas in 1913 the Russian Empire produced little more than one-tenth of the United Kingdom's output, she now produces more than five times as much as Britain and considerably more than the United States.

Soviet coal production is heavily concentrated on a small number of fields, four of which supply a large proportion of the higher grades of coal, including practically all the coking coal. These four, the Donbass, Kuzbass, Karaganda and Pechora fields, are considered to be of "all-Union" importance in that they provide large surpluses, over and above the requirements of local industry, for use in other regions. At present they account for some 60 per cent of the total output (Table 10). The remaining fields are generally of local importance only. They are usually poor in coking coal (e.g. the Urals) and in some cases a large part of their production is in the form of lignite (e.g. the Moscow basin). Some areas which appear as major producers in Table 10 are in fact composed of a number of relatively small and scattered mining districts (e.g. the Far East).

TABLE 10. *Coal Production, 1913–75 (millions of metric tons (figures in brackets indicate percentage of Soviet total))*

	1913		1950		1960		1975†	
U.S.S.R.	29.1	(100.0)	261	(100.0)	510	(100.0)	701	(100.0)
Donbass	25.3	(86.9)	95	(36.4)	188	(36.9)	221	(31.5)
Kuzbass	0.8	(2.7)	39	(14.9)	84	(16.5)	134	(19.1)
Urals	1.2	(4.1)	32	(12.3)	62	(12.2)	38	(5.4)
Moscow	0.3	(1.0)	31	(11.9)	43	(8.4)	35	(5.0)
Karaganda	—	—	16	(6.1)	26	(5.1)	44	(6.3)
Ekibastuz	—	—	—	—	6	(1.2)	48	(6.8)
Pechora	—	—	9	(3.4)	18	(3.5)	23	(3.3)
East Siberia	0.8	(2.7)	16	(6.9)	37	(7.3)	65	(9.3)
Far East	0.4	(1.4)	13	(5.0)	22	(4.3)	35	(5.0)
Central Asia	0.2	(0.7)	4	(1.5)	8	(1.6)	9	(1.3)
Georgia	0.1	(0.3)	2	(0.8)	3	(0.6)	2	(0.3)
Others	—	—	2	(0.8)	13	(2.5)	47	(6.7)

† Estimated

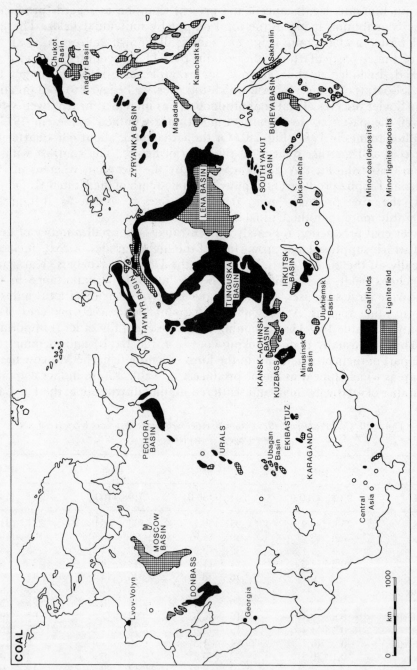

FIG. 27. Distribution of coal and lignite resources. Shaded areas are the main basins; dots indicate smaller deposits.

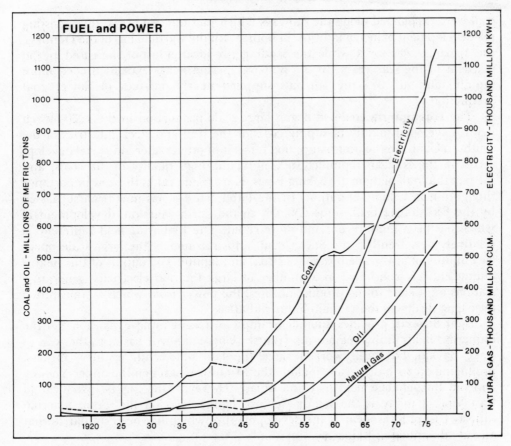

Fig. 28. Changes in the production of coal, oil, natural gas and electricity, 1910–77.

The Donbass, which has always been the most important field, still accounts for just below one-third of the total production, though this marks a decline in its relative importance over the inter-war period, when it accounted for more than half. The volume of production continues to increase, albeit slowly, despite the difficulties presented by the rather thin seams which reduce productivity per worker well below the average for the country as a whole. The high quality of the coal, and the proximity of the field to major centres of population and industry have made it worth while to repair the great damage which occurred here during the Second World War and to continue the expansion of output from this field. Production from the Donbass has more than doubled since 1950.

The Kuznetsk Basin (Kuzbass) is now the second largest producer, the output including a large proportion of coking coal. Productivity is high mainly because of the thick, easily worked nature of the seams: output per worker is nearly twice that of the Donbass. The Kuzbass was virtually unworked before the Revolution and its development on a large scale dates from the establishment in the 1930s of the Urals–Kuznetsk Combine, whereby Urals iron and Kuzbass coal were exchanged along the railways which join the two areas, thus assisting the development of heavy industry in both. With the wartime loss of the Donbass, the Kuzbass was for a while the leading producer. Output increased by 50 per cent in the war years. In the post-war period it has expanded even more rapidly, and in 1975 the Kuzbass supplied nearly one-fifth of Soviet coal production.

The **Karaganda** coalfield began large-scale production in the 1930s when it was developed mainly to supply coal for the iron and steel industries of the southern Urals. In the post-war period it has supported major industrial developments in the Kazakh republic. In view of the high quality of the coals, and the fact that half of them are coking types, Karaganda ranks third in importance though not in volume of output. In the latter sense it has now been surpassed by the **Ekibastuz** field, some 250 km to the north-west, the development of which has been more recent and more rapid. The Ekibastuz field represents a relatively new trend in the Soviet coal industry, namely the large-scale open-cast mining of low-grade bituminous coal and lignite. The output of this field is almost entirely consumed in a number of large thermal electricity generating stations built close to the production sites, the power from which is transmitted over long distances to the main industrial areas.

East Siberia provides another example of recent rapid expansion. Of the numerous fields in this region, the Irkutsk (Cheremkhovo) basin, to the west of Lake Baykal, has been worked since the late nineteenth century. Others, producing on a smaller scale, include the Minusinsk basin on the upper Yenisey and the Bukachacha field in Chita oblast. However, the biggest producer in East Siberia today is the Kansk-Achinsk lignite field on the Trans-Siberian railway east of Krasnoyarsk, the development of which has been similar to that already described at Ekibastuz.

The **Pechora** field provides the only example of large-scale coal mining in the Arctic and production costs are high. Output remained at a very low level until 1941, when the loss of the Donbass stimulated the development of this remote field. Its exploitation involved the building of a railway some 1200 km long from Vorkuta to Kotlas, linking Pechora with the European industrial areas. Today this field supplies coking coal to the Cherepovets steel works and to other sites in the north-western region. Output has increased only very slowly in recent years and, with its limited reserves and high-cost production, it is unlikely to expand in the foreseeable future. The technological experience of high-latitude mining gained in the development of this field may well be of value in the future if and when it becomes necessary to exploit the resources of the Tunguska and Lena basins.

The **Urals** coalfields rank high in the list of producers, but are a good deal less important than production figures suggest. The region contains a number of scattered, relatively small fields, organized into the four mining combines of Perm, Chelyabinsk, Sverdlovsk and Bashkiria. Three-quarters of the output is in the form of lignite and there is very little coking coal, hence the heavy reliance of the Urals on other sources, notably the Kuzbass and Karaganda, for this vital fuel. After a period of rapid growth in the 1940s and 1950s, production has declined quite rapidly: reserves are now very limited and this decline is expected to continue.

The **Moscow Basin** shows a similar trend. Production is entirely in the form of lignite and expansion was rapid in the inter-war and early post-war years, the aim being to lessen the dependence of local industries on coal brought in from other regions. Since 1960 the output of this field has declined by nearly 20 per cent, partly as a result of dwindling reserves but mainly because of the growing use of oil and gas piped into the region.

Remaining areas are of minor importance. The **Far East** contains a large number of scattered fields. The main producing areas are close to the Chinese frontier and in the island of Sakhalin. The **Central Asian** and **Georgian** fields have some local significance but supply only a fraction of their regions' requirements. Their output is in fact little greater than that of the **L'vov–Volynsk** field, transferred from Poland in 1945, which now produces nearly 10 million tonnes annually.

Despite the major developments which have taken place in the eastern regions, coal production and consumption, particularly the latter, remain heavily concentrated in the western half of the country. Some of the most important industrial districts, notably the Moscow Basin and the Urals, are poor in coal, which has to be carried in large quantities over long distances. The need to lessen the strain on the transport system has been one reason why Soviet economic planners have paid great attention to the development of alternative sources of energy.

Oil

This is by far the most important of these alternative energy sources, and the last 25 years have witnessed a rapid growth in Soviet oil production. As Table 11 shows, while output trebled between 1913 and 1950, since the latter date it has increased approximately fourteenfold. The 1977 production of 546 million tonnes represented nearly one-fifth of world output and made the U.S.S.R. the world's leading producer, significantly ahead of the United States. Oil and natural gas together accounted for 67 per cent of Soviet energy production in 1976, compared with only 19 per cent in 1950: over the same period, the share contributed by coal declined from 65 to 29 per cent. The current (1976–80) five-year plan envisages a continuation of these trends, with oil contributing 45.5 per cent, gas 25.5 per cent and coal 27 per cent by 1980. Beyond the latter date, however, the position is uncertain and there are signs that coal may achieve a comeback in subsequent decades.

Oil reserves are even more difficult to estimate than those of coal, and published figures are constantly revised as new discoveries are made. It now seems to be established that the Soviet Union has larger resources than any other single country and that these may amount to more than a quarter of total world reserves. This may be compared with nearly 50 per cent for the Middle East

TABLE 11. *Oil Production, 1913–76 (millions of metric tons (figures in brackets indicate percentage of Soviet total))*

	1913		1950		1960		1976	
U.S.S.R.	10.3	(100.0)	37.9	(100)	148.0	(100.0)	520.0	(100.0)
Baku and								
N. Caucasus	9.0	(87.4)	20.8	(54.9)	29.9	(20.2)	40.0	(7.7)
Volga–Ural	—	—	11.0	(29.0)	104.0	(70.3)	215.0	(41.3)
West Siberia	—	—	—	—	—	—	181.7	(34.9)
Central Asia	0.1	(1.0)	3.4	(9.0)	7.4	(5.0)	16.6	(3.2)
Kazakhstan	0.1	(1.0)	1.1	(2.9)	1.6	(1.1)	23.3	(4.5)
Ukraine	1.1	(10.6)	0.3	(0.8)	2.2	(1.5)	11.6	(2.2)
Belorussia	—	—	—	—	—	—	6.2	(1.2)
Sakhalin	—	—	0.6	(1.6)	1.6	(1.1)	2.5	(0.5)
Others	—	—	0.7	(1.8)	1.3	(0.9)	23.1	(4.4)

as a whole, 12 per cent for North America and about 6 per cent for Latin America. These figures are, of course, for known reserves only and fresh discoveries may change the situation at any time. Until the early 1960s known oil reserves and the great bulk of production were heavily concentrated in the European part of the country, but since then, as with many other industrial resources, major discoveries have been made in the Asiatic regions, which now contribute a large and growing share of total production. At present, more than 80 per cent of total output comes from three main areas (Fig. 29): Baku and the North Caucasus, the Volga–Ural district and Western Siberia. Each of these in turn has been the

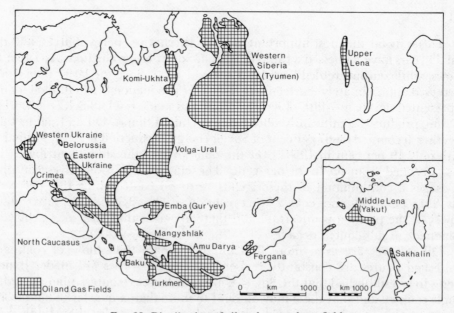

FIG. 29. Distribution of oil and natural gas fields.

main area of activity, but the first two have now passed their production peak.

Baku and the North Caucasus. The Baku field of Azerbaydzhan, together with the smaller fields on the north flank of the Caucasus around Maykop and Groznyy, have a relatively long history of exploitation. They were producing on a large scale (by the standards of the time) in the late nineteenth century and were the leading producers until the 1940s, supplying three-quarters of Soviet oil throughout the inter-war period. Since the Second World War, however, the importance of these fields has diminished in relative and, more recently, in absolute terms. Most of the known reserves lie either at great depth beneath the ground or under the waters of the Caspian, making their exploitation both difficult and expensive. Output is now declining, particularly in the Baku field, and this zone now accounts for less than 8 per cent of Soviet production.

The **Volga–Ural** field, often referred to as the "Second Baku", is at present the largest producer and still supplies rather more than 40 per cent of Soviet oil. The area was little developed before the Second World War. As late as 1940 its output was less than 2 million tonnes (6 per cent of the total); its present production is well in excess of 200 million tonnes. Development here was accelerated in the war years when the Caucasian fields were threatened by the advancing German armies, and the Volga–Ural field supported most of the great upsurge in production which occurred during the 1950s and 1960s. Over the past few years there has been little growth—in some districts output has started to decline—and this field has clearly passed its peak.

The **West Siberian** (Tyumen) field has been developed only over the past decade: oil was first struck in the West Siberian Lowland in 1959 and commercial production did not begin until 1964. Since then, output has risen by leaps and bounds to reach 182 million tonnes (more than one-third of the Soviet total) in 1976, an amount equivalent to the entire Soviet output in the early 1960s. The 1976–80 plan envisages that by 1980 annual production will be 300 million tonnes—nearly half the planned total.

Minor fields. The sequence of discovery, rapid development, a levelling out of production and subsequent decline can be seen in the numerous minor fields which now account for less than 20 per cent of total output. Prior to the Second World War, the **Emba** field, on the north-eastern shores of the Caspian, was the only other producer of any significance. Even so, although output continued to rise until the mid-1960s it never exceeded 3 million tonnes a year. In the 1950s it was outstripped by the rapidly expanding fields in western **Turkmeniya**. These began production in the late nineteenth century but only became important after the Second World War. Peak production of 16 million tonnes was achieved in 1973, since when output has declined and the Turkmen fields now account for less than 3 per cent of the total. Other Central Asian fields are those of Uzbekistan (**Fergana**), Tadzhikistan and Kirgiziya, but total output from these three republics is less than 2 million tonnes and no expansion is envisaged. Kazakhstan, on the other hand, although producing only about 23 million tonnes in 1976, now ranks fourth, and output has expanded rapidly during the last decade. This has been due mainly to the development of the **Mangyshlak** field on the Caspian, discovered in the early 1960s. Like the

Tyumen field, though in a very different way, this region lies in a zone of great environmental difficulty. Water must be obtained by distillation from the Caspian and an atomic power station has been built to provide electricity for the distillation process. Despite the large investment involved, however, the Mangyshlak field has not come up to expectation and production seems to have passed its peak.

The oil resources of the Transcaucasus (other than Baku) would appear to be even smaller than those of Central Asia. Production in **Georgia** now exceeds 1 million tonnes and is planned to reach 3 million by 1980, but this field will never be of more than local importance.

Output is considerably greater in the **Ukraine** and **Belorussia**, where there are three producing districts—along the northern hill-foot of the Carpathians (an area transferred to the U.S.S.R. from Poland at the end of the Second World War), north of the Dnepr in Kremenchug oblast, and at Rechitsa in Belorussia. Oil production in the Ukraine was negligible before 1950 but increased steadily over the next 20 years to a peak of 15 million tonnes in 1972, since when there has been a marked decline. Production in Belorussia began only in 1965, reached 8 million tonnes in 1975, but is now falling. There seems to be little future for these fields. Reserves appear to be bigger in the northerly **Komi–Ukhta** field which has an annual output of some 10 million tonnes.

All the fields mentioned so far lie in the western half of the country, west of the Yenisey river. To the east of the Yenisey, the only producer is the small **Sakhalin** field, which has had a stable production of about 2.5 million tonnes a year for several decades and by no means supplies all the needs of the Far East region.

Given the major changes in the location of Soviet oil production since the Second World War, it is interesting to speculate on likely future developments. The 1976–80 five-year plan aims at a 23 per cent increase in output to reach 640 million tonnes in 1980. This objective can be achieved from fields already in production, practically the whole of the planned increase coming from the West Siberian field, but maintaining a high rate of growth into the 1980s and 1990s may present problems. Large oil-bearing districts exist in East Siberia and the Far East, mainly in the Lena basin; whether their reserves measure up to those of West Siberia remains to be seen. Beyond that, the best hope probably lies in offshore resources. As yet, except in the Caspian, there has been no development of offshore areas. Large reserves may well exist in continental shelf areas of the Arctic and Pacific Oceans and in the latter case a joint Soviet-Japanese exploration programme is now under way in the Sea of Okhotsk. In 1978 British Petroleum held discussions with Soviet officials on the possibility of joint exploration in the Barents Sea. What appears certain is that the search for new sources of oil and gas will, as has already occurred in West Siberia and Kazakhstan, involve exploration and development under progressively more difficult conditions, and it will become increasingly expensive to sustain the growth of production. Under these circumstances, the large coal reserves of Siberia may well become economically more attractive.

Natural Gas

An even more rapid expansion has taken place in the production of natural gas (Table 12). As late as 1950, total output was less than 6000 million cubic metres, by 1965 it had reached 128,000 million and in 1977 stood at 346,000 million cubic metres. Current plans envisage a growth more rapid than that of any other energy source; the 1980 target is 435,000 million cubic metres, 50 per cent above the 1975 level.

TABLE 12. *Natural gas production by republics, 1940–75 (millions of cubic metres (figures in brackets indicate percentage of Soviet total))*

	1940		1950		1960		1975	
U.S.S.R	3219	(100.0)	5761	(100.0)	45,303	(100.0)	289,268	(100.0)
R.S.F.S.R.	210	(6.5)	2867	(49.8)	24,412	(53.9)	115,217	(39.8)
Ukraine	495	(15.4)	1537	(26.7)	14,268	(31.5)	68,703	(23.8)
Belorussia	—		—		—		568	(0.2)
Uzbekistan	1	(n)	52	(0.9)	447	(1.0)	37,211	(12.9)
Kazakhstan	4	(0.1)	7	(0.1)	39	(0.1)	5,199	(1.8)
Azerbaydzhan	2498	(77.6)	1233	(21.4)	5,841	(12.9)	9,890	(3.4)
Kirgiziya	—	—	—	—	41	(0.1)	285	(0.1)
Tadzhikistan	2	(0.1)	2	(n)	3	(n)	419	(0.1)
Turkmeniya	9	(0.3)	63	(1.1)	234	(0.5)	51,776	(17.9)

As in the case of oil, the massive rise in output over the past 25 years has been supported by the successive discovery and exploitation of a series of new fields, several of them in remote locations. In the earlier stages of its development, natural gas came mainly from producing oilfields. In 1940 more than three-quarters of the small output came from the Baku district of Azerbaydzhan and in the early post-war years the Volga–Ural field became a major producer. Since the mid-1950s, however, a progressively greater proportion has come from districts which, although within the broad oil/gas zones shown on Fig. 29, have often been quite separate from those producing oil. By the early 1960s major producers included not only the Baku, Volga–Ural, Komi–Ukhta and West Ukraine oilfields but also new sources, of gas rather than oil, at Shebelinka in the eastern Ukraine and in the Krasnodar and Stavropol' districts of the North Caucasus. Since then, major sources have been developed in more easterly areas, notably in the desert zone of Uzbekistan and Turkmeniya (first in the Amu Dar'ya valley and then further west), in the northern part of the West Siberian Lowland and in the Orenburg oblast of the Ural region.

Since most Soviet sources record production on the basis of republics rather than individual fields, it is difficult to be precise about the relative importance of the various districts. In 1975 the ranking was roughly as follows: Uzbekistan and Turkmeniya 30 per cent, Ukraine 24 per cent, West Siberia 14 per cent, North Caucasus and Baku 9 per cent, Komi–Ukhta 7 per cent, Orenburg 6 per cent. The most rapid expansion at present is in the Orenburg and West Siberian gasfields and these are destined to support the great bulk of increased production until 1980.

Pipelines and Refineries

The great increase in the production of oil and gas over the past 25 years has necessitated the construction of a complex system of pipelines (Fig. 30), since producing areas are increasingly far removed from the main centres of population and industry. By 1975 the U.S.S.R. had 75,000 km of oil pipeline and nearly 100,000 km of gas pipeline. Particularly noteworthy in the case of the oil pipeline network are the pipelines which carry the products of the Volga–Ural and West Siberian fields eastwards across Siberia and westwards across the European plain. The former has now reached beyond Irkutsk and may eventually be extended to the Pacific coast, whence export to Japan could take place. The scale of production of both oil and gas is now such as to permit large-scale export of both commodities not only to other members of COMECON but also to western Europe. In order to achieve this, oil pipelines have been constructed not only to the industrial areas of European U.S.S.R. but also to several Baltic and Black Sea ports, while the "Friendship" pipeline system carries Soviet oil across the western frontier into Poland, East Germany, Czechoslovakia and Hungary. A similar sequence of events has followed upon the upsurge of natural gas production. Pipelines now carry the products of the Central Asian fields not only to the major cities of that region but also northwards to the Urals and north-westwards into the European part of the country, where a growing network supplies European and Central Asian gas to most major cities. Gas is also supplied by pipeline to the Soviet Union's east European neighbours, and links are now being established with several west European countries. The biggest projects under way at present include the construction of gas pipelines from the West Siberian and Orenburg fields to link with the European network. At the same time, a certain amount of gas is fed into the Soviet pipeline system from Iran and Afghanistan.

The availability of oil and gas at an ever-increasing number of industrial centres has been of major significance in the location of industrial activity. Areas such as the Industrial Centre, with a poor local energy base, now have an assured supply for both domestic and industrial use, and the building of oil refineries and gas-processing plant at points served by the pipeline system as well as on the oil and gas fields has permitted not only a rapid growth of the chemical industry but also its establishment in many new areas. Thus the growth of the oil and gas industries has a greater significance than even their contribution to energy supplies would suggest.

Minor Sources of Power

Coal, oil and natural gas together make up more than 90 per cent of the energy produced in the Soviet Union (Table 13). Of the remainder, more than half comes from hydroelectric power (see below) and the rest from wood, peat

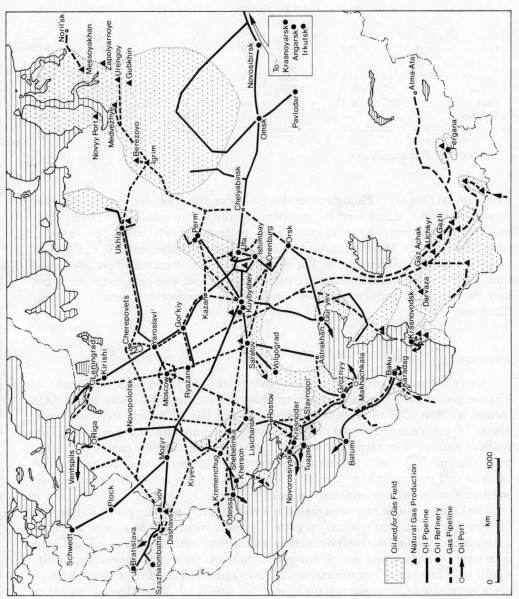

Fig. 30. Oil and natural gas pipelines completed by 1977.

TABLE 13. *Power supplies, 1913–76 (millions of metric tons of conventional fuel**
(figures in brackets indicate percentage of total power supply) (see also Fig. 29))

	1913		1950		1960		1976	
All sources	48.4	(100.0)	313.8	(100.0)	723.3	(100.0)	1746.5	(100.0)
Coal	23.1	(47.7)	205.7	(64.5)	373.1	(51.6)	479.0	(27.4)
Oil	14.7	(30.4)	54.2	(17.0)	211.4	(29.2)	743.1	(42.5)
Natural gas	—	—	7.3	(2.3)	54.4	(7.5)	380.3	(21.8)
Hydroelectricity	0.2	(0.4)	7.6	(2.4)	30.5	(4.2)	97.2	(5.6)
Wood	9.7	(20.0)	27.9	(8.8)	28.7	(4.0)	24.6	(1.4)
Peat	0.7	(1.4)	14.8	(4.6)	20.4	(2.8)	11.3	(0.6)
Oil shale	—	—	1.3	(0.4)	4.8	(0.7)	11.0	(0.6)

* One tonne = 7000 kilocalories.

and oil shale (Fig. 31). Though these three have greatly declined in their relative importance, the quantities of material involved remain very large. The production of peat, for example, used mainly for electricity generation, particularly in the Moscow basin, totalled 54 million tonnes in 1976 and that of oil shale about 25 million tonnes. The widespread use of these relatively low-grade fuels serves to emphasize the uneven distribution of coal and petroleum resources and the desire to reduce the costs involved in transporting them over long distances.

Electricity

Soviet economic planning has devoted much effort to the development of electric power and the total generated has risen from little more than 2000 million kWh in 1913 to 1,150,000 million kWh in 1977. Of the latter total, only about 14 per cent is derived from hydroelectric and barely 2 per cent from nuclear stations. The target for 1980 is 1,380,000 million kWh, nearly one-third more than in 1975; the hydroelectric proportion will remain unchanged and the nuclear will rise to only 6 per cent, leaving four-fifths of all electricity to be produced in thermal-generating stations.

Coal is the most widely used fuel in thermal plant. Over the past 20 years the contribution of oil and gas has, of course, greatly increased, but there are now indications that solid fuel will be used to a greater extent in coming years. There is a large and growing use of low-grade fuels in electricity generation. Peat, lignite and low-grade bituminous coals have long been used on a large scale in areas deficient in high-energy fuels, such as the Urals and Moscow basin; a more recent development, already mentioned, has been the construction of large thermal-generating plant at sources of cheap low-grade fuel, as at Ekibastuz or on the Kansk–Achinsk field, and the transmission of electricity over long distances.

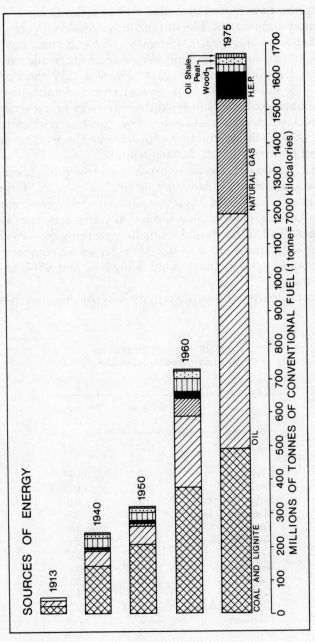

Fɪɢ. 31. Changes in the sources of energy production, 1913–75.

Although hydroelectric sources supply less than one-sixth of the electricity used, their exploitation has involved some of the most impressive pieces of engineering in the country. This is particularly the case where barrages have been built to tap the power of such major rivers as the Dnepr, Volga, Kama, Irtysh, Ob', Yenisey and Angara. The stations at Kuybyshev (Volga), Volgograd, Krasnoyarsk (Yenisey) and Bratsk (Angara), for example, have generating capacities of 2.3, 2.5, 2.4 and 4.5 million kW respectively, while even larger ones are being built at Ust–Ilim on the Angara (5 million kW) and Sayan, on the upper Yenisey (6.5 million kW). On several rivers, notably the Dnepr and Volga, strings of barrages have converted the waterway into a series of artificial lakes, and hydroelectricity generation has been part of multipurpose projects concerned not only with the production of power but also with the improvement of navigation and the irrigation of the steppelands.

The massive expansion of electricity production which has taken place in the U.S.S.R. is, of course, by no means unique to that country. Other industrial countries have greatly increased their output in recent years, and the Soviet Union still lags behind other major industrial nations in the availability of electric power per head of the population, though the gap is closing. In 1975 the total supply was equivalent to 4102 kWh *per capita* compared with 9358 in the United States, 4844 in the United Kingdom and 4887 in the Federal Republic of Germany.

A major problem connected with electricity is its transmission from generating

TABLE 14. *Regional distribution of electricity generation by economic regions, 1975*

	Million kWh	Per capita kWh
U.S.S.R.	1,039	4,102
North-west	52	4,079
Centre	115	4,070
Volga–Vyatka	15	1,816
Black Earth Centre	15	1,926
Volga	102	5,380
North Caucasus	39	2,599
Urals	112	7,317
West Siberia	70	5,655
East Siberia	97	12,393
Far East	22	3,419
Ukraine/Moldavia	208	3,952
Belorussia	27	2,894
Baltic	29	3,636
Transcaucasus	36	2,704
Kazakhstan	53	3,741
Central Asia	47	2,054

station to consuming area. Unfortunately for the Soviet Union, her greatest potential sources of energy, both hydroelectric and thermal, lie in Siberia. Even her developed sources of power are very unevenly distributed as Table 14 indicates: *per capita* output in East Siberia, for example, is three times as great as in the Centre. Thus it has been necessary to invest large amounts of capital in the development of an electricity grid, including the construction of very high voltage lines from Siberia to the European regions.

METALLIC MINERALS

With a few exceptions the Soviet Union is now self-sufficient in metallic minerals, though in several cases this position was not achieved until the 1960s. The distribution of the main worked deposits is shown in Fig. 32. **Iron** ore, which despite the increasing use of other metals remains the essential basis of modern industry, is widely distributed, but the bulk of Soviet production, which in 1977 reached 240 million tonnes, comes from a relatively small number of sources. Of these, by far the most important have been the ores at Krivoy Rog in the Ukraine and at various places in the Urals, notably Magnitogorsk and Nizhniy Tagil; the two regions together still account for two-thirds of the total output. Secondary producing districts of some importance include Kerch in the Crimea, Olenogorsk in the Kola peninsula, Atasu and Karazhal in Kazakhstan, the Kuzbass, Korshunovo on the Angara river and Dashkesan in the Trans-caucasus. Until the late 1950s, the iron ores worked in the Soviet Union were nearly all of high quality with an iron content above 40 per cent, but depletion of the richer reserves and continuing increase in output has made it necessary to pay more attention to lower-grade sources. Among these the most important by far are the enormous reserves of the Kursk Magnetic Anomaly (KMA), which lies midway between Moscow and the Donbass and includes some high-grade ores as well as a virtually inexhaustible supply of ores with a 20–25 per cent metal content. KMA ores already provide about one-third of Soviet output and are vital to the future growth of the steel industry. Other deposits, which have recently become of major importance as the richer ores of the Urals are used up, include those at Kachkanar in the northern Urals and Rudnyy in north-western Kazakhstan.

Other metals used in the steel industry are also in plentiful supply. The U.S.S.R. is one of the world's leading producers of **chrome** ore, mined chiefly in the Urals, and of **nickel**, which comes mainly from the Kola peninsula and the southern Urals. The mining of nickel (together with copper and platinum) at Noril'sk, near the mouth of the Yenisey, is one of the few inroads so far made into the mineral riches of the Siberian Platform. Major deposits of **manganese** at Nikopol' in the Ukraine and Chiatura in the Transcaucasus support a Soviet production equivalent to nearly one-third of the world total. **Molybdenum** and **tungsten** are mined in the Caucasus, Urals and Central Asia.

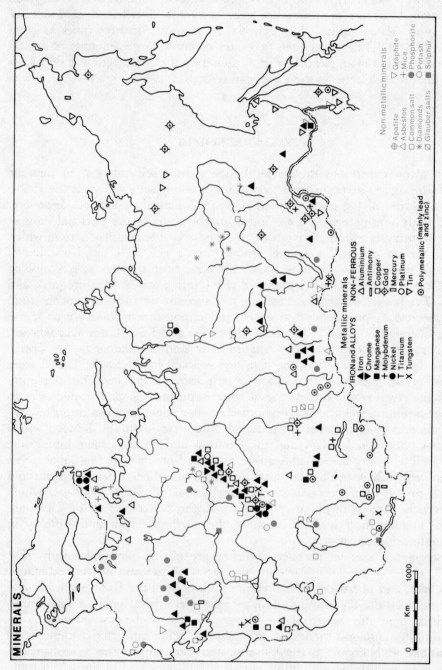

Fig. 32. Worked deposits of economic minerals.

There is also a wide range of non-ferrous metal ores. **Copper,** of which the U.S.S.R. is now the world's second producer, is mined at numerous sites in the Urals and Kazakhstan, which are the two main producers, in the Transcaucasus and the Kola peninsula and at Norilsk. **Aluminium** ores, which include nephelite, alunite and kaolinite as well as bauxite, are widely dispersed: major producers include Boksitogorsk south-east of Leningrad, Plesetsk in the Onega valley, Kamensk–Ural'skiy and Serov in the Urals, Krasnooktyabr'skiy in Kazakhstan, Belogorsk near Achinsk and Kirovabad in Azerbaydzhan. **Lead** and **zinc,** commonly associated with other metals in "polymetallic ores", come mainly from the Leninogorsk district of eastern Kazakhstan, but are also mined at several other places, mainly in the Central Asian republics. East Siberia and the Far East are particularly noteworthy as producers of **gold** and **tin.**

As Table 15 shows, the U.S.S.R. now takes first or second place in world output of the majority of major minerals and is the leading producer of coal

TABLE 15. *Soviet mineral production (figures for 1974 or 1975)*

Commodity	Units	Production World	Production U.S.S.R.	U.S.S.R. Per cent	U.S.S.R. Rank
Antimony	Sb content, tonnes	71,700	7,300	10.2	4
Asbestos	000 tonnes	5,210	1,350	25.9	2
Bauxite	000 tonnes	79,442	6,000	7.6	4
Chrome ore	Cr_2O_3 content, tonnes	3,310	820	24.8	2
Coal	000 tonnes	2,311,000	526,226	22.8	2
Lignite	000 tonnes	862,000	174,738	20.3	2
(Coal and lignite)	000 tonnes	(3,173,000)	(701,004)	(22.1)	(1)
Cobalt	Co content, 000 tonnes	25.3	1.7	6.7	3
Copper ore	Cu content, 000 tonnes	7,538	1,100	14.6	2
Diamonds	000 carats	45,920	9,800	21.3	2
Gold	kilograms	1,027,000	400,000	38.9	2
Iron ore	Fe content, 000 tonnes	520,000	139,824	26.9	1
Lead ore	Pb content, 000 tonnes	3,183	600	18.9	1
Magnesite	Crude $MgCO_3$, 000 tonnes	11,810	1,570	13.3	3
Manganese ore	Mn content, 000 tonnes	9,530	2,848	29.9	1
Mercury	tonnes	9,444	2,400	25.4	1
Molybdenum	Mo content, tonnes	88,490	8,800	9.9	4
Nickel ore	Ni content, 000 tonnes	733	125	17.1	3
Oil (crude)	000 tonnes	2,706,400	491,004	18.1	1
Natural gas	million m^3	1,298,000	288,996	22.3	2
Phosphate rock	P_2O_3 content, 000 tonnes	117,000	22,500	19.2	2
Potash	K_2O content, 000 tonnes	24,240	6,100	25.2	1
Salt	000 tonnes	154,200	15,556	8.7	3
Silver	Ag content, tonnes	9,442	1,550	16.4	1
Sulphur	000 tonnes	—	2,400	—	3
Tin concentrates	Sn content, tonnes	205,500	14,000	6.8	6
Tungsten ore	WO_3 content, tonnes	46,100	9,600	20.8	2
Vanadium ore	V content, tonnes	20,180	3,900	19.3	3
Zinc ore	Zn content, 000 tonnes	5,892	1,010	17.1	2

Source: *Geographical Digest 1977*, George Philip & Son, Ltd., pp. 37–41.

and lignite (combined), lead, manganese, mercury, oil, potash and silver. Her limited output of bauxite is partially compensated by the use of alternative sources of aluminium (nephelite, alunite, kaolinite), but still necessitates some import, as does her shortage of tin. Otherwise, the Soviet Union would appear to be self-sufficient in all the minerals required by modern industry.

CHAPTER 9

INDUSTRIAL DEVELOPMENT

Industrial development in the Soviet Union since 1917 has involved not only large-scale expansion of output but also major changes in the location of industry, including its development in areas where it was previously non-existent. To see the effects of these changes we must turn to a consideration of individual forms of industrial activity. One way in which the relative importance of different branches of industry can be assessed is by a consideration of the available data on employment. In 1975, out of a total population of 253 million, approximately 127 million were in some form of employment. Of these, some 35 million (28 per cent) were employed in agriculture and a slightly smaller number were in industry. The allocation of the 34 million industrial workers among the major sectors of industry is shown in Table 16 and Fig. 33.

TABLE 16. *Industrial employment, 1940–75, by major branches of industry*
(see also Fig. 33)

	1940		1950		1965		1975	
	000's	%	000's	%	000's	%	000's	%
Fuel and power	774	(7.8)	1,173	(9.6)	2,119	(7.7)	2,120	(6.2)
Ferrous metallurgy	405	(4.1)	605	(4.9)	1,236	(4.5)	1,369	(4.0)
Engineering and metal-working	2,576	(25.8)	3,343	(27.3)	9,905	(36.1)	13,816	(40.6)
Chemicals	299	(3.0)	355	(2.9)	1,251	(4.6)	1,753	(5.1)
Timber industries	1,594	(16.0)	1,834	(15.0)	2,819	(10.3)	2,795	(8.2)
Building materials industries	295	(2.9)	600	(4.9)	1,716	(6.3)	2,151	(6.3)
Light industries	2,332	(23.4)	2,150	(17.6)	4,308	(15.7)	5,109	(15.0)
Food industries	1,161	(11.6)	1,268	(10.4)	2,592	(9.4)	3,015	(8.9)
Unclassified	535	(5.4)	898	(7.3)	1,501	(5.5)	1,926	(5.7)
Total	9,971	(100.0)	12,226	(100.0)	27,447	(100.0)	34,054	(100.0)

The most striking change revealed by these figures is the overall growth of industrial employment, which now stands at about ten times its 1913 level, although over the same period the population has increased by little more than 50 per cent. The number of workers in industry has risen by more than a quarter since 1965. Changes in employment structure were most marked in the inter-war period, when the numbers employed in engineering and metal working

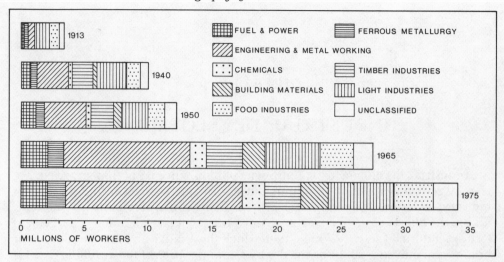

FIG. 33. Changes in the number of workers in the major branches of industry, 1913–75.

increased more than fivefold while those in light industry and food processing increased by less than 90 per cent. In the last decade (1965–75), growth of employment was most rapid (some 40 per cent) in the engineering and chemical branches; in light industry and food processing it amounted to about 17 per cent, while in the basic industries (fuel and power, ferrous metallurgy) there was very little change.

THE IRON AND STEEL INDUSTRY

Despite the increasing importance attached to other materials, steel remains the fundamental basis of modern industry and the view that a country's economic strength can be assessed by its steel output is by no means obsolete. In the Soviet Union a prime objective of economic planning has been the establishment of a heavy industrial base and the steel industry has been accorded high priority throughout the period since the Revolution. As Table 18 shows, steel production rose more than four-fold between 1913 and 1950; even more striking is the fact that it has increased fivefold since the latter date (Fig. 34). A 1977 output of 147 million tonnes made the U.S.S.R. the world's leading producer and further growth is envisaged with a 1980 target of 169 million tonnes. This continuous growth has involved some major changes in the location of the industry, but a persistent feature has been the dominance of two major areas, often referred to as the first and second metallurgical bases, in the Ukraine and Urals respectively, which still produce about two-thirds of all Soviet steel.

The Ukraine

We have already seen that, in 1913, more than two-thirds of Russia's pig iron (Table 17) and well over half her steel came from the Ukraine. This region

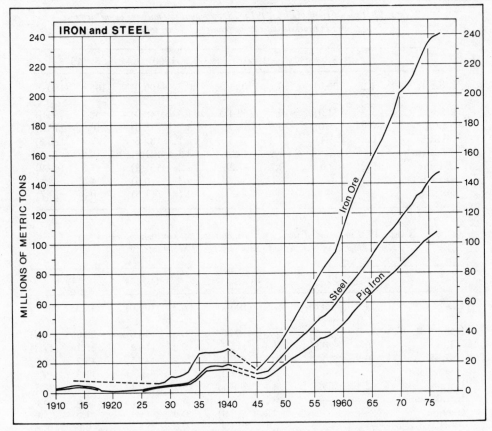

FIG. 34. Changes in the production of iron ore, pig iron and steel, 1910–77.

remains the most important, though its relative significance has declined appreciably: today it is responsible for less than half the pig-iron output and 37 per cent of the steel, though it produces more than twenty times as much steel as in 1913. This relative decline is due entirely to the growth of the industry in other parts of the Soviet Union, notably in the Urals.

The iron and steel works of the Ukraine occur in a number of districts, with different locating factors in each area. The most important (Fig. 35) are on the Donbass coalfield at Donetsk (formerly Stalino) and Makeyevka. When first established in the 1860s, these works relied on local coal-measure iron ores, but now draw mainly from the large deposit of high-grade ore at Krivoy Rog in the Dnepr bend; future growth will increasingly depend on the ores of the Kursk Magnetic Anomaly. Once rail links were established between the Donbass and Krivoy Rog in the late nineteenth century, interchange of coking coal and iron ore between the two areas began. This not only had the effect of stimulating iron and steel production in the Donbass but also resulted in the establishment of large works at Krivoy Rog and in the Dnepr bend cities of Dnepropetrovsk, Dneprodzerzhinsk and Zaporozh'ye. A similar, though smaller scale, interchange

TABLE 17. *Production of pig iron, 1913–76, by republics (millions of metric tons (figures in brackets indicate percentage of Soviet total))*

	1913		1950		1960		1976	
U.S.S.R.	4.2	(100.0)	19.2	(100.0)	46.7	(100.0)	105.4	(100.0)
R.S.F.S.R.	1.3	(31.0)	10.0	(52.1)	21.5	(46.0)	52.7	(50.0)
Europe	0.4	(9.6)	0.9	(4.7)	3.1	(6.6)	16.0	(15.2)
Urals	0.9	(21.4)	7.2	(37.5)	15.1	(32.3)	27.7	(26.3)
Siberia	—	—	1.9	(9.9)	3.3	(7.1)	9.0	(8.5)
Ukraine	2.9	(69.0)	9.2	(47.9)	24.2	(51.8)	47.3	(44.9)
Kazakhstan	—	—	—	—	0.3	(0.6)	4.6	(4.4)
Georgia	—	—	—	—	0.7	(1.5)	0.8	(0.7)

TABLE 18. *Production of steel, 1913–76, by republics (millions of metric tons (figures in brackets indicate percentage of Soviet total))*

	1913		1950		1960		1976	
U.S.S.R.	4.3	(100.0)	27.9	(100.0)	65.3	(100.0)	144.5	(100.0)
R.S.F.S.R.	1.8	(41.9)	18.5	(66.3)	36.6	(56.0)	82.6	(57.2)
Europe	0.9	(20.9)	4.4	(15.7)	9.2	(14.1)	25.1	(17.4)
Urals	0.9	(20.9)	10.7	(38.4)	21.9	(33.5)	43.2	(29.9)
Siberia	—	—	3.4	(12.2)	5.5	(8.4)	14.3	(9.9)
Ukraine	2.4	(55.8)	8.4	(30.1)	26.2	(40.1)	53.1	(36.7)
Kazakhstan	—	—	0.1	(0.4)	0.3	(0.5)	5.6	(3.9)
Georgia	—	—	0.8	(2.9)	0.9	(1.4)	1.5	(1.0)
Azerbaydzhan	—	—	n.	n.	0.8	(1.2)	0.8	(0.6)
Latvia	0.1	(2.3)	n.	n.	0.1	(0.2)	0.5	(0.3)
Uzbekistan	—	—	0.1	(0.3)	0.3	(0.5)	0.4	(0.3)

between the Donbass and the Kerch ore field in the Crimea led to iron and steel plant at Kerch (destroyed in the Second World War and not rebuilt) and at Zhdanov, the main trans-shipment port on the Sea of Azov.

The Ural Region

This is now the Soviet Union's "second metallurgical base". We have already noted the importance of the Ural region as an iron-smelting area in the eighteenth century and its decline when coke smelting was introduced in the Donbass in the nineteenth. A phase of renewed development began during the first five-year plan with the establishment of the Urals–Kuznetsk combine. This involved the interchange of Urals iron and Kuzbass coking coal by rail over a distance of 1800 km. At a later stage a similar arrangement was made with respect to the Karaganda coalfield of Kazakhstan.

The decision to undertake the establishment of a second metallurgical base in the Urals was motivated by strategic as well as by economic considerations.

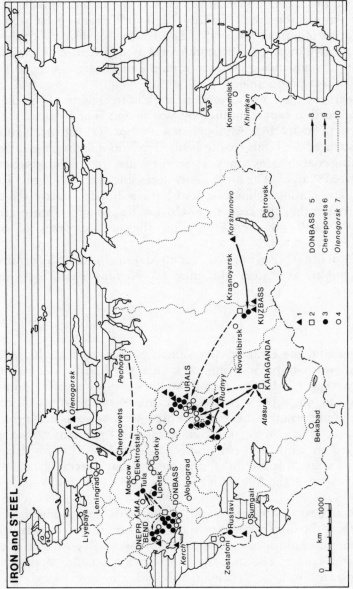

Fig. 35. Distribution of the iron and steel industry. 1, main sources of iron ore; 2, main sources of coking coal; 3, integrated iron and steel plant; 4, other steel works; 5, major areas of iron and steel production; 6, secondary areas; 7, outlying sources of iron ore and coking coal; 8, main movement of iron ore; 9, main movements of coking coal; 10, boundaries of Major Economic Regions.

Soviet industrial development in general aimed at a wider dispersal of industry, and in this instance it was considered particularly undesirable that so large a part of the country's steel capacity should be concentrated in the Ukraine, rather close to the vulnerable western frontier. By 1940 the Urals had become a major steel area, producing about 20 per cent of the national total. The large deposits of high-grade iron ore at Nizhniy Tagil and Magnitogorsk were among the biggest sources of iron in the world. The wisdom of developing this region was amply illustrated during the Second World War, when the Ukrainian steel area was lost to the advancing German armies and the Urals carried the main burden of Soviet war production.

The war years therefore saw a rapid increase in steel output from the region, which has continued to expand in the post-war period. The Urals now turn out some 30 per cent of Soviet steel. Although new methods of coke production make it possible for some of the Urals coal to be used in iron smelting, the dependence on outside coking coal remains heavy. In recent years, iron ore production in the Urals has declined sharply. The more easily accessible ores at Nizhniy Tagil and Magnitogorsk are nearing exhaustion and have only been partly replaced by new sources from within the region, notably at Kachkanar; future growth of steel production will rely increasingly on the ore resources of northern Kazakhstan.

There are nearly a score of important iron- and steel-producing centres in the Urals: the biggest are at or near Magnitogorsk, Nizhniy Tagil, Sverdlovsk and Chelyabinsk.

Other Regions

The Ukraine and the Urals between them produce at least 70 per cent of Soviet pig iron and two-thirds of the steel. Compared with these two regions, remaining districts are of relatively minor, though steadily increasing, importance to the national economy. These secondary districts have a variety of locational factors. The most important is the *Kuzbass* which, with its works at Novokuznetsk (formerly Stalinsk) and Gur'yevsk, produces about 9 per cent of Soviet steel. Formerly relying on Urals iron ore, the Kuzbass steel works now draw much of their iron from the hills around the basin and have recently begun to use ore from Korshunovo on the Angara. Coking coal is, of course, available in large quantities on the spot.

The *Industrial Centre* (Moscow Basin) now rivals the Kuzbass as a steel producer. Some of the ore comes from the Tula district, where ironworks were established before the industrial revolution, but at present a good deal of pig iron comes from the Ukraine. The steel plants of this region, the largest of which are near Moscow and Gorkiy, also depend heavily on scrap from local engineering industries. The situation in this part of the country is now being transformed by the rapid development of the Kursk Magnetic Anomaly ores, which are being used to support increased steel production both in the Industrial Centre and the *Central Black Earth* region, where a large integrated plant has been built at Lipetsk. The much smaller production of the *Leningrad* district depends wholly on pig iron brought in from other regions. An important addition to the steel capacity of the north-western part of the U.S.S.R. is the integrated plant built in the 1950s at *Cherepovets* on the Rybinsk reservoir. This, like the majority of steel works in the region, is market-oriented in its location and draws its raw materials from a great distance: coking coal comes from the Vorkuta field, iron ore from the Kola peninsula and scrap from the engineering industries of Moscow and Leningrad.

Republics other than the Ukraine and R.S.F.S.R. contribute only about 6 per cent of Soviet steel production. Nearly 4 per cent comes from *Kazakhstan,* where the plant at Temir-Tau, near Karaganda, has recently been expanded to produce about 5 million tonnes a year. This plant is located primarily with respect to local coking coal and originally received its ore from the Urals. It is now supported by iron ore production in the Kazakh republic itself.

A number of steel works have been established in various regions to supply some of the local demand for steel, to support the growth of engineering industries in their regions and to consume the scrap produced by those industries. Such pig iron as is used is brought in from other districts. Steel works in this category are those at *Bekabad* in Soviet Central Asia, at *Petrovsk-Zabaykal'skiy* east of Lake Baykal, at *Komsomol'sk-na-Amure* in the Far East and at *Liyepaya* on the Baltic; all these are very small-scale producers. In *Transcaucasia* the small supplies of coking coal in Georgia and the considerable manganese and iron ore deposits of the region support iron and steel production at Rustavi and steel works at Zestafoni (Georgia) and Sumgait (near Baku). Finally, in at least one case, that of *Volgograd*, a major steel works has been established on the basis of excellent rail and water transport facilities rather than on local resources of either iron or coal.

Numerous developments, some of them involving individual works of large capacity, have thus taken place in many parts of the Soviet Union. Important though some of these developments may be, it is important to remember that the industry remains heavily concentrated in the west; Siberia, Kazakhstan and Central Asia combined produce only about 20 million tonnes of steel a year. While this is equivalent to the entire Soviet annual output in the 1940s, it represents only 14 per cent of present production. In the early 1960s plans were proposed for the development of a "third metallurgical base" in the eastern regions, involving an integrated development of the coal and iron resources of a zone from Karaganda to Lake Baykal. In the event, although steel production in this zone has increased, growth has been less rapid than in the European part of the country and the 1976–80 five-year plan envisages no additional plant east of the Urals. The virtual abandonment of the planned third base may be attributed mainly to the exploitation of the KMA ores, which offer new possibilities for the growth of the steel industry in the European regions.

NON-FERROUS METALLURGY

As might be expected in a country possessing a great range of metallic minerals (see pages 105–108) and aiming at industrial self-sufficiency, non-ferrous metallurgy is well-developed in the U.S.S.R. Precise details of its scale and location are less easy to obtain than for industries discussed so far, but a number of major aspects are clear. In the first place, because of the great range of raw materials involved and the various processes to which these are subjected, non-ferrous metallurgy is a widely dispersed activity and there are different location patterns for each process and each metal. Secondly, owing to the different geological conditions under which they occur, the sources of non-ferrous metals are often distant from those of, say, coal or iron, frequently in more remote parts of the country, and non-ferrous metallurgy shows a very different pattern from that of ferrous metallurgy. The only major overlap is in the Urals, which are of outstanding importance in both types of metal production; the Ukraine or the Centre, on the other hand, are of minor significance in the non-ferrous sector. Finally, non-ferrous metallurgy is one of those branches of industry which were rather poorly developed in the U.S.S.R. prior to the 1950s but have undergone rapid expansion in the last 25 years. This growth has taken the industry into outlying regions, and non-ferrous metallurgy has been a major element in the industrial development of Siberia, Kazakhstan, Central Asia and the Caucasus.

In each branch of non-ferrous metallurgy there are at least three main processes: the mining of the ore, some form of concentration which may or may not take place near the mines, and the conversion of concentrate into metal. Mining has already been dealt with and attention in this section is focused on ore concentration and metal production.

Aluminium production is the largest of the non-ferrous metal industries of the U.S.S.R. The output of this metal remained at a low level until 1950, when it was only about 150,000 tonnes, but now exceeds 2 million tonnes a year, about 14 per cent of world output and second only to that of the U.S.A. The Soviet Union's rather limited bauxite resources have led to the development, not without considerable difficulty, of new technologies for the production of alumina from alternative sources such as nephelite, alunite and kaolinite. The conversion of alumina to aluminium requires large quantities of electric power, and the process is therefore attracted to sites, particularly hydroelectric sites, where this is readily available. Prior to the 1950s, aluminium was produced mainly in the western regions, at Volkhov, on the Dnepr bend, and in the Urals; since then, however, the most important developments have been in Siberia, where large, hydroelectricity-based aluminium plant at Bratsk, Krasnoyarsk and Shelekhov (near Angarsk) are responsible for nearly half the total output. Smaller aluminium-producing districts occur in the Kuzbass, Transcaucasia and Central Asia.

Copper production now stands at about 1.3 million tonnes a year, 17 per cent of the world total and the same as in the United States. Although most of the growth to this level has occurred in the post-war period (output in 1940 was only 146,000 tonnes), copper smelting has a long history going back to the establishment of plant in the Urals in the late seventeenth century. Today, smelting and refining of copper are carried on mainly in mining districts. The two most important regions are the Urals, with smelters and/or refineries at

Krasnouralsk, Kirovgrad, Revda, Verkhnyaya Pyshma, Chelyabinsk and Mednogorsk, and Kazakhstan, where the producing centres are Karsakpay, Dzhezkazgan (at present the biggest in the U.S.S.R.), Balkhash and in the upper Irtysh valley at Glubokoye. Smaller-scale copper production takes place at Almalyk in Central Asia, Alaverdi in the Transcaucasus and Norilsk in northern Siberia.

The Soviet Union is now the world's leading producer of **zinc** (1 million tonnes) and the second producer of **lead** (660,000 tonnes). These are produced mainly in the mining districts of the upper Irtysh valley, at Leninogorsk and Ust'–Kamenogorsk, and on the north flank of the Caucasus at Ordzhonikidze; in addition, there is zinc production in the Donbass, lead production in the Kuzbass and at Tetyukhe in the Sikhote Alin' mountains of the Far East, and both metals are produced on a modest scale in Central Asia.

The rapid development of non-ferrous metallurgy in the Soviet Union during the 1960s and 1970s denotes progress towards a more technologically advanced, varied and sophisticated industrial structure, characterised also by rapid growth in the production of such items as oil, natural gas, electricity and chemicals.

ENGINEERING INDUSTRIES

Before the Revolution, the engineering industries of Russia were poorly developed. With the exception of shipbuilding and railway engineering, production was on a very small scale and most machinery was imported. The position has been greatly improved over the past 60 years. Engineering now employs about 40 per cent of the Soviet industrial labour force and imports of machinery have fallen to a low level. In the Soviet Union today, as in all industrially developed countries, the distribution of the engineering industry is closely related to markets, that is to the manufacturing industries which use its products, as well as to sources of iron and steel, non-ferrous metals and power. The U.S.S.R. has been particularly concerned with the expansion of its heavy industrial base; consequently the heavier branches of engineering, producing equipment for the mining, metallurgical and power industries have undergone the most rapid expansion. Heavy engineering is most developed in the major industrial areas of the Donbass, Urals and Kuzbass. Another item of particular importance has been the production of transport equipment, especially railway locomotives and rolling stock. This branch of engineering is widely dispersed throughout the country, but the bulk of production again occurs in major industrial regions. More highly specialized and highly skilled types of engineering producing, for example, electrical equipment, machine tools and motor vehicles are heavily concentrated in the Leningrad–Gor'kiy–Moscow region, though they are by no means absent from other parts of the country. These activities, in the Industrial Centre at least, are based on a long tradition of manufacturing and a highly skilled labour force rather than on local physical resources. Agricultural engineering is a widely dispersed branch of industry occurring in all agricultural regions. The biggest works are usually found at sites having access to large supplies of steel and/or power; some of the most important being in the eastern Ukraine and in the great cities along the Volga such as Kazan', Saratov and Volgograd.

Although the various branches of engineering show concentration into a number of major regions as indicated above, the industry is represented, albeit on a small scale, in virtually all towns of any size. As one Soviet writer puts it, "clusters of machine-building enterprises have been created in all parts of the country, depending on the industrial specialization of the given regions; this is done with the aim of making the economy of the region more complete".

THE CHEMICAL INDUSTRY

This is a modern branch of industry which has made rapid strides in all developed countries during the twentieth century. Soviet progress in this sphere was until quite recently a good deal less impressive than in some other countries, for example Germany, the United States or the United Kingdom. Expansion was slow down to the Second World War but in the post-war period the growth of the Soviet chemical industry has been greatly accelerated and, during the 1960s and 1970s, this has been the most rapidly expanding sector. Chemical industries are based on a great variety of raw materials: prior to the 1950s, the most important were: naturally occurring minerals of various kinds, notably the mineral salts; agricultural products, particularly grain and potatoes as sources of industrial alcohol; and the byproducts of coke manufacture and metallurgy. Over the past 20 years, a major new resource element has been added in the shape of oil and natural gas, which have largely, though not entirely, replaced the traditional raw materials and have permitted not only the growth but also the diversification of the chemical industry.

The variety of raw materials used, the many different processes to which these are subjected and the wide range of products render it impossible to identify a simple distribution pattern for the industry as a whole. Some processes take place near the raw material source, which may be a mine, coke oven, smelter, oil refinery, gas-processing plant or even an agricultural collecting point, while others are carried out in market areas. The many different products, which have many different markets, include industrial chemicals (which are in turn consumed by other chemical industries), mineral fertilizers, synthetic rubber, plastics, artificial and synthetic fibres, dyes, paints, pharmaceuticals and photo-chemicals.

Industrial Chemicals

The most important items in this category are sulphuric acid and soda. In the U.S.S.R., *sulphuric acid* is derived mainly from the mineral iron pyrites, mined chiefly in the Urals, but some is made from natural sulphur and from the sulphides produced in non-ferrous metallurgy and oil refining. Because sulphuric acid is difficult to transport, and because by far its most important use is in the manufacture of phosphatic fertilizers (see below), the most common situation is for these raw materials to be moved to sulphuric acid plants built in close proximity to the fertilizer plants.

Soda is derived from common salt (sodium chloride) and limestone. Production of *soda ash* takes place mainly in the Donbass and Urals, where these commodities, together with coal, are readily available. *Caustic soda* is for the most part manufactured from soda ash in these two areas, but a newer process, involving the electrolysis of salt, is carried out at electric power sites, notably Kuybyshev, Irkutsk and Pavlodar.

Mineral Fertilisers

In terms of volume of output, these are by far the most important chemical products. Output remained very low until 1950 (5.5 million tonnes) but then increased rapidly as part of the drive to increase agricultural production. Production of mineral fertilizers in 1977 totalled 96.7 million tonnes, including 43 million tonnes of nitrogenous fertilizers, 28 million tonnes of phosphatic fertilizers (plus 4 million tonnes of ground phosphate rock) and 22 million tonnes of potassic fertilizers. These different types are, of course, combined in various proportions in the fertilizers actually used on the land. While fertilizer manufacture depends on a variety of raw materials, the bulky nature of the end product means that fertilizer plants are widely dispersed at major distributing points in all agricultural regions.

The production of *nitrogenous fertilizers* involves complex chemical processes. The basic raw material is ammonia produced by the synthetic ammonia process in which atmospheric nitrogen is combined with hydrogen; thus the availability of hydrogen is a major factor. The traditional process was to obtain hydrogen from coal or from coke-oven gases so that synthetic ammonia plants were established in mining and metallurgical areas such as the Donbass and Urals, whence synthetic ammonia was supplied to fertilizer factories throughout the main agricultural areas. More recently, increasing use has been made of hydrogen derived from natural gas, and many new fertilizer plants have been built at widely dispersed points on the natural gas pipeline system.

Phosphatic fertilizers are obtained rather more simply by the treatment of a phosphatic raw material with sulphuric acid to give superphosphates. The main source of phosphate is the apatite deposit at Kirovsk, in the Kola peninsula; the material is concentrated before being distributed to fertilizer plants throughout the European agricultural regions. A second, more recently developed major source, is the phosphorite deposit at Karatau, near Dzhambul in southern Kazakhstan, which supports fertilizer plants in Central Asia. An additional source of phosphates is ground phosphatic rock: this is extracted at numerous sites, mainly in the European regions, and either applied direct to the land or mixed with apatite in superphosphate plants.

Potash fertilizers are produced from potassium salts, mainly in the Solikamsk–Berezniki district of the Urals, in the Lvov area of the western Ukraine and at Soligorsk in Belorussia.

Synthetic Rubber

Over the world as a whole, the main source of rubber is the rubber tree *Hevea brasiliensis* but, for obvious climatic reasons, this is not grown in the U.S.S.R. At one time it was hoped that the problem could be solved by the cultivation of other latex-producing species such as kok-sagyz (*Taraxacum kok-saghyz*), tau-sagyz (*Scorzonera tau-saghyz*), guayule (*Parthenium argentatum*) and milkweed (*Asclepias*). These were introduced on a large scale in the 1930s, mainly in Central Asia. The experiment proved much less successful than had been hoped, hence the growth of a synthetic rubber industry which is expanding rapidly as the use of road transport increases. The first process to be used involved the distillation of ethyl alcohol from potatoes, and plant using this process were established in the 1930s at Yaroslavl', Voronezh, Yefremov (Tula oblast), Kazan' and Leningrad. Nowadays the bulk of synthetic rubber production is based on the byproducts of oil refining: the majority of the older plants have been converted to this process and additional plants have been built, for example at Sumgait (near Baku), Sterlitamak, Tolyatti and Volzhskiy. The majority of synthetic rubber production now occurs in oil-refining districts.

Plastics

This is a branch of the chemical industry which has developed mainly over the past 25 years in association with the growth of oil and gas production. In 1950 the U.S.S.R. produced only 67,000 tonnes of "synthetic resins and plastics", most of this in the form of thermo-setting resins of the bakelite variety. In 1977, output was about 3,300,000 tonnes, produced mainly from the by-products of oil refining. Regions with a tradition of chemical manufacture and a high level of technology, notably the Centre, have attracted the great bulk of the plastics industry, but it also occurs in several other oil-refining areas, for example at Groznyy, near Kuybyshev, at Guryev and at Novopolotsk.

Artificial and Synthetic Fibres

Here, too, growth has been relatively recent: total output in this sector has risen from 24,000 tonnes in 1950 to just over a million tonnes in 1977. There are two main branches: the production of cellulose fibres derived from timber and cotton, and that of wholly synthetic fibres made by chemical processes. Before the Second World War, practically all the Soviet output of manmade fibres was of the first type, mainly rayon which was produced in half a dozen plants within the traditional textile region of the European forest zone. In the 1940s and 1950s, additional plants were built in the Urals, Siberia and Central Asia as well as in the European regions.

Since the 1950s, however, wholly synthetic fibres have made up an increasing proportion—now nearly 40 per cent—of production in this sector. These are the Soviet equivalent of nylon, dacron, orlon and other fibres familiar in the West.

The plant producing these materials are found mainly within the textile-manufacturing districts which are their markets, and close to oil refineries and gas-processing plant from whence they obtain their raw materials.

Other Chemical Industries

The remaining chemical industries, producing such diverse items as dyes, paints, pharmaceuticals and photochemicals, are situated mainly in the towns of the European U.S.S.R., particularly those of the Industrial Centre.

TIMBER INDUSTRIES

More than 700 million hectares, nearly one-third of the total area of the U.S.S.R., are forest-covered and timber is a major natural resource, industrial raw material and export commodity. Industries based on timber employ nearly 3 million people, some 8 per cent of the industrial labour force, and another 400,000 are employed in forestry. Of the 380 million cubic metres produced each year (30 per cent of the world output) at least a quarter is still used for fuel, being particularly important in areas remote from sources of coal, oil or gas. The remainder goes to paper-making, to a variety of timber-based industries or for export.

Although an estimated 80 per cent of Soviet timber reserves are in Siberia, nearly two-thirds of the timber produced comes from the European section of the country, which is also the market for three-quarters of the timber products. While the timber industries are located, in a general sense, in the market areas, individual processing centres are usually located where there are good transport facilities, timber being a major item carried by the railways and making up nearly half the volume of goods carried by inland waterways. The general arrangement is one whereby felled timber is transported to saw-milling centres from which the sawn timber is distributed to market areas. Sawmilling is thus carried on not only in many of the towns of the forested zone of European Russia and at a smaller number of centres in southern Siberia but also outside the forest belt at such places as Saratov, Volgograd, Rostov and Dnepropetrovsk, all of which receive their timber by waterway. Such activities as furniture making, on the other hand, are more concentrated into a few large cities, the most important centres being Moscow, Leningrad and Kiyev. Paper production, one of the largest consumers of timber, is especially important in the North-west and Ural regions though the biggest single centre is at Pravdinsk, near Gorkiy, whence comes the paper for *Pravda* and other leading publications.

At the moment, there is a notable lack of balance in the timber industry between sources of supply and areas of demand. Both are mainly in European Russia, but are usually separated by long distances over which timber must be transported, thus greatly increasing costs. The rate of cutting in European Russia now exceeds that of natural growth by a considerable margin and it is intended to accelerate the exploitation of the huge Siberian reserves where current rates of cutting are equivalent to less than 10 per cent of the natural growth rate. The movement of the industry eastward across the Urals will, of course, place a still heavier burden on transport facilities as areas of exploitation will become still more distant from the main manufacturing districts. The timber industry provides one of the best illustrations of a major problem in Soviet economic geography, namely the great distance which often separates rich raw material resources from the districts in which they are required.

TEXTILE INDUSTRIES

The textile industry was one of the few branches of manufacturing which were at all well developed before the Revolution. Traditional domestic linen manufacture in the mixed forest zone of European Russia was succeeded, in the nineteenth century, by mechanized textile production, mainly of cotton, which was heavily concentrated in the Moscow basin. Cotton has remained by far the most important branch of textile manufacture in the U.S.S.R., though its predominance has slightly declined in recent years. Of all types of cloth produced, 67 per cent is still cotton, compared with 83 per cent in 1913.

The rate of growth of the textile industry in the inter-war years and during the 1940s was a good deal less rapid than that of the heavier branches. Between 1913 and 1950 output of all types of cloth rose by less than 60 per cent (Table 19). Since 1950, however, growth has accelerated and total

TABLE 19. *Textile production, 1913–76 (millions of square metres (figures in brackets are index numbers relating production to that of 1913))*

	1913		1950		1960		1976	
Cotton	1817	(100)	2745	(151)	4838	(266)	6779	(373)
Woollen	138	(100)	193	(140)	439	(318)	764	(554)
Linen	121	(100)	257	(212)	516	(426)	807	(667)
Hemp and jute	81	(100)	73	(90)	168	(207)	153	(189)
"Silk"*	35	(100)	106	(303)	675	(1929)	1599	(4569)
Total	2192	(100)	3374	(154)	6636	(303)	10,102	(461)

* Including artificial and synthetic textiles.

production trebled by 1976. The output of cotton textiles has expanded less rapidly than that of other branches: the biggest growth has been achieved in the case of "silk", but it should be noted that this includes artificial and synthetic fibres, which now make up the bulk of the production in this category.

Cotton

The production of cotton cloth is largely divorced from the main cotton-growing areas, a state of affairs which has persisted since the mechanization of the industry in the nineteenth century. The R.S.F.S.R., which grows very little if any cotton, still produces nearly 80 per cent of the Soviet Union's cotton cloth, much the same proportion as in 1913. 65 per cent comes from the Industrial Centre alone. Central Asia and Transcaucasia, the main cotton-growing districts, still produce less than 10 per cent.

The great cotton towns of the Centre lie mainly to the north-east of Moscow, between the capital and the upper Volga: the industry is carried on in more than thirty towns in this district, of which Ivanovo is the most important. Cotton manufacture also takes place on a smaller scale in several towns in Belorussia, the Baltic and North-western regions, the Ukraine and the Urals. Since the Revolution, new mills have been established at Leninakan, Kirovabad and Baku in Transcaucasia, at Tashkent, Fergana, Ashkhabad and Dushanbe in Central Asia and at Barnaul in West Siberia. Current plans envisage further expansion of the industry in cotton-growing districts; even so the Centre is expected to continue producing two-thirds of the country's cotton cloth. One major advance has been achieved: whereas before the Revolution half the raw cotton was imported, the present, much larger industry is supplied entirely from internal resources.

Wool

Although the production of woollen cloth is more than five times that of 1913, the actual quantity is still less than one-ninth that of cotton. The woollen branch is rather more widely dispersed. The Centre is again the most important single region, but woollen textiles are also produced in a number of towns in the North-west, Belorussian, Black Earth Centre, Volga, Ural, Ukraine, Georgia and Central Asian regions.

Linen

Linen manufacture is, as might be expected, a speciality of the Centre and North-west. It is carried on in a number of towns of the cotton-manufacturing belt, where Kostroma is the leading producer, as well as in Belorussia and the Baltic republics.

Silk and Artificial Fibres

These are made in three regions, Central Asia and Transcaucasia (where the main product is natural silk), and the Centre, which accounts for over 70 per cent of the total and where production is almost entirely of artificial and synthetic textiles.

It will be observed that the textile industry as a whole is heavily concentrated in the Centre, which is the dominant producer in all branches. Conversely, the industry is poorly represented in such major industrial areas as the Donbass, Urals and Kuzbass, where its introduction might well be encouraged in order to produce a more varied employment structure.

OTHER INDUSTRIES

With the single exception of textiles, only passing reference has so far been made to the production of consumer goods, the large-scale output of which is such a characteristic feature of the economies of Western Europe and North America. As has already been suggested, Soviet economic planners, in their desire to develop the heavy industrial base, have devoted a relatively small proportion of the capital funds available to investment in the consumer goods industries, and the output of these has risen much more slowly than in the case of the heavier branches. Over the past twenty years, however, rather more attention has been paid to the production of consumer goods and output has accelerated.

Soviet sources frequently distinguish between "Group A" industries, producing energy, raw materials and capital equipment (the "means of production"), and "Group B" producing items for consumption. Since the inception of the first five-year plan in 1928, it is claimed, total industrial production has increased 110-fold. Within this total, however, the output of Group A industries has multiplied by 288 and that of Group B industries by 46, a ratio of more than 6 to 1 in favour of Group A. The discrepancy was most marked down to the mid-1950s; between 1928 and 1955, total production increased twenty-onefold, Group A by 39 times and Group B ninefold, a ratio of 4.3 to 1. Between 1955 and 1970, however, when total industrial production increased 3.7-fold, Group A output multiplied 4.1 times and Group B 3.1 times a ratio of 1.4 to 1. Finally, between 1970 and 1975, total industrial output rose by 43 per cent, Group A production by 46 per cent and Group B by 37 per cent, a ratio of only 1.25 to 1. Thus, although it is true that producer goods industries still receive the lion's share (at least 80 per cent) of capital investment in industry, the growth rates of the two sectors are closer to each other than ever before.

As a result of these trends, recent years have witnessed a rapid rise in most types of consumer goods production. To give a few examples, in 1977 (1955 figures in brackets) the U.S.S.R. produced 2,088,000 (445,000) motor vehicles, 7 million (495,000) television and 8.7 (3.5) million radio receivers, 3.6 million (87,000) domestic washing machines, 5.8 million (151,000) refrigerators, 1 million (235,000) motorcycles, 61 (20) million clocks and watches, 735 (270) million pairs of leather footwear and 1,511,000 (432,000) pieces of knitwear. Despite these increases, *per capita* production of most consumer goods is still well behind that of other industrially advanced powers, though the gap is undoubtedly closing.

INDUSTRIAL REGIONS (Fig. 36)

Soviet industry is a good deal less concentrated in its distribution than that of most European countries, partly as a result of its planned dispersal and the

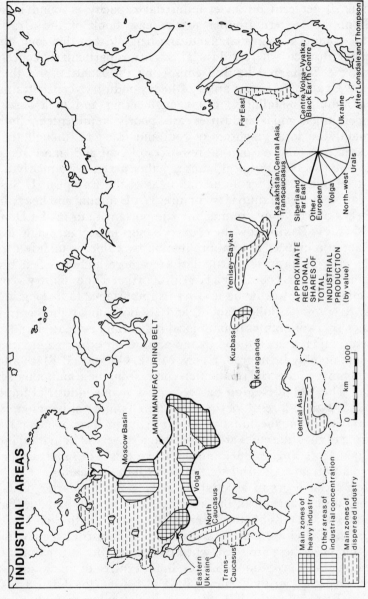

Fig. 36. Industrial regions (based on a map by R. E. Lonsdale and J. H. Thompson, *Economic Geography*, 36, no. 1, Jan. 1960, p. 42; modified by the author).

policy of establishing some industrial capacity in each of the Major Economic Regions. As a result, industrial regions are by no means easy to define. However, there are a number of areas which make a major contribution to Soviet industrial production and may thus be identified as industrial regions; Fig. 36 attempts to show their present distribution.

More than 70 per cent of Soviet industrial capacity is found in an area stretching from the western frontier to the east flank of the Urals which constitutes the country's main manufacturing belt. Within this zone, there are several extensive districts where industrial activity is particularly concentrated. Two of these, the **Eastern Ukraine** embracing the Donbass and the Dnepr Bend, and the **Urals,** are major areas of heavy industry, concentrating their attention on mining, metallurgy, heavy engineering and to a lesser extent chemicals; consumer goods industries are poorly represented. Both have depended mainly on local resources of coal and iron ore, though the Urals, as we have seen, rely also on outside resources of coal and, more recently, of iron as well. The two metallurgical bases together account for nearly a fifth of Soviet industrial output. Other industrial areas of the European U.S.S.R. are much more varied in their industrial structure. While mining and heavy industry are by no means absent, they are much less important than in the Donbass or Urals. The **Moscow Basin,** now the country's most important single industrial region with about a quarter of total production by value, is mainly concerned with textiles, with engineering, particularly the more highly skilled branches, and with chemicals, and accounts for a large proportion of the country's consumer goods production. The Moscow basin owes its importance to its long industrial tradition, its reservoir of skilled labour and its position at the centre of the communications network rather than to local industrial raw materials. A similar situation, on a smaller scale, is found in and around the other major cities of the European plain, notably Leningrad, Kiyev, Minsk, Odessa and Riga; altogether about a fifth of Soviet industrial production comes from these and other scattered urban centres. The **Volga Region** has become of major industrial importance over the past 25 years as a result of the rapid development of its resources of oil and hydroelectricity and the function of the river itself as a major transport artery. Its string of riverside cities are engaged in a variety of activities, including oil refining, food processing, engineering and chemicals. The same may be said of the much less important industrial zone of the **North Caucasus.**

Asiatic regions as a group account for only about a quarter of industrial output, rather more than half of this coming from Siberia and the Far East. Only the **Kuzbass** and possibly the **Karaganda** district, with their coal-mining and metallurgical activities, can be considered as industrial regions of major significance, and even these are small when compared with the major industrial concentrations of the European U.S.S.R. Small centres of heavy industry are found, as we have seen, in the Yenisey–Baykal district, the Far East, Central Asia and the Transcaucasus, but these are of local rather than national importance. These districts also carry on a variety of other manufacturing industries which are now rapidly expanding but are as yet of limited significance to the industrial economy as a whole.

CHAPTER 10

TRANSPORT

In a country the size of the Soviet Union, any attempt at developing the available natural resources must obviously involve vast capital investment in the development of transport systems that permit the carriage of large volumes of raw materials and finished goods over great distances. The discovery and exploitation of new sources of raw materials, the building up of new industrial areas and the expansion of agriculture into new lands have all involved both a strengthening of inter-regional transport links and a rapid rise in the volume of freight and passenger movement by all the transport media. Over the past sixty years, the amount of passenger traffic within the U.S.S.R. has increased nearly twenty-fourfold, while the movement of freight has multiplied more than forty times (Tables 20 and 21).

This great increase in the volume of transport within the U.S.S.R. has been accompanied by striking changes in the relative importance of the various transport media. Prior to the Revolution, three-fifths of the freight traffic was carried by rail and the remainder was moved almost entirely by inland waterways and by coastwise shipping routes. In the inter-war years, the railways' share of goods traffic continued to increase steadily while the significance of water transport diminished and that of roads increased but little. Since the 1950s the relative, though not the absolute, importance of the railways has declined. Roads are becoming much more significant, though their position is still a relatively minor one in comparison with the situation in western Europe or North America. There has been a notable revival of coastwise shipping as a

TABLE 20. *Principal Forms of Freight Transport within the U.S.S.R.*
(Thousand Million Tonne-Kilometres (Figures in Brackets Indicate Percentages of Total Freight Traffic))

	1913		1950		1960		1976	
Railway	76.4	(60.6)	602.3	(84.4)	1504.3	(79.8)	3295.4	(60.7)
Road	0.1	(0.1)	20.1	(2.8)	98.5	(5.2)	354.8	(6.5)
Inland waterway	28.9	(22.9)	46.2	(6.5)	99.6	(5.3)	222.7	(4.1)
Sea	20.3	(16.1)	39.7	(5.6)	131.5	(7.0)	762.1	(14.0)
Air	—	—	0.1	(n)	0.6	(n)	2.7	(n)
Pipeline	0.3	(0.2)	4.9	(0.7)	51.2	(2.7)	794.6	(14.6)
Total	126.0	(100.0)	713.3	(100.0)	1885.7	(100.0)	5432.3	(100.0)

TABLE 21. *Principal Forms of Passenger Transport within the U.S.S.R.*
(Thousand million passenger-kilometres (figures in brackets indicate percentages of
total passenger traffic))

	1913		1950		1960		1976	
Railway	30.3	(92.7)	88.0	(89.5)	170.8	(68.5)	315.1	(40.4)
Road	*	*	5.2	(5.3)	61.0	(24.4)	325.3	(41.7)
Inland waterway	1.4	(4.3)	2.7	(2.7)	4.3	(1.7)	6.0	(0.8)
Sea	1.0	(3.0)	1.2	(1.2)	1.3	(0.5)	2.4	(0.3)
Air	—	—	1.2	(1.2)	12.1	(4.8)	130.8	(16.8)
Total	32.7	(100.0)	98.3	(100.0)	249.5	(100.0)	779.6	(100.0)

* Not recorded.

means of freight movement, and pipelines now make a significant contribution. The dominance of the railway has been even more striking in the case of passenger movement, some 90 per cent of which was still by rail as late as 1950. Over the past twenty years, however, an increasing volume of short-distance movement has taken place by road, and airlines now account for a large number of the longer journeys.

RAILWAYS

Although the building of railways began rather late in the Russian Empire— the first trunk line, from Moscow to St. Petersburg, was not in operation until 1851—the Soviet régime inherited a fairly extensive network of 71,700 km and this has been nearly doubled to reach 138,500 km in 1976. The Soviet network is at its densest in the European part of the country, particularly to the west of the Volga (Fig. 37). There is a distinct radial pattern of trunk routes centred on Moscow, while the closest network is in the Ukraine, especially on the Donbass coalfield. Beyond the Volga, the pattern is one of a few major trunk routes from which run numerous branch lines; only in the Ural region is there anything approaching a network.

The bulk of the railway system west of the Volga was built before the Revolution, and Soviet construction in this part of the country has consisted mainly of "short cuts" giving more direct connections between major cities, and short branch lines. A large part of the railway building during the Soviet period has been in the Asiatic regions, most of it in a middle zone extending across southern Siberia and northern Kazakhstan from the Urals to Lake Baykal. In addition, links with such outlying regions as Central Asia and Transcaucasia have been greatly improved. In these areas, several major trunk lines have been built, notably the Turksib (Turkestan–Siberia) railway, which links Central Asia with the Trans-Siberian, the Yuzhsib (South Siberian) and Sredsib (Middle Siberian) lines, which run eastwards from the Urals south of and parallel to the Trans-Siberian, and the line to the south-east of the Aral Sea providing a

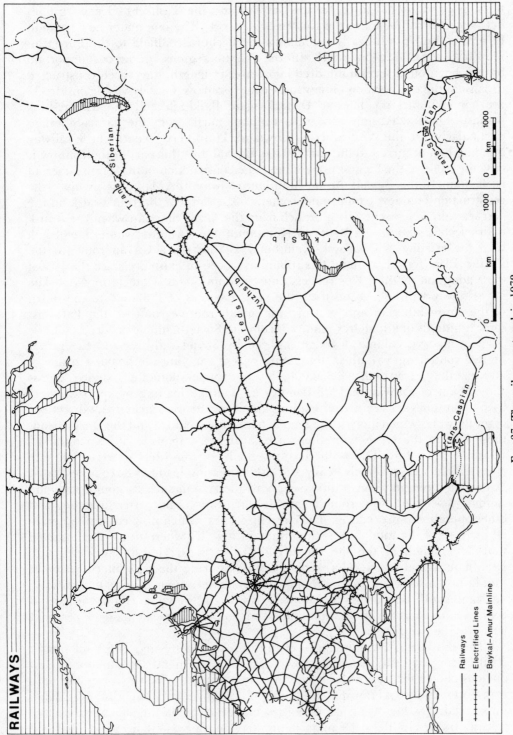

RAILWAYS

Railways ——————
Electrified Lines ++++++++
Baykal–Amur Mainline — — —

FIG. 37. The railway network in 1978.

third link (additional to the Trans-Caspian and the Tashkent–Orenburg line) between Central Asia and the European network. The one major new route in Europe is the Vorkuta railway, linking the Pechora coalfield to the European industrial areas (see page 94). In the Asiatic regions, numerous important branch lines, often several hundred kilometres in length, have been constructed to assist in the exploitation of new industrial resources. Clearly visible on Fig. 37 are, for example, the lines to Dzhezkazgan, Balkhash and the Mangyshlak peninsula in Kazakhstan and those running north from the Trans-Siberian, particularly into the West Siberian Lowland. Until very recently, little railway building had occurred to the east of Lake Baykal, but this part of the country is now the scene of the biggest project since the construction of the Trans-Siberian itself, namely the Baykal–Amur Mainline railway (BAM). This involves the construction of a new trunk route, some 3000 km in length, from Bratsk on the Angara (already reached by a branch from the Trans-Siberian when the Bratsk hydroelectric station was built) to Komsomol'sk-na-Amure, where it will link with the existing Khabarovsk–Komsomol'sk–Sovetskaya Gavan route to the Pacific. Plans for a line along this route have been in existence since the 1930s; their adoption in the 1970s reflects both economic and strategic motives. The new railway will help to open up the vast resources of the zone to the north of the Trans-Siberian and will provide an alternative route to the Far East some hundreds of kilometres removed from the Soviet-Chinese border.

The massive volume of freight carried by Soviet railways and the rather limited route length result in the Soviet system carrying the heaviest traffic of any in the world: the 3,330,000,000,000 tonne-kilometres carried across 138,500 km of railway in 1976 denotes an average loading of approximately 24 million tonnes. Even higher loadings occur on the most heavily used sections of the network, which include the lines between the Donbass and the Dnepr bend, those linking the Urals with the Kuzbass and Karaganda, the Novosibirsk–Irkutsk section of the Trans-Siberian, and the lines from Moscow to the Ukraine and Urals. These extremely heavy and still increasing loadings have necessitated large-scale investment in improvements to the system such as double-tracking (about 30 per cent of the route length), electrification and better signalling and other operational procedures. The electrified lines, which now constitute nearly 30 per cent of the total, are distinguished in Fig. 37, where it may be observed that these include all the lines already identified as carrying the heaviest loads. Elsewhere, diesel traction has replaced steam during the past fifteen years. It should be emphasized that, although the relative importance of the railways has significantly declined in recent years (Table 20) the volume of traffic carried continues to increase at a rapid rate and rose by no less than 65 per cent between 1965 and 1975.

The continuing predominance of the railways in the movement of freight results from positive decisions by Soviet transport planners, but is in any case an obvious choice for the Soviet economy, the nature of which involves the bulk transport of industrial raw materials and products over very long distances. High bulk, relatively low-value commodities make up by far the greatest part of railway traffic. In 1976 the main items were (on a tonne-km basis): coal and coke (17 per cent), ores and metals (15 per cent), petroleum products (15 per cent), mineral building materials (13 per cent), timber (9 per cent), grain (4 per cent) and mineral fertilizers (3 per cent).

Passenger movement by rail, although still increasing, may be considered of secondary importance and is now barely 40 per cent of the total (Table 21). In recent years it has been overtaken by road travel for short journeys, while an increasing proportion of long-distance travellers go by air.

INLAND WATERWAYS

Rivers and canals have long been of great importance in the economic life of Russia and, although they now carry only about 4 per cent of internal goods traffic compared with 23 per cent in 1913, the actual volume carried has increased nearly eightfold since the Revolution. In Asiatic Russia, north of the Trans-Siberian railway, the great rivers which flow to the Arctic are the main transport arteries for a vast area, but the volume of traffic which they carry is small and the European waterways are far more important (Fig. 38). The low relief of the European plain with its large, slow-flowing rivers whose headwaters are close to each other and separated by low watersheds, provides ideal conditions for water transport. As we saw in Chapter 3, the rivers were used as trading arteries in early times and some of the canals between them were built in the days of Peter the Great. A great deal of capital has been invested in canal construction and river improvement during the Soviet period. The most important system is that based on the Volga, which now carries two-thirds of all water-borne traffic. The upper Volga is joined through the Rybinsk reservoir and Lakes Onega and Ladoga to the Baltic and to Moscow via the Moscow canal. This system is linked to the White Sea by the White Sea–Baltic Canal and to the Black Sea by way of the Volga–Don Canal, opened in 1952. The Kama and its tributaries give access to the western flank of the Urals. The development of the Volga waterways has been a major achievement of the Soviet period. Apart from the actual building of the canals, there has been much widening and deepening of rivers, particularly in the section between the upper Volga and the Baltic, where the Rybinsk reservoir serves as a regulating water body. Navigation improvements have often been accompanied by the installation of major hydroelectric plant, as for example at Kuybyshev and Volgograd and at Tsimlyansk on the Don. Many other rivers of European Russia are navigable over long distances, at least by small vessels, though none is comparable in importance to the Volga. The Dnepr has been much improved, particularly by the construction of the Zaporozh'ye and Kakhovka dams. The Dnepr is also joined, by a canal through the Poles'ye, to the Bug, a tributary of the Vistula.

One major drawback to the use of waterways throughout practically the whole of the Soviet Union is, of course, the winter freeze which lasts for periods ranging from four to six months according to latitude.

Of the 485 million tonnes of freight carried by the inland waterway system in 1976, building materials accounted for 289 million, timber 68 million, petroleum products 38 million and coal and coke 24 million tonnes.

Fig. 38. Inland waterways. Canals and major hydroelectric stations are named in red.

SEA TRANSPORT

Quite apart from its importance in the foreign trade of the U.S.S.R., maritime transport also plays a significant role in the movement of goods from one part of the U.S.S.R. to another. In fact, on a tonne-kilometre basis, more than three times as much "internal" goods traffic is carried by sea as by river and canal. Traffic is heaviest between the various ports of the Black Sea and across the Caspian, these routes working in conjunction with the river and canal systems already mentioned. As might be expected, petroleum products make up about half the traffic. The Northern Sea Route through the Arctic Ocean serves as an outlet for the limited traffic of the Siberian rivers and is even used for trade with the Far Eastern Region, though it is only open in its entirety for ten or twelve weeks in the year. The Far East also depends to some extent on the lengthy sea route from the Black Sea via the Dardanelles and Suez Canal.

ROAD TRANSPORT

Road transport in the Soviet Union is still a good deal less developed than in Western Europe or North America, though major expansion has taken place over the last twenty years. In 1950 the U.S.S.R. produced only 362,900 motor vehicles of which a mere 65,000 were cars. In 1977 output was 1,280,000 cars, 734,000 lorries and 74,000 public service vehicles. While this increase in production denotes the establishment of a large-scale motor-vehicle industry; the number of vehicles on the roads remains rather low; probably fewer than 12 million. The road network is also somewhat limited, with 1,407,000 km of motor road, of which about 700,000 km are hard-surfaced. The latter figure does, however, indicate considerable progress in the post-war period: in 1945 there were less than 150,000 km in this category. Obviously the network of main roads is a very open one, even in the European part of the country. In the European regions most of the traffic is over quite short distances. Roads are much more important for long-distance traffic in areas where railways are not available, though the actual volume of traffic in such areas is small. Some of the biggest Soviet road-building projects have been concerned with such outlying regions. The Aldan Highway, for example, from Never (near the Chinese border) to Yakutsk, is one of several roads running northwards from points along the Trans-Siberian railway, and there has been a good deal of construction in Transcaucasia and Central Asia. During the 1960s and 1970s, much attention has been paid to the improvement of the system in the European part of the country, and modern highways now link the major cities.

Road transport, however, still accounts for only 6.5 per cent of all freight movement and the great bulk of this is over very short distances to or from the nearest railway station. Passenger travel by road has grown very rapidly over the last twenty years and (on a passenger-kilometre basis) now surpasses that on the railways. While much of this increased road travel will be short-distance commuting into and within the major urban areas, it does include a growing volume of movement by bus between the cities of the European U.S.S.R.

AIR TRANSPORT

Aircraft at present play a negligible role in the movement of freight and are most important in this respect in remote parts of Siberia, where small consignments of high value goods are carried by air. As a means of passenger transport, however, airways are of rapidly growing importance for long journeys and now account for 17 per cent of all passenger movement. Fares over long distances are generally little higher than on the railways. The national airline, *Aeroflot*, has an internal network of some 860,000 km serving well over 3000 airports, by which most major cities can be reached from Moscow within twelve hours. In 1976, over 100 million passengers were carried on internal flights.

CHAPTER 11

POPULATION

POPULATION GROWTH

Although a great deal of information concerning the population of the Russian Empire and the Soviet Union can be gathered from a variety of sources, it is difficult to present a concise summary of population growth for a number of reasons. In the first place, only five complete censuses have ever been taken, in 1897, 1926, 1939, 1959 and 1970. For the period before 1897 and for years between the censuses, it is necessary to have recourse to various estimates and partial enumerations, the accuracy of which must always be open to some doubt. The profound effects on population growth of the First World War, the Revolution and its aftermath, and the Second World War, together with the several major boundary revisions which have taken place during the past sixty years, add to the problems involved. Nevertheless, it is possible to give at least a general picture of population growth and change since the early eighteenth century and this will provide, in many senses, a commentary on the historical and economic developments discussed in earlier chapters.

1724–1897

Some of the earliest population estimates available were made during the reign of Peter the Great. These do not cover the entire population within the Russian Empire as it then existed, but are concerned with the "Russian population" only, that is to say, with the whole population, regardless of ethnic origin, living in the European part of the territory under Peter's control, together with such Russians, Ukrainians and Belorussians as lived in the Asiatic part. Figures on this basis are available for 1724 and in Table 22 these are compared with the equivalent totals (i.e. covering the same areas and the same classes of people) for 1859 and 1897.

In addition to the rapid natural increase indicated by a population growth of more than 400 per cent in 173 years, these figures show a major redistribution of the Russian population over that period. Most striking is the movement from north to south in European Russia involving large-scale colonization of the steppe. Whereas in 1724 nearly two-thirds of the Russian population lived in the forested central and northern parts of the European plain, by 1897 this proportion had fallen to less than one-third. While the actual numbers living in the centre and north increased nearly threefold over the 173-year period, the

134

TABLE 22. *The Growth and Distribution of the "Russian Population", 1724–1897*
(Millions (Figures in brackets indicate percentage of total))

	1724		1859		1897		1897 as % of 1724
Total	17.9	(100.0)	58.6	(100.0)	94.3	(100.0)	527
European Russia	17.5	(97.8)	55.2	(94.2)	87.4	(92.7)	498
Centre and North	1.3	(63.2)	20.4	(34.8)	30.7	(32.6)	272
South*	6.2	(34.6)	34.8	(59.4)	56.7	(60.1)	915
Asiatic Russia	0.4	(2.2)	3.4	(5.8)	6.9	(7.3)	1725

* Essentially the European steppelands.

population of the south rose to nearly nine times its 1724 level. Most of this redistribution took place before the middle of the nineteenth century, by which time most of the steppe had been brought under cultivation. The most rapid population increase occurred in the Asiatic part of the country which in 1724 contained only 400,000 settlers of European origin. This number had multiplied eightfold by 1859 and doubled again between 1859 and 1897. The proportion of the total Russian population living in Asia, however, remained small.

1897–1913

The total population of the Russian Empire in 1897, including all ethnic groups within its boundaries at that date, was 125.7 million. By 1913 this had risen to 165.7 million, an increase of 32 per cent in 16 years (Table 23).

TABLE 23. *Population of the Russian Empire, 1897–1913*
(Millions (Figures in brackets indicate percentage of total))

	1897		1913		1913 as % of 1897
Total	125.7	(100.0)	165.7	(100.0)	132
European Russia	103.6	(82.4)	136.1	(82.1)	131
Siberia and Far East	7.2	(5.7)	10.0	(6.0)	139
Asiatic Steppe	2.5	(2.0)	2.0	(2.4)	160
Turkestan	7.5	(6.0)	9.6	(5.8)	128
Transcaucasia	4.9	(3.9)	6.0	(3.6)	122

During this short period, the distribution of the population among the major divisions of the country changed but little. The most rapid increases were in the Asiatic steppe region (the provinces of Ural'sk, Turgay, Akmolinsk and Semipalatinsk, now part of Kazakhstan) and in Siberia and the Far East, these areas together increasing their population from 9.7 to 14 million. Growth in

Turkestan and Transcaucasia, on the other hand, was appreciably below the national average. Although regional variations in the rate of natural increase may well have played some part in bringing about these differences, there can be little doubt that the main factor at work was migration from European Russia into Siberia. This movement had been in progress since the seventeenth century but remained on a small scale until the latter part of the nineteenth. Between 1800 and 1860, some 566,000 migrants settled in Asiatic Russia and of these at least 60 per cent were convicts or exiles. The liberation of the serfs in 1861 was followed by a rapid increase of peasant colonization in Siberia, and in the next forty years more than 2 million people moved from Europe to Asia, an annual average more than five times that of the preceding period. Migration became still more rapid in the early part of the twentieth century, totalling 3 million between 1900 and 1914 and including only a small proportion of forced migrants. Thus, between the beginning of the nineteenth century and the outbreak of the First World War, some 5.5 million people moved from European Russia into the Asiatic parts of the Empire. In the areas most affected, namely Siberia and the Far East, the natives were soon outnumbered and the population became predominantly Russian. Russians and Ukrainians accounted for 85 per cent of the people of these regions as a whole and were in the majority in all parts except Yakutia and Kamchatka. In the Asiatic steppe, where the native population was more numerous, Russians and Ukrainians accounted for some 40 per cent of the 1914 total. Turkestan, on the other hand, received relatively few settlers: the 400,000 Russians and Ukrainians living in that region in 1914 amounted to only 6 per cent of the total.

1913–26

The period between 1913 and the first Soviet census of 1926 was one of great internal upheaval and thus of confusion as regards the details of population growth. The 1926 census revealed a total of 147 million people within the frontiers of the U.S.S.R. as they were at that date, 18.7 million less than the figure for the Russian Empire in 1913. It should be remembered, however, that in the intervening period the Soviet Union had lost control of Finland, the Baltic States, Poland and other western territories with a total 1913 population of 26.4 million. Thus the figure which should be compared with the 1926 total is 139.3 million (165.7 − 26.4), indicating a growth of 7.7 million or 5.6 per cent in the thirteen-year period. Such an increase was a good deal less rapid than the pre-war average, an obvious result of the special events of the period. Had pre-war rates of increase been maintained, the 1926 population should have been at least 175 million, 28 million more than was in fact the case. The allocation of this "population deficit" to its various causes is a complicated process and many different views have been expressed. The most likely suggestion is as follows: emigration 2 million, military deaths in the First World War 2 million, deaths in the civil war, epidemics and famine 14 million, deficit of births due to reduced fertility during this period 10 million.

1926–39

In the years between the 1926 census and that of 1939 there were no significant changes in the boundaries of the U.S.S.R. and the results are therefore strictly comparable. Over this period of thirteen years, the Soviet population rose from 147 to 170.5 million, an increase of 16 per cent. This represents a rate of growth nearly three times as rapid as that for the period 1913–26 but still well below the rate for 1897–1913, reflecting slow natural increase in the difficult years of the late 1920s and early 1930s. Once again, migration from European to Asiatic areas was an outstanding feature (Table 24).

TABLE 24. *Population of the U.S.S.R., 1926–39*
(Millions (figures in brackets indicate percentage of total))

	1926		1939		1939 as % of 1926
Total	147.0	(100.0)	170.5	(100.0)	116
European U.S.S.R.	114.3	(77.7)	129.3	(75.8)	113
Siberia and Far East	12.5	(8.5)	16.6	(9.7)	133
Central Asia	7.6	(5.2)	10.5	(6.2)	138
Kazakhstan	6.1	(4.1)	6.1	(3.6)	100
Transcaucasia	6.6	(4.5)	8.0	(4.7)	121

Rates of growth well above the national average were recorded in Central Asia and Transcaucasia as well as in Siberia and the Far East. In the former, essentially non-Russian areas, declining death rates as well as an appreciable migration from European areas were responsible for the rapid growth while in Siberia and the Far East migration gain was the dominant factor. Between 1926 and 1939 there was a net migration gain of 1.2 million in the Ural region, 1.2 million in Siberia and 900,000 in the Far East.

1939–59

The census of 1939 was followed, in 1940, by the addition of large territories in the west, which raised the population of the U.S.S.R. by more than 20 million to a total of 190.7 million and it is with the latter figure that post-war data must be compared. The situation regarding population change in the Soviet Union during and immediately after the Second World War is very obscure and a number of conflicting estimates have been made for 1945–6. The lowest of these puts the 1945 total at only 173 million, 20 million below that of 1940. Had pre-war rates of natural increase continued during the war years, the population would have reached at least 203 million by 1945, suggesting a wartime population deficit of some 30 million. When we consider that military deaths, at a conservative estimate, numbered well over 5 million, that civilian losses were at least as great and that high mortality and low fertility must have affected the whole population during the war years, this estimate appears not at all unreasonable. Furthermore, if the 1945 estimate of 173 million is accepted, then the 1958 census total of 208.8 million indicates an increase of 21 per cent in the first fourteen years of the post-war period. This would seem to be a likely rate of growth in view of official birth-rate and death-rate figures which give a natural increase rate of 1.7 per cent in 1950.

Whatever confusion may exist concerning the events of the 1940s, the 1959 census figure of 208.8 million may be taken as having a high degree of accuracy. This total indicates a population growth of only 9.5 per cent in the twenty years since 1939, comprising an actual decline during the war and an accelerated increase in the post-war period. For comparison with earlier dates, a simplified regional breakdown of the census figures is given in Table 25, while Table 26 gives a more detailed picture.

TABLE 25. *Population of the U.S.S.R., 1939–59*
(Millions (figures in brackets indicate percentage of total))

	1939		1959		1959 as % of 1939
Total	190.7	(100.0)	208.8	(100.0)	109.5
European U.S.S.R.	149.5	(78.4)	151.7	(72.7)	101.5
Siberia and Far East*	16.6	(8.7)	24.6	(11.8)	148.2
Central Asia	10.5	(5.5)	13.7	(6.6)	130.5
Kazakhstan	6.1	(3.2)	9.3	(4.4)	152.5
Transcaucasia	8.0	(4.2)	9.5	(4.5)	118.8

* Including the Kurgan and Tyumen oblasts which, in 1959, were part of the Ural economic region.

These figures reveal striking contrasts between the various economic regions (Fig. 39). The population within the present boundaries of the Soviet Union increased by 9.5 per cent between 1939 and 1959. The majority of economic regions in the European part of the country experienced population growth below this national average, exceptions being the North Caucasus region, where there was considerable agricultural expansion in the post-war years, and the Donets–Dnepr region of the Ukraine in which further industrial development took place after the massive reconstruction of war-damaged plant. An actual decline in numbers occurred in the Centre, Black Earth Centre and Volga–Vyatka regions, in the South-west region of the Ukraine and in the Belorussian republic. In contrast to the situation in these western regions, the Urals, West Siberia, East Siberia and the Far East all recorded increases well above the national average at 29, 28, 34 and 70 per cent respectively, as did Kazakhstan (53 per cent), the Central Asian republics (30 per cent) and Transcaucasia (18 per cent). In terms of absolute numbers, the five regions of decline noted above lost rather more than 4 million people while the Urals and the three Siberian regions gained nearly 10 million, Kazakhstan and the Central Asian republics more than 3 million each and Transcaucasia 1.5 million.

TABLE 26. *Population of the U.S.S.R. by Economic Regions, 1939–59*
(Thousands (figures in brackets indicate percentage of total))

	1939		1959		1959 as % of 1939
U.S.S.R.	190,678	(100.0)	208,827	(100.0)	109.5
R.S.F.S.R.	108,379	(56.8)	117,534	(56.3)	108.4
North-west	11,169	(5.7)	11,474	(5.5)	102.7
Centre	25,308	(13.3)	24,789	(11.9)	97.9
Volga–Vyatka	8,698	(4.6)	8,253	(4.0)	94.9
Central Black Earth	10,439	(5.5)	8,698	(4.2)	83.3
Volga	12,125	(6.4)	12,454	(6.0)	102.7
North Caucasus	10,512	(5.5)	11,786	(5.6)	112.1
Ural	14,444	(7.6)	18,613	(8.9)	128.9
West Siberia	7,937	(4.2)	10,159	(4.9)	128.0
East Siberia	5,185	(2.7)	6.961	(3.3)	134.3
Far East	2,562	(1.3)	4,347	(2.1)	169.7
Ukraine	40,469	(21.2)	40,869	(20.0)	103.5
Donets–Dnepr	14,760	(7.7)	16,548	(7.9)	112.1
South-west	20,856	(10.9)	20,255	(9.7)	97.1
South	4,852	(2.5)	5,066	(2.4)	104.4
Baltic Republics	5,817	(3.1)	6,002	(2.9)	103.2
Transcaucasian Republics	8,028	(4.2)	9,505	(4.6)	118.4
Central Asian Republics	10,530	(5.5)	13,668	(6.5)	130.5
Kazakhstan	6,094	(3.2)	9,310	(4.6)	152.8
Belorussia	8,910	(4.7)	8,055	(3.6)	90.4
Moldavia	2,452	(1.3)	2,884	(1.4)	117.6

A variety of factors were responsible for these regional variations in rates of population growth. One such reason was the continued movement of population from rural areas to towns. Between 1939 and 1959, while the urban population increased by 65 per cent, that of rural areas declined by 15 per cent. Rural population decline was most marked in a number of European regions, where it amounted to more than 25 per cent and was great enough to offset the urban increases in those regions. At the same time, urban populations increased much less rapidly in the European zone than they did in Siberia, Kazakhstan and Central Asia, where rural populations, as well as urban ones, experienced considerable growth, due mainly in this case to the exceptionally high birth rates of those regions. Mention should also be made of the special effects of the Second World War, which caused abnormally high mortality in the European U.S.S.R. and accelerated the movement of population towards the east.

1959–75

Although a further census was held in 1970, it is more satisfactory to treat this sixteen-year period as a single unit rather than dividing it into two parts of very unequal length. Consequently, this section begins with an examination

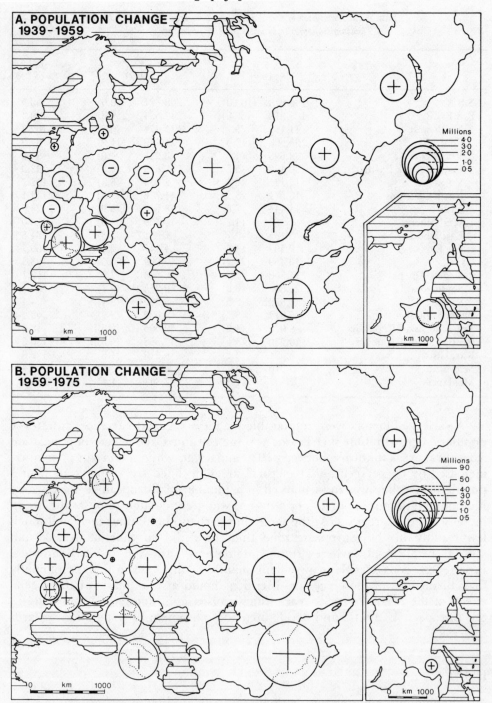

Fig. 39. Population gains and losses by economic regions. (A) 1939–59, and (B) 1959–75.

of population changes between 1959 and 1975 (the last year for which detailed data were available at the time of writing) and concludes with a discussion of current trends as exemplified by the last five years, 1970–5.

In the period between 1959 and 1975, the population of the Soviet Union increased by a further 44.5 million or 21.3 per cent, an increase appreciably greater than that achieved during the preceding twenty years. The urban population grew by 53.1 million (53.1 per cent), while that of rural areas declined by 8.6 million (7.9 per cent). Contrasts between the major geographical divisions are indicated in Table 27 and Figure 39 and a more detailed picture of regional change is given in Table 28.

TABLE 27. *Population of the U.S.S.R., 1959–75*
(Millions (figures in brackets indicate percentages of total, urban and rural populations))

	1959		1975		Change, 1959–1975	
					Millions	Per cent
Total	208.8	(100.0)	253.3	(100.0)	+ 44.5	+ 21.3
Urban	100.0	(100.0)	153.1	(100.0)	+ 53.1	+ 53.1
Rural	108.8	(100.0)	100.2	(100.0)	− 8.6	− 7.9
European U.S.S.R.	153.7	(73.6)	176.3	(69.6)	+ 22.6	+ 14.6
Urban	74.3	(74.3)	111.1	(72.6)	+ 36.7	+ 49.3
Rural	79.4	(73.0)	65.2	(65.1)	− 14.2	− 17.9
Siberia and Far East	22.6	(10.8)	26.6	(10.5)	+ 4.0	+ 17.7
Urban	12.4	(12.4)	18.3	(12.0)	+ 5.9	+ 47.6
Rural	10.2	(9.4)	8.3	(8.3)	− 1.9	− 18.6
Kazakhstan	9.3	(4.6)	14.2	(5.6)	+ 4.9	+ 52.7
Urban	4.1	(4.1)	7.6	(5.0)	+ 3.5	+ 85.4
Rural	5.2	(4.8)	6.6	(6.6)	+ 1.4	+ 26.9
Central Asia	13.7	(6.5)	22.9	(9.0)	+ 9.2	+ 67.2
Urban	4.8	(4.8)	9.0	(5.8)	+ 4.2	+ 87.5
Rural	8.9	(8.2)	13.9	(13.8)	+ 5.0	+ 56.2
Transcaucasia	9.5	(4.5)	13.3	(5.3)	+ 3.8	+ 40.0
Urban	4.4	(4.4)	7.1	(4.6)	+ 2.7	+ 61.4
Rural	5.1	(4.6)	6.2	(6.2)	+ 1.1	+ 21.6

Note: A number of changes in the boundaries of economic regions occurred between 1959 and 1975. The data in the above table are based on those for economic regions within their 1975 boundaries. Consequently the figures for 1959 differ, in some cases, from those given for 1959 in Table 25.

The population changes which have occurred since 1959 display both similarities and contrasts with those of 1939–59. Perhaps the most striking contrast is that, in the more recent period, every Major Economic Region experienced some growth, though in several cases this was very small. Once again, the European part of the country showed a growth rate (14.6 per cent) well below and the Asiatic regions a rate of growth (40 per cent) well above the national average (21.3 per cent), though this discrepancy was less marked than in the earlier period. Particularly slow rates of growth were recorded in the Volga-Vyatka, Black Earth Centre, Centre and Ural regions, where many

TABLE 28. *Population of the U.S.S.R. by Economic Regions,* 1959–75*
(Thousands (figures in brackets indicate percentage of the Soviet total))

	1959		1975		Growth 1959–75	
					000	%
U.S.S.R.	208,827	(100.0)	253,261	(100.0)	44,434	21.3
R.S.F.S.R.	117,534	(56.3)	133,741	(52.8)	16,207	13.8
North-west	10,865	(5.2)	12,749	(5.0)	1,884	17.4
Centre	25,718	(12.3)	28,255	(11.2)	2,537	9.9
Volga–Vyatka	8,252	(4.0)	8,261	(3.3)	9	0.1
Central Black Earth	7,769	(3.7)	7,787	(3.1)	18	0.2
Volga	15,975	(7.7)	18,960	(7.5)	2,985	18.7
North Caucasus	11,601	(5.6)	15,003	(5.9)	3,402	29.3
Ural	14,184	(6.8)	15,306	(6.0)	1,122	7.9
West Siberia	11,252	(5.4)	12,379	(4.9)	1,127	10.0
East Siberia	6,473	(3.1)	7,827	(3.1)	1,354	20.9
Far East	4,834	(2.3)	6,435	(2.5)	1,601	33.1
Ukraine	41,869	(20.0)	48,817	(19.3)	6,948	16.6
Donets–Dnepr	17,766	(8.5)	20,729	(8.2)	2,963	16.7
South-west	19,028	(9.1)	21,265	(8.4)	2,237	11.8
South	5,075	(2.4)	6,823	(2.7)	1,748	34.4
Baltic	6,612	(3.2)	7,976	(3.1)	1,364	20.6
Transcaucasia	9,505	(4.6)	13,315	(5.3)	3,810	40.1
Central Asia	13,682	(6.5)	22,880	(9.0)	9,198	67.2
Kazakhstan	9,295	(4.5)	14,168	(5.6)	4,873	52.4
Belorussia	8,056	(3.9)	9,331	(3.7)	1,275	15.8
Moldavia	2,885	(1.4)	3,812	(1.5)	927	32.1

Note: A number of changes in the boundaries of economic regions occurred between 1959 and 1975. The data in the above table are those for economic regions within their 1975 boundaries. Consequently, in several cases, the figures for 1959 differ from those given for 1959 in Table 26. The figures for Kaliningrad oblast (611,000 in 1959, 779,000 in 1975) are included in the totals for both the R.S.F.S.R. and the Baltic economic region.

* For the boundaries of these regions, see Fig. 18.

districts recorded an actual decline. Of all the European regions, only the North Caucasus, Moldavia and the South-west showed a growth rate above the national average, though several districts in the Volga region grew quite rapidly.

A striking change, however, occurred in the more easterly parts of the R.S.F.S.R., that is in the Urals, West Siberia, East Siberia and the Far East. Between 1939 and 1959 these regions experienced very rapid population growth but, after 1959, the populations of the Urals, West Siberia and East Siberia expanded at rates below the national average, while that of the Far East, though increasing at an above-average rate, was less striking in this respect than was formerly the case. The four regions together increased their population between 1959 and 1975 by only 5.2 million (14.2 per cent compared with a national average of 21.3 per cent) as compared with a growth between 1939 and 1959 of about 10 million (33 per cent compared with a national average of 9.5 per cent). The annual addition to the population of these regions showed a marked decline from the earlier period (325,000 as against 500,000), despite the fact that the population growth of the Soviet Union as a whole had greatly increased. Clearly, the eastern regions are no longer attracting or retaining the large number of migrants from the west who had helped to build up their populations in earlier decades. Furthermore, the rate of natural increase in these regions underwent a marked decline (see below).

The areas of most rapid population growth, by a considerable margin, were the Central Asian republics, Kazakhstan and Transcaucasia, whose populations grew by 67.2, 52.4 and 40.1 per cent respectively during the sixteen-year period. These represent annual growth rates even more rapid than those experienced between 1939 and 1959. From 1959 to 1975 the population of these regions increased by nearly 18 million, a figure representing about 40 per cent of the U.S.S.R.'s total increase. Such rates, in Central Asia and Kazakhstan at least, were too high to be sustained by natural increase alone, and indicate considerable in-migration from other parts of the country.

A more detailed picture of recent change is given in Figs. 40–42, which show total, urban and rural change respectively for 1970–5 on the basis of the smallest administrative areas for which population data are available. From these maps it will be seen that, whereas urban populations have increased in every case, rural numbers have declined over a very wide area and this has been sufficient to bring about a decline in the total population of several administrative divisions. Consequently, there are certain similarities between the map of total population change (Fig. 40) and that showing the strength of the urban element (see Fig. 46).

As the maps indicate, there was a marked population decline over a large central area of the East European Plain. This decline was most marked in the less-favoured agricultural areas in the northern part of the forest zone but also occurred in some of the more productive and more densely settled agricultural areas of the Black Earth Centre and the western Ukraine. Practically the whole of the area to the west of the Volga showed rates of increase below the national average, including not only those districts in which the rural element is dominant but also such highly urbanized areas as the Donetsk and Voroshilovgrad oblasts of the Donbass and the Yaroslavl' and Vladimir oblasts of the Centre. Elsewhere, as in the Moscow, Leningrad, Minsk and Kiyev oblasts, urban growth has been sufficient to give a total population increase above the national average, despite rural decline. The latter situation also occurs in Moldavia, the southern Ukraine and much of the North Caucasus region, where rural decline has been less than the national average, and there has been agricultural expansion as well as some industrialization. Thus, over the European zone as a whole, the main process at work has been rural depopulation, which in many areas has been on a scale so great as to cause a decline in total numbers. At the same time, the rate of urban growth has, in the majority of cases, been below the national average. Other factors at work were out-migration to other parts of the country and a low rate of natural increase.

The Volga and Ural regions show a rather different situation. Rural populations have declined in all areas but urban growth has been above the

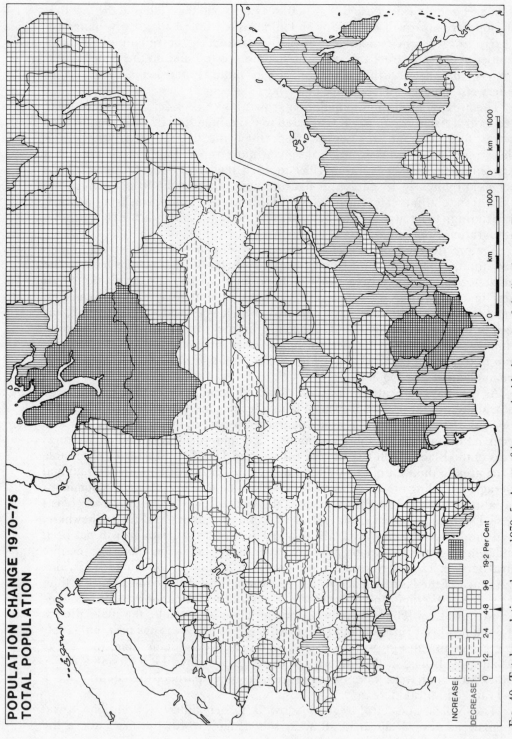

**POPULATION CHANGE 1970-75
TOTAL POPULATION**

INCREASE

DECREASE

0   1·2   2·4   4·8   9·6   19·2 Per Cent

Fig. 40. Total population change, 1970–5. Areas of increase in black, areas of decline in red. The arrowhead on the scale indicates the average gain of 4.8 per cent.

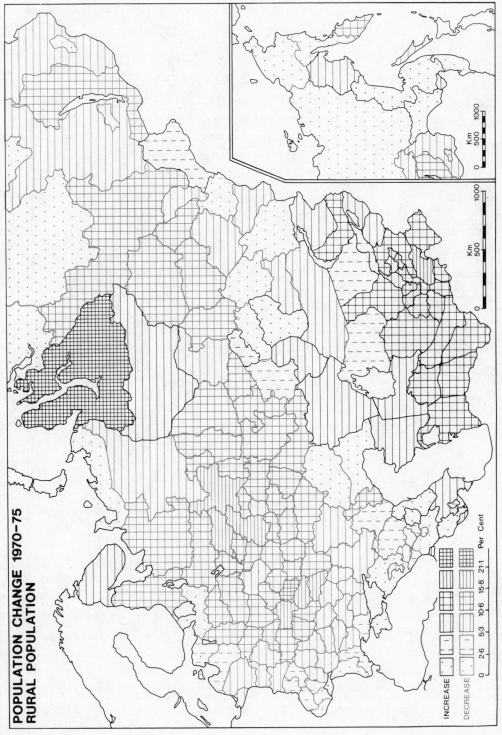

Fig. 41. Rural population change, 1970–5. Areas of increase in black, areas of decline in red. The arrowhead on the scale indicates the average decline of 5.3 per cent.

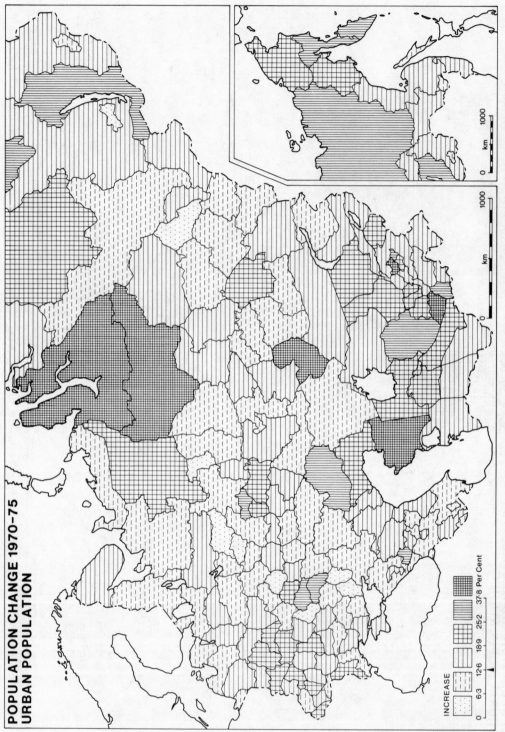

POPULATION CHANGE 1970–75
URBAN POPULATION

INCREASE

0	6·3	12·6	18·9	25·2	37·8 Per Cent

Fig. 42. Urban population change, 1970–5. The arrowhead on the scale indicates the average gain of 12.6 per cent.

national average in several cases; the net result has been to give above-average total growth in three areas: the Kuybyshev and Saratov oblasts and the Tatar A.S.S.R.

Most areas of the Transcaucasus experienced rapid increase of total population. Urban growth was generally above average and, overall, there was rural growth as well. However, rural decline set in in several districts, mainly in Georgia. In Kazakhstan and Central Asia, both rural and urban elements grew rapidly, and total growth was more rapid here than in any other part of the country. Rural decline has, however, started to affect northern Kazakhstan, mainly in the Virgin Lands.

The three Siberian regions show a good deal of variety. With few exceptions these are now areas of rural decline, most rapid in West Siberia. Urban growth is generally above average except in some western areas. Since 1970 total growth has been rapid in most districts to the east of Lake Baykal: some of the highest growth rates in the U.S.S.R. were recorded in certain northern districts, though in numerical terms such increases are of little significance. The population of the Chukotskiy A.Ok., for example, increased by 21 per cent in five years, from 101,000 to 122,000.

DEMOGRAPHIC TRENDS

The variations in national and regional population growth rates discussed in the previous section result from various combinations of the two components of population change, which are migration and natural increase. As far as migration is concerned, the population of the U.S.S.R. may be treated as a closed system in that movements of people between the Soviet Union and other countries take place only on a very small scale and have a negligible effect on national population growth. Internal migration, however, occurs on a large and increasing scale. Two forms of movement are involved, that from rural areas into towns, which influences local distribution and growth rates, and longer-distance migrations between regions, which have a major effect on regional growth rates. As already indicated, the most important migration flows are those from the European part of the country to the Asiatic regions. In the past, these were most significant to population growth in Siberia and the Far East; today they are more towards Kazakhstan and Central Asia, especially to the towns in those regions which consequently have a growing "European" element.

Recent population change must also be viewed against major demographic trends, which are significant not only at the national level but also as a major element in regional contrasts in population growth rates. Figure 43 displays such data as are available at the national level on birth, death and natural increase rates. Broken sections of the graphs denote generalized trends over periods for which annual figures have not been published; significantly, the missing data are for the periods of upheaval—the First World War, the Revolution, the Civil War, the early and mid-1930s (the period of forced collectivization of agriculture), the Second World War and the early post-war years. A complete annual series is available only from 1950.

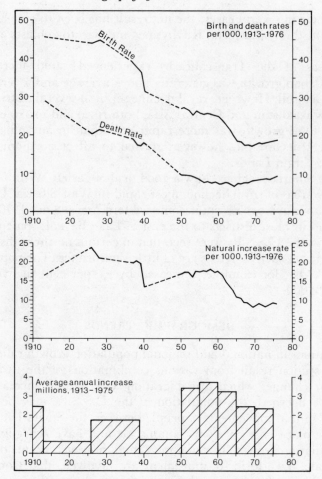

FIG. 43. Demographic trends, 1913–76.

The Soviet birth rate, which in 1913 was 45.5 per 1000, had declined to 26.7 by 1950. Over the same period, however, the death rate had fallen even more rapidly from 29.1 to 9.7 per 1000. Thus the rate of natural increase in 1950 stood at 1.7 per cent per annum, somewhat above the 1913 level (1.64 per cent) and well above the natural increase rates of western Europe. This simple statement masks considerable fluctuations in the intervening years; the periods of upheaval for which no data have been published were undoubtedly times when the birth rate was low and the death rate high, giving slow natural increase, and there must have been several single years in which deaths were more numerous than births.

From 1950 to 1960 the natural increase rate remained steady at around 1.7 per cent per annum; the birth rate fell only slowly to 24.9 per 1000 in 1960 and was balanced by a further decline in the death rate to 7.6 per 1000. During the 1960s, however, a dramatic change occurred. The birth rate fell sharply to a low point of 17.0 per 1000 in 1969, while the death rate showed a slight rise, owing to the ageing of the population. Thus, in 1969, the natural increase rate of 0.89 per cent was the lowest ever recorded (though not the lowest ever experienced by the Soviet population) and barely half the rate of the late 1950s. While part of this fertility decline can be attributed to a shortage of women of child-bearing age resulting from the reduced number of births during the Second World War, this is by no means the whole story. During the 1960s a large proportion of the Soviet population adopted the small-family habit already characteristic of western Europe.

Since 1970 the rate of natural increase rate has again been steady, but now at the much reduced level of 0.8 to 0.9 per cent per annum. The birth rate recovered slightly to 18.4 per 1000 in 1976, but the continued ageing of the Soviet population as a whole produced a rise in the death rate to 9.5 per 1000. The latter trend is likely to continue and, in the absence of factors favouring a rise in fertility, the natural increase rate seems set to decline further. The Soviet population appears to have passed its peak of growth and, in this connection, we may note that the numerical addition to the population in 1976 was only 2.3 million as against a peak of 3.9 million in 1960. As a result of these trends, the annual addition to the Soviet labour force is now much less than in the past, and increasing emphasis is laid by Soviet economic planners on the need to raise labour productivity. In this new demographic situation, a major problem will be that of building up a larger population in Siberia and the Far East, where the greatest untapped resources are now to be found.

As well as influencing total population growth, birth and natural increase rates show marked regional contrasts. The fertility decline just described began first and has been most marked among the European nationalities of the U.S.S.R., whereas the peoples of Central Asia and Transcaucasia, particularly those with a Moslem cultural heritage, continue to exhibit very high fertility. Data on birth and death rates are not published on the basis of nationalities, but figures for individual republics indicate the wide range of variations now existing in the U.S.S.R. In 1976, when, as already indicated, the birth, death and natural increase rates for the Soviet population as a whole were 18.4, 9.5 and 8.9 per 1000 respectively, the R.S.F.S.R. recorded 15.9, 10.0 and 5.9, while, at the other extreme, the figures for Tadzhikistan were 38.2, 8.5 and 29.7. Such vast differences in the rate of natural increase are a major component in regional differences in population growth rates.

DISTRIBUTION AND DENSITY

Despite the changes in distribution outline above, the population of the Soviet Union remains only slightly less heavily concentrated in the European part of the country than in earlier periods. Siberia and the Far East, which together make up nearly 60 per cent of the country, have quadrupled their population over the last hundred years, but still have only 27 million inhabitants, 10.5 per cent of the total. Kazakhstan, Central Asia and Transcaucasia, with a combined population of some 50 million, show a more even balance between territory and numbers, having about 20 per cent of the Soviet total in each case. This leaves close on 70 per cent of the population, about 176 million people, in the European part of the Soviet Union.

The map of population density (Fig. 44) serves to emphasize the uneven distribution of the Soviet people. The average density for the country as a whole in 1975 was 11.4 per sq km and administrative areas with a density above that average are enclosed by a thick line on Figure 44. Such areas are clearly confined to two distinct zones. By far the largest of these embraces the whole of the European U.S.S.R. south of the latitude of Leningrad, extending eastwards across the Urals and West Siberia to the Kuzbass and southwards into the Transcaucasus. A much smaller area of above-average densities occurs in the foothill and basin zone of Soviet Central Asia. Areas with densities above 45.6 per sq km, four times the Soviet average but still well below much of western Europe, are more restricted in extent. The largest of these high-density zones covers Moldavia and virtually the whole of the Ukraine, where a maximum of 193 per sq km occurs in the Donetsk oblast. Others include Moscow (292 per sq km) and the oblasts to the east along the upper Volga, Leningrad oblast (70 per sq km), Lithuania and parts of Belorussia, much of the Caucasus and Transcaucasia and the Tashkent–Fergana Basin area of Central Asia. At the other end of the scale, much of Kazakhstan, north European Russia, Siberia and the Far East have densities below 5 per sq km. The lowest densities of all, less than 1 per sq km, are found in the northern parts of the West Siberian Lowland and Central Siberian Plateau and in the far north-east of the country. The Yakut A.S.S.R., for example, with a territory of 3,103,000 sq km, covers nearly one-seventh of the Soviet Union, but has only 779,000 inhabitants, 0.03 per cent of the total, living at an average density of roughly one person to every 4 sq km.

Although Fig. 44 makes no distinction between urban and rural populations, showing simply the density of population as a whole, its general pattern closely reflects the distribution and quality of agricultural land as described in Chapter 6. The zones of above-average density correspond fairly well to the *Main Agricultural Belt* (Zone II) and the *Southern Areas of High Agricultural Value* (Zone IV) on the map of agricultural regions (Fig. 23). It is, of course, true that some of the highest oblast densities reflect the presence of major urban agglomerations but, since oblast boundaries are designed to include a strong urban element in each case, differences between oblasts in their degree of urbanization (see below) are less great than might be expected. This, together with the fact that some 40 per cent of the Soviet population still lives outside the towns, results in a fairly close correspondence between the pattern of rural densities and that of overall population density.

URBANIZATION

A steady income in the size of the urban element has been a characteristic of population change throughout the present century. Whereas in 1913 only 18 per cent lived in urban areas, this proportion had reached 61 per cent by

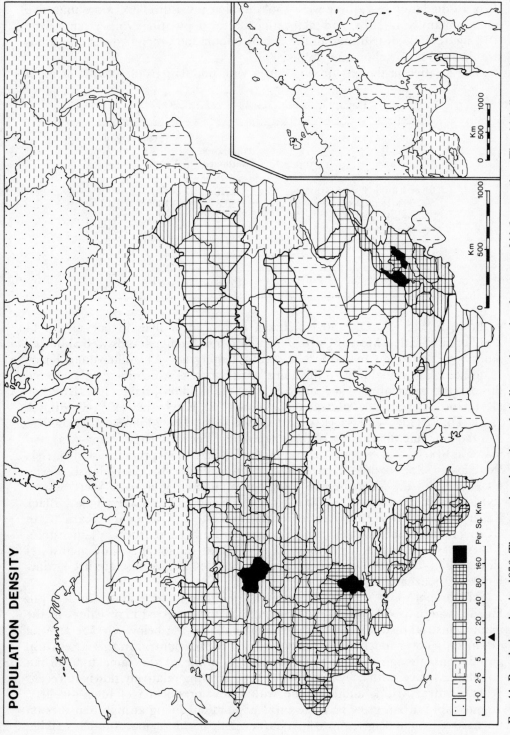

Fig. 44. Population density 1976. The arrowhead on the scale indicates the national average of 11.6 per sq km. The thick line encloses areas of above-average density.

1976. In the latter year, there were 156.6 million town-dwellers, more than five times as many as in 1913, and 98.9 million rural population, 75 per cent of the 1913 figure. The distribution of the urban population among towns of various sizes in 1976 was as shown in Table 29.

The location of the 254 urban centres with populations of 100,000 or more

TABLE 29. *Urban Centres by Size Groups, 1976*

Size	Number	Population (millions)	Percentage of Urban	Percentage of Total
Over 1 million	14	27.7	17.7	10.9
500,000–1,000,000	28	20.8	13.3	8.1
250,000–499,999	57	19.7	12.6	7.7
100,000–249,999	155	24.1	15.4	9.4
50,000–99,999	219	14.9	9.5	5.8
Below 50,000	5313	49.4	31.6	19.3
Total	5786	156.6	100.0	61.2

is shown in Fig. 45. One Soviet citizen in nine now lives in one of the 14 "millionaire" cities. Moscow, with 7.7 million inhabitants, stands well above all other Soviet cities in size and is followed by Leningrad (4.4 million) and Kiyev (2 million). The remaining "millionaire" cities, most of which have only entered this category since about 1960, are Tashkent (1.6 million), Baku (1.4), Kharkov (1.4), Gor'kiy (1.3), Novosibirsk (1.3), Minsk (1.2), Kuybyshev (1.2), Sverdlovsk (1.2), Tbilisi (1.0), Odessa (1.0) and Omsk (1.0). The 28 cities of 500,000 to 1 million include the capitals of three republics (Yerevan, Riga, Alma-Ata) and major industrial and regional centres in the Ukraine (Dnepropetrovsk, Donetsk, Yenikayevo, Zaporozhye, Krivoy Rog, Lvov), the Urals (Chelyabinsk, Perm, Ufa, Izhevsk), the Volga region (Volgograd, Kazan', Saratov), West Siberia (Krasnoyarsk, Novokuznetsk, Barnaul), the Centre (Yaroslavl', Tula), Black Earth Centre (Voronezh), North Caucasus (Rostov, Krasnodar), Kazakhstan (Karaganda), East Siberia (Irkutsk) and the Far East (Khabarovsk, Vladivostok). The remaining centres with more than 100,000 inhabitants show a distinct clustering in such major industrial areas as the Moscow basin, eastern Ukraine, Urals and Kuzbass.

The proportion of the population living in urban areas is shown in detail in Fig. 46, where it will be seen that, apart from the expected high values in the main industrial districts, the most striking feature is the below-average level of urbanization over much of the European part of the country. In this zone, rural populations, though declining, are still large, while at the same time urban populations have, with a few exceptions, been growing relatively slowly in recent years. Central Asia is another zone with a low proportion of town-dwellers, despite rapid urban growth; large rural populations living at high densities on the basis of irrigated agriculture are characteristic of this region. Another striking

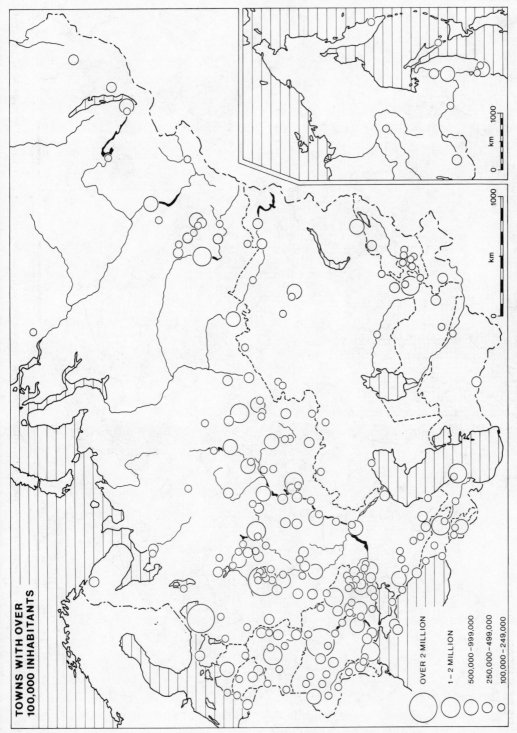

TOWNS WITH OVER
100,000 INHABITANTS

OVER 2 MILLION

1 – 2 MILLION

500,000 – 999,000

250,000 – 499,000

100,000 – 249,000

Fig. 45. Towns with populations over 100,000 in 1977.

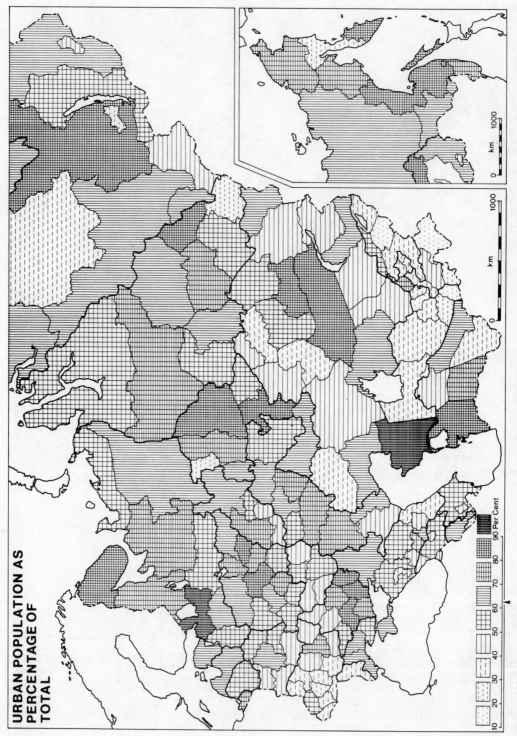

URBAN POPULATION AS PERCENTAGE OF TOTAL

Fig. 46. Urban population as a percentage of total population, 1976. The arrowhead on the scale indicates the national average of 62 per cent.

feature is the high level of urbanization in much of Siberia and the Far East, particularly in remote northern areas, where the possibilities for agriculture are extremely limited and the population lives mainly in ports, mining towns and lumbering centres.

Despite the large-scale movement from rural to urban areas which has taken place over the past sixty years, the U.S.S.R. still has an appreciably smaller proportion of town-dwellers than is usually associated with a major industrial power, and it was not until quite recently that the number of city-dwellers exceeded those living in rural areas. As late as 1940 only one-third of the Soviet population was classed as urban and the 50-per-cent level was not reached until 1961. The rural population continued to grow in numbers until the late 1960s, and it is only over the past decade that an actual decline in rural numbers has taken place. Even now, the agricultural labour force remains very large. Of a total working population of 127 million, about 28 per cent (35 million) are employed in the agricultural sector of the economy as against 27 per cent in extractive and manufacturing industry. These figures probably underestimate the proportion of the population which is directly or indirectly dependent on farming for a livelihood.

POPULATION STRUCTURE

The events described in this chapter have had a fundamental effect on the age and sex structure of the Soviet population (Fig. 47). At the 1970 census, the last date for which detailed information is available, there was a marked excess of females over males, the former numbering 130.3 million and the latter 111.4 million, a sex ratio of 85 males to 100 females. This imbalance was visible in all age groups born before 1945, reaching its maximum among those born between 1905 and 1925, most of whom were of military age during the Second World War. Among the population aged 45–49 in 1970 (15–19 in 1940) there were only 63 men per 100 women and in the 50–59 age group (20–29 in 1940) only 57. The low birth rate of the war years was reflected in the small numbers of both sexes in the 25–29 age group, while the large numbers between the ages of 10 and 20 were a product of accelerated population growth in the post-war years. The relatively small numbers below the age of 5, however, indicate the low level of fertility in the late 1960s.

The Soviet population in 1970 was still a relatively youthful one, with 92 million people (38 per cent) below 20 years of age and no fewer than 45 million (18.6 per cent) below 10. However, the population was ageing as a result of the lower birth rate and a longer expectation of life. The under-5's constituted only 8.5 per cent of the total in 1970 as against 11.6 per cent in 1959, while the proportion aged 60 or more had risen from 9.4 to 11.8 per cent. Since 1970 this ageing process has undoubtedly continued, though precise details will not be available until the next census. Annual figures for males and females are published, however, and these show that, by 1976, the sex ratio had risen slightly to 87; there were 118.7 million men and 136.8 million women. It will be some decades

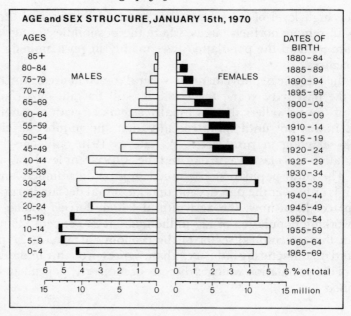

Fig. 47. The age and sex composition of the Soviet population in 1970. The black sections of each bar indicate the surplus of males or females in that age group.

yet before the imbalance between the sexes, resulting mainly from the upheavals of the period before 1945, is completely removed. This long-standing feature is one of the factors responsible for the large-scale employment of women in the U.S.S.R., who make up more than 40 per cent of the total labour force.

CONCLUSION

In several ways, the population of the Soviet Union has in recent years, become more like those of other developed countries. The birth rate overall has fallen to "western" levels, though the U.S.S.R. has not experienced the dramatic birth rate decline which affected, for example, the United Kingdom, in the early 1970s and is still far from a "zero growth" situation. The natural increase remains far above that of western Europe, where birth rates are much lower and death rates a good deal higher, and about 50 per cent above that of the United States, which has a lower birth rate but a similar death rate to that of the Soviet Union (total growth rates in the two countries are now very similar, the lower natural increase in the United States being compensated by large-scale immigration). The large excess of women and the youthful age structure still distinguish the population of the Soviet Union from those of other developed countries.

In the decades ahead, further change may be expected. The death rate will continue to rise as the population becomes less youthful and the birth rate is more likely to fall than otherwise as rates among the high-fertility ethnic groups decline towards those of the majority. As a result, the natural increase and thus the total growth rate of the Soviet population will come yet closer to those of the rest of the developed world.

This slow-down in population growth will have serious implications in the economic field. In the past, rising production, especially in industry, was to a large extent supported by additions to the labour force, and the productivity of Soviet workers remained well below that of other advanced countries, particularly the United States. A large and sustained increase in labour productivity is now absolutely essential if the Soviet Union is to achieve the economic growth envisaged in her long-term development plans.

BIBLIOGRAPHY

The volume of literature on all aspects of the Soviet Union increases annually and selection becomes ever more difficult. As a first step in the selection process, the list which follows is (except in the special case of atlases) confined to works in English.

BOOKS

Several full-scale geographical texts by Western writers appeared during the 1960s, some of which have more recent editions:

COLE, J. P., *Geography of the U.S.S.R.*, Penguin Books, Harmondsworth, 1967.

COLE, J. P. and GERMAN, F. C., *A Geography of the U.S.S.R.—The Background to a Planned Economy*, Butterworths, London, 1961, 2nd edn., 1970.

GREGORY, J. S., *Russian Land, Soviet People*, Harrap, London, 1968.

HOOSON, D. J. M., *The Soviet Union—A Systematic Regional Geography*, London University Press, London, 1966.

HOWE, G. M., *The Soviet Union*, Macdonald & Evans, London, 1968.

JORRÉ, G., *The Soviet Union—The Land and its People*, Longmans, London, 3rd edn., 1967 (tr. E. D. Laborde, revised by C. A. Halstead).

LYDOLPH, P. E., *Geography of the U.S.S.R.*, Wiley, New York, 1964; 2nd edn., 1970; 3rd edn., 1977.

MELLOR, R. E. H., *Geography of the U.S.S.R.*, Macmillan, London, 1964.

Shorter works from which additional insight and information may be obtained include:

EAST, W. G., *The Soviet Union*, Searchlight Book No. 15, Van Nostrand, Princeton, 1963.

HOWE, G. M., *The U.S.S.R.*, Hulton, Amersham, 1972.

SHABAD, T., The Soviet Union, in *A Geography of Europe* (G. W. Hoffman, ed.), Ronald Press, New York, 1961.

Older texts of some interest for the picture which they provide of the situation in the 1940s and 1950s are:

EAST, W. G. and SHABAD, T., Chapters XIV–XVIII in *The Changing World* (W. G. East and A. E. Moodie, eds.), Harrap, London, 1956.

GREGORY, J. S., *Land of the Soviets*, Penguin Books, London, 1946.

GREGORY, J. S. and SHAVE, D. W., *The U.S.S.R.—A Geographical Appraisal*, Harrap, London, 1944.

MIROV, N. T., *Geography of Russia*, Wiley, New York, 1951.

SHABAD, T., *The Geography of the U.S.S.R.*, Columbia University Press, New York, 1953.

For a wide variety of comparisons between the Soviet Union and the United States, see:

PARKER, W. H., *The Super-Powers: The United States and the Soviet Union Compared*, Macmillan, London, 1972.

Soviet publishing houses commonly produce English-language editions of standard Russian texts, mainly at an introductory level, which give an idea of the way in which Soviet geographers describe their own country:

MINTS, A. A., *The Geography of the U.S.S.R.—An Introductory Survey*, Novosti, Moscow, 1975.
POKSHISHEVSKIY, V. V., *The Geography of the Soviet Union*, Progress Publishers, Moscow, 1974.

In addition to the general geographies listed above, a great amount of material has been published on the various systematic aspects. Physical geography is covered mainly by translations of Soviet books, e.g.:

BERG, L. S., *The Natural Regions of the U.S.S.R.*, Macmillan, New York, 1950.
BORISOV, A. A., *Climates of the U.S.S.R.*, Oliver & Boyd, Edinburgh, 1966 (trans. R. A. Ledward; ed. C. A. Halstead).
GERASIMOV, I. P., ARMAND, D. L. and YEFRON, K. M., *Natural Resources of the Soviet Union: Their Use and Renewal*, Freeman, San Francisco, 1971.
NALIVKIN, D. V., *The Geology of the U.S.S.R.*, Pergamon Press, Oxford, 1960.
SUSLOV, S. P., *Physical Geography of Asiatic Russia*, Freeman, San Francisco, 1961.

Problems of resource management are dealt with in:

PRYDE, P. R., *Conservation in the Soviet Union*, Cambridge University Press, London, 1972.

while relationships between the physical environment and the development of the Soviet economy form the main theme of:

PARKER, W. H., *The World's Landscapes: 3, The Soviet Union*, Longman, London, 1969.

A dozen aspects of Soviet geography are covered individually in:

SYMONS, L. J. (ed.), *Geography of the U.S.S.R.*, Hicks, Smith & Sons Ltd., Wellington, N.Z., 1969–70: a series of 12 booklets: *The Evolution of the State* (L. J. Symons), *Population* (J. C. Dewdney), *Transport* (R. E. H. Mellor), *Soils and Vegetation* (W. W. Newey), *Collectivised Agriculture* (L. J. Symons), *Industrial Development* (R. E. H. Mellor), *Physiography* (J. C. Dewdney), *Mineral Resources* (W. W. Newey), *Water* (W. W. Newey), *Climate and Man* (D. J. M. Hooson), *Cities and Villages* (R. E. H. Mellor), *The Regions* (J. C. Dewdney).

Not surprisingly, economic affairs have received particular attention. Modern economic geographies by western writers in the 1960s and 1970s include:

CRESSEY, G. B., *Soviet Potentials—A Geographical Appraisal*, Syracuse University Press, Syracuse, N.Y., 1962.
MATHIESON, R. S., *The Soviet Union: An Economic Geography*, Heinemann, London, 1975.

Important Soviet economic geographies available in translation are, in chronological order:

BALZAK, S. S., VASYUTIN, V. F. and FEIGIN, Ya., *Economic Geography of the U.S.S.R.*, Macmillan, New York, 1949.
BARANSKY, N. N., *Economic Geography of the Soviet Union*, Foreign Languages Publishing House, Moscow, 1956.
LAVRISHCHEV, A., *Economic Geography of the U.S.S.R.*, Progress Publishers, Moscow, 1969.

Works by economists, economic historians and others on the nature and development of the Soviet economy include:

CAMPBELL, R. W., *Soviet Economic Power: Its Organization, Growth and Challenge*, Macmillan, London, 1967.
CAMPBELL, R. W., *The Soviet-type Economies: Performance and Evolution*, Houghton Mifflin, Boston, 1974.
DOBB, M., *Soviet Economic Development since 1917*, Routledge and Kegan Paul, London, 1948, 2nd edn., 1966.
HUTCHINGS, R., *Soviet Economic Development*, Blackwell, Oxford, 1971.
NETTL., J. P., *The Soviet Achievement*, Thames & Hudson, London, 1967.
NOVE, A., *The Soviet Economy*, Allen & Unwin, London, 1961, 2nd edn., 1968.
NOVE, A., *An Economic History of the U.S.S.R.*, Lane/Penguin, London, 1969.
SCHWARTZ, H., *The Soviet Economy since Stalin*, Lippincott, Philadelphia, 1965.

SHERMAN, H. J., *The Soviet Economy*, Little, Brown & Co., Boston, 1969.

TREML, V. G. and FARRELL, R. (eds.), *The Development of the Soviet Economy: Plan and Performance*, Praeger, New York, 1968.

Numerous books have also been published on specific sectors of the Soviet economy:

CAMPBELL, R. W., *The Economics of Soviet Oil and Gas*, Johns Hopkins, Baltimore, 1968.

DEWDNEY, J. C., *The U.S.S.R.* (Studies in Industrial Geography), Dawson, Folkestone, 1976.

DIENES, L., *Locational Factors and Locational Developments in the Soviet Chemical Industry*, University of Chicago, Chicago, Department of Geography, 1969.

ELLIOT, I. F., *The Soviet Energy Balance*, Praeger, New York, 1974.

HEMY, G. W., *The Soviet Chemical Industry*, Hill, London, 1971.

HODGKINS, J. A., *Soviet Power—Energy Resources, Production and Potentials*, Prentice-Hall, London, 1961.

SHABAD, T., *Basic Industrial Resources of the U.S.S.R.*, Columbia University Press, New York, 1969.

SHIMKIN, D. B., *Minerals: A Key to Soviet Power*, Harvard University Press, Cambridge, Mass., 1953.

STRAUSS, E., *Soviet Agriculture in Perspective: A Study of its Successes and Failures*, Allen & Unwin, London, 1969.

SYMONS, L., *Russian Agriculture*, Bell, London, 1972.

SYMONS, L. and WHITE, C., *Russian Transport: An Historical and Geographical Survey*, Bell, London, 1975.

Works on other aspects of human geography and on Soviet society in general include:

HARRIS, C. D., *Cities of the Soviet Union: Studies in their Functions, Size, Density and Growth*, Rand McNally, Chicago, 1970.

LORIMER, F., *The Population of the Soviet Union—History and Prospects*, League of Nations, Geneva, 1946.

MATTHEWS, M., *Class and Society in Soviet Russia*, Lane/Penguin, London, 1972.

MILLER, J., *Life in Russia Today*, Batsford, London, 1969.

PARKER, W. H., *An Historical Geography of Russia*, London University Press, London, 1968.

SMITH, H., *The Russians*, Times Books, London, 1976.

A wide range of statistical information on economic and human aspects is now readily available from statistical yearbooks published annually in Russian. Much of this material has been consolidated in:

CLARKE, R. A., *Soviet Economic Facts, 1917–1970*, Macmillan, London.

Works in English on specific regions of the Soviet Union deal mainly with the Asiatic parts of the country:

CONOLLY, V., *Beyond the Urals—Economic Developments in Soviet Asia*, Oxford University Press, London, 1967.

CONOLLY, V., *Siberia Today and Tomorrow*, Collins, London, 1975.

HOOSON, D. J. M., *A New Soviet Heartland?*, Searchlight Book No. 21, Van Nostrand, Princeton, 1964.

KIRBY, E. S., *The Soviet Far East*, Macmillan, London, 1971.

NOVE, A. and NEWTH, J. A., *The Soviet Middle East: A Communist Model for Development*, Allen & Unwin, London, 1967.

THIEL, E., *The Soviet Far East*, Methuen, London, 1967.

A recent work on the U.S.S.R.'s most important city region is:

HAMILTON, F. E. I., *The Moscow City Region*, Problem Regions of Europe, Oxford University Press, London, 1976.

PERIODICALS

No attempt is made in this bibliography to list even the more recent of the many articles on diverse aspects of the geography of the U.S.S.R. which have appeared in the various periodicals published by learned societies in the Soviet Union and the Western world. Special mention must be made, however, of the journal *Soviet Geography: Review and Translation*, published ten times a year by the American Geographical Society. In addition to translations of major articles from Soviet geographical journals and occasional contributions by Western geographers, the "News Notes" contributed to each issue of *Soviet Geography* by the editor (Theodore Shabad) report regularly on recent developments, particularly in the industrial field, and are invaluable as a source of up-to-date information on many of the topics covered in this book. Mention should also be made to the series of eight articles on the Soviet Union contributed by Soviet geographers to the February–September (inclusive) 1976 issues of the *Geographical Magazine* (I.P.C. Magazines Ltd.).

ATLASES

Soviet atlases are generally of very high quality and can be of considerable value even to those with a limited knowledge of the Russian language. The best and most recent are:

FIZIKO-GEOGRAFICHESKIY ATLAS MIRA (Physical-Geographical Atlas of the World), Moscow, 1964. A full translation appears in *Soviet Geography*, May–June, 1965.

ATLAS S.S.S.R. (Atlas of the U.S.S.R.), Moscow, 1969.

ATLAS SELSKOGO KHOZYAYSTVA S.S.S.R. (Atlas of the Agriculture of the U.S.S.R.), Moscow, 1960.

ATLAS RAZVITIYA KHOZYAYSTVA i KULTURY S.S.S.R. 1917–1967 (Atlas of the Growth of the Economy and Culture of the U.S.S.R., 1917–1967), Moscow, 1967.

ATLAS OBRAZOVANIYE i RAZVITIYE SOYUZA S.S.R. (Atlas of the Formation and Development of the U.S.S.R.), Moscow, 1972.

Atlases in English include:

U.S.S.R. AGRICULTURE ATLAS, Central Intelligence Agency, Washington, D.C., 1974.

OXFORD REGIONAL ECONOMIC ATLAS OF THE U.S.S.R. AND EASTERN EUROPE, Oxford University Press, London, 1956; revised edn., 1960.

TAAFFE, R. N. and KINGSBURY, R. C., *AN ATLAS OF SOVIET AFFAIRS*, Methuen, London, 1965.

INDEX

Figures in *italics* refer to a map, diagram or table on the specified page